A YEAR IN THE WHYTE HOUSE

A NOVEL

ARMAND L. WELLER

PLUS: A ONE-ACT CHRISTMAS PLAY

FOR CHURCH GROUPS

A Year in the Whyte House

Trilogy Christian Publishers A Wholly Owned Subsidary of Trinity Broadcasting Network

2442 Michelle Drive Tustin, CA 92780

Rights Department, 2442 Michelle Drive, Tustin, CA 92780.

Trilogy Christian Publishing/TBN and colophon are trademarks of Trinity Broadcasting Network.

For information about special discounts for bulk purchases, please contact Trilogy Christian Publishing.

Trilogy Disclaimer: The views and content expressed in this book are those of the author and may not necessarily reflect the views and doctrine of Trilogy Christian Publishing or the Trinity Broadcasting Network.

Manufactured in the United States of America

10 9 8 7 6 5 4 3 2 1

Library of Congress Cataloging-in-Publication Data is available.

ISBN: 979-8-88738-365-1

E-ISBN: 979-8-88738-366-8

Endorsements

This book is an entertaining read for anyone, but as a church secretary, I particularly liked the pleasantly embedded insights into how a church is run— something that any church pastor, leader, or even member, will particularly enjoy.

—Pennsylvania

As a pastor and homeschool dad, this book provided some very valuable lessons and insights for me in both areas.

—Pennsylvania

I would highly recommend this book to anyone who is affiliated with a church in any capacity. I'm a church children's director and found it a good way to learn something new while engaging in a thoroughly delightful leisure-time activity.

—Florida

I grew up as a pastor's kid and remember many fun experiences similar to the ones in this book. It brought back many good memories.

—Virginia

ACKNOWLEDGMENTS

This book draws loosely on my own experiences as a father and pastor who had to depend heavily on the Lord. Many of the stories are drawn from my own memory. The three sisters were real members of my church, and my middle daughter did play a role in their story. There really was a "Frank's Place" similar to a lunch counter where I spent many pleasant morning tea breaks.

There are many people to acknowledge, particularly my wife, Barbara, who has been a wonderful partner and editor in this endeavor, not to mention the talented folks at Trilogy Publishing.

This book also serves as my tribute to several people who were influential in my life and who have already transitioned to their homes in heaven. Pastor Jack was named after my brother, Jack Weller, who died in a scuba diving accident while I was in seminary. Pastor Jack's wife, Connie, honors a pastor friend's wife and my wife's best friend, Connie Reeser, who also died much too young from cancer. Jack's parents are named after Tom and Janet Garner to honor my first senior pastor and mentor, who taught me much of what I know (and share in this book). Ron Young was based on my good friend and church council president, Ronnie Hughes, who also recently graduated to heaven.

Pastor Jack's Weaverton church secretary is named for two of my fantastic church secretaries, Linda Demusz and Linda Siewak, who are still friends. I could not have run the churches I served without them. Alex and Kate Hartley honor real church members, Terry and Kathy Lister, both former actors who diligently continue to serve the church in many capacities. Pastor David and Jessica Julian and their twins, Owen and Laina, provided much-needed guidance on homeschooling.

All of the above-named people, as well as too many others to mention, have blessed my life in various ways, and I hope reading this book will bless yours.

TABLE OF CONTENTS

SEASON I

SUMMER VACATION

Chapter 1

ALMOST ARRESTED

Pastor Jack and Connie did not at first notice the red and blue lights flashing behind them. They were too engrossed in surveying the inside of the little church building on the corner of Church Street and Weaver Road. There they stood, both of them with their noses pressed against the old windows like little kids, hands making a kind of cup around their faces so they could see through the reflections from the early afternoon sun on the windows.

The outside of the quaint church resembled the old German ecclesiastical architecture common to southeast Pennsylvania. It was a traditional red brick building with tall, clear windows, white trim, and a gray slate roof, all apparently in good condition. But the inside looked as though someone had miraculously and carefully lowered an old New England-style sanctuary inside the rough, red brick walls of the church building.

There were white pews and an altar, all with mahogany trim. Wainscoting matched the pews. In the chancel, above the altar on a shelf protruding from the wall, were four large golden candlesticks set in front of a rich blue and gold *fleur-de-lis* wall pattern. And between them was a large white cross, at least six feet high, with gold trim.

Jack excitedly commented to his wife, without removing his nose from the windowpane, "This is lovely. I could really worship here." In fact, they were so intrigued that they were completely oblivious to those red and blue flashing lights.

It must have been the voices of their five children squealing, "Daddy! Daddy!" from the open windows of the Dodge minivan a few yards behind them that finally caught their attention. That and the much deeper, gruff voice, speaking with firm authority, that said, "What do you think you're doing here?" That's when they turned to see the foreboding figure of a big (really big), burly man in uniform with an unsmiling face and glaring eyes.

"We received a concerned call from a neighbor that someone was snooping around the church and asked us to check it out. So...I would like an answer.... What do you think you're doing here?"

"Oh, I'm so sorry, officer," said Pastor Jack. "Excuse me a moment." And to the children, he said, with his own voice of authority, "Children, you can stop yelling now. This kind officer and I are having an important conversation, and we really could do without all the chatter for a few minutes." He figured a few complimentary words about the officer couldn't hurt.

"Sorry, Daddy," came the quiet response from the children.

"I'll go talk to them," said their mother as Connie worked her way over to the gray, weathered van, happy to leave the conversation with the officer to her husband.

"I'm sorry, officer. There's really a simple explanation for all of this. You see, I'm a pastor, and next Sunday, a few people from Grace Church here are coming to see me preach at Trinity Church in Overland. They want to see if I might be the right choice to be the next pastor of this congregation. And I was nosy. I wanted to see what the church facilities looked like. We really are not trying to break in, although I can imagine some neighbors might be alarmed. I'm truly sorry. They must have thought we were 'casing the joint,'" he concluded with a nervous laugh.

Pastor Jack's words and sincere demeanor, and even his weak attempt at humor, apparently made sense to the officer because he gradually relaxed his stance, and the tension in his craggy face began to ease into something close to a smile. "Well, that certainly seems to explain things. But some ID would help even more."

While Pastor Jack carefully removed his wallet from his back pocket to retrieve his driver's license for the officer, the man continued, "You might be the luckiest man in the county today. You see, I'm a member here at Grace. And fortunately for you, I recently heard that someone might be preaching nearby in a neutral pulpit who might be our next pastor. But you know how church talk is. Lots of opinions but very few facts. Count your lucky stars," he went on, "that it was me and not one of our other officers who answered this call."

As Pastor Jack surrendered his photo ID and clergy card to the officer, he hesitantly said, "Sir, I was wondering if it might be all right for you to turn off those flashing lights. I think my wife might have more success in calming down our five youngsters."

"Sure, be happy to, Mr. John Patrick Whyte from Bradford, Connecticut," he replied, reading from the driver's license in his hand. Returning the items to Pastor Jack, he turned to his patrol car, and quickly, all the flashing ceased. When he came back to the clergyman, he said, with a genuine smile, "You know, it would have been better to plan a visit to the church with a member of the pulpit committee. We could have avoided this whole scene."

"You're right. You are absolutely right," admitted the pastor. "But we didn't want to appear presumptuous about the possibility of being called to fill the pulpit of Grace Church. That's why we sort of...sneaked around like this."

"I understand. Tell you what," said a much more mellow officer of the law, "while you're here, you might as well check out the parsonage next door while you're at it. I don't have a key, and I'm sure it's locked, but feel free to wander around a bit. I'm sure your kids would like to check out the backyard and the pond nearby. And you seem to be good at looking through windows," he added with a little twinkle in his eyes.

"Meanwhile, I'll call the neighbor who was concerned about your activity to assure her everything is just fine. If you do become our pastor, I'm sure you'll meet her soon enough. She's old Mrs. Weaver, one of the descendants of the family that settled Weaverton back in the late 1700s. Her home is just across Church Street. She loves this old church but can't get out like she used to. So she keeps an eye on all the happenings in and around this building."

"I hope she doesn't have negative thoughts about me because of what we've been doing here," said a deeply concerned Pastor Jack.

"Don't think that'd be a problem. I'll explain it all to her. She may be nosy, but she's got a good heart. So why don't you nose around a little more? If you don't mind, I'll just hang around in case someone else stops by and wonders about seven people scurrying around our little country church," he said with a grin in his voice. "So, Reverend Whyte, you just go ahead and do some scurrying."

"Thanks a lot, officer. And by the way, you don't have to call me Reverend. My name is John, but everyone calls me Jack or Pastor Jack. I always tell people to just call me whatever they feel most comfortable calling me. I really have never needed fancy titles."

"Okay," said the officer. "And my name is Officer Harold Bender, but most folks just call me Harry. Now, why don't you folks go on and do some more investigating? If you have any questions about the church or the property, if I have an answer, I'll be happy to give it to you."

"Thanks, Officer Bender, err, Harry. We'll do that." And then to his family, "Let's go, gang. This nice officer said we could wander around some more. Connie, let's check out that big old brick house next door. It's the parsonage."

"The parsonage? I didn't know they had a parsonage. It sure looks large enough to handle our big brood. Come on, kids. Let's look around." That was followed by lots of squeals of excitement as five members of the Whyte family scampered out of the old van and ran next door with their mom and dad for another adventure.

The five children headed to the backyard to do some exploring on their own while Jack and Connie headed left and up the gently sloping bank to the front of the house. Right next to the road that passed in front of the parsonage was a small stand of three elegant, white birch trees standing straight and tall. If they moved here, thought Connie, those trees would be a friendly reminder of Connecticut's familiar landscape and their current home.

There was a concrete walkway that went from the road, where a mailbox shaped like a small church stood, past the birch trees to a huge wrap-around porch beginning on the front of the old house and continuing around to the left side of the parsonage.

"Ohhh," sighed Connie, "look at this beautiful wrap-around porch. I've always wanted one of these. Why Jack, it's big enough that we could put lots of chairs and a table out there. I can already see our whole family gathered here for lots of fun things. You could even have an informal Bible study for teens right there. And we could hang a big old porch swing right there in the corner. Oh, Jack, I can just imagine..."

"Hey, wait, hold on there, Connie. Don't get all excited and start decorating things. We might not come here. I don't want to see you get disappointed. What if this isn't God's place for us? Just don't get carried away, okay?"

"Jack Whyte. How long have we been married?'

"Almost fifteen years."

"And haven't you learned by now how much I just love to decorate and arrange things and imagine how things might look, given the opportunity? If this isn't God's place for us, although I think it is," she said with a twinkle in her eyes, "I won't be devastated. I'll just have fun thinking about possibilities for the next house."

"I know. I know. Well, then, go ahead and enjoy yourself. I'm going to see what the kids are doing in the back of the house. I don't want them getting too close to that pond."

"Okay. I'm going to stick my nose against some more windows and check out the inside of this lovely home. Officer Bender is right. We're pretty good at that." And with a little smile on her face that caused some lovely wrinkles to form around her eyes, Connie went off to explore on her own.

As Jack worked his way around to the back of the huge house, he glanced over to his right at the church parking lot. There nonchalantly stood Officer Bender, a smile now on his face, arms crossed in front of his chest, leaning against his patrol car and seemingly enjoying the investigation the Whytes were conducting. Catching Pastor Jack's eye, Harry waved and gave him a warm nod as if to say, "Just enjoy yourself. Take your time. I'll just hang out here till you're finished."

It was a big, three-story brick house, probably built in the 1920s. It sat a few feet up the hill from the church building. Attached to the back of the house and at the top of the sloping, green backyard was a large, screened-in porch with a roof that sloped up to the second-floor windows.

Jack wondered how many bedrooms it had up there. *Would there be enough for all of his children? I'm sure it has an attic. All these old houses did, and that basement, too, just to the right of the garage. I wonder if all of the basement is finished. Oh my, I'm starting to think like Connie. Take it easy, Jack. One day at a time. You might not know for many weeks whether this is the church God has for you.... Now, what are my five kids doing back here?*

The pastor surveyed the backyard where his children were having a ball. There were Sarah, Megan, and Paul doing their best to climb the branches of a low maple tree. That seemed safe enough. There was an apple tree near the house, then that maple tree. And at the bottom of the yard, where the driveway curved around, was a big old black walnut tree.

Just behind the house, to the right of the screened-in porch, was a beautiful weeping willow being watered generously by a small stream on the far side of the parsonage yard. That stream flowed gently with quiet ripples down to the pond. And down by the pond was his oldest son, Johnny, skipping stones across the silvery, smooth surface of the water. His youngest, Suzy, gazed in awe at her big brother so cleverly making stones seem to float and fly across the pond. Ah, the wonder of a five-year-old for the skills of a teenager.

For a while, Pastor Jack just stood and marveled at how God had blessed him with such a wonderful family. His three middle children were helping one another with the challenges that come with trying to conquer the branches of that maple tree. *I think they're going to get a bit dirty from that adventure. Oh, well, that's why we have a washer and dryer at our vacation rental in Ocean City, New Jersey. And there's Johnny taking time to teach his little sister how to skip stones across the pond. Where did he develop such patience in only thirteen years of life? I don't think Suzy is getting the knack yet. But she sure is trying. Such a determined five-year-old. Just like her mother. I think she just enjoys being with her big brother, even if she never masters that stone-skipping skill.*

No one seems to have even noticed the small group of cows off to the left of the pond. If they had, I'm sure they'd be leaning on the fence to check them out and maybe even pet them. Oh, there is so much my children could enjoy if the Lord allowed us to come here. I don't want to get too excited, but I think this might be part of His plan for my family and me. It just seems to feel right.

Just then, Connie rounded the far side of the house and the screened-in porch and was coming toward him as he stood next to the old apple tree. She had a huge smile on her face as she crossed to where Jack was standing. Whenever she smiled like that, her face just seemed to light up. Oh, how much he loved his wife.

"Oh, Jack, I just love this old house. From what I could see, there's so much we could do here for the children. And there's a bed of roses on the far side of the house near that huge willow. Just think. Fresh, fragrant flowers in the spring. I tried to see what it was like inside the house, but there were off-white Venetian blinds at each window. And they were in the closed position."

At that moment, she saw the children and their escapades, and her smile quickly turned to concern. "Jack, look at those three climbing that tree. They are so dirty they...they look like homeless waifs."

"Yeah, they do, don't they? But they're our homeless waifs. And they sure are having fun. We never had this kind of place for them to play in the city. Anyway, it's all harmless." Then with a sneaky grin, he said, "And if people think they are homeless kids, think about how much they'll admire you and me for taking those poor, disadvantaged children into our home and cleaning them up and feeding them."

"Ja-ack," lamented Connie. She never could resist his good nature. "Oh, I suppose you're right. It will all come out in the wash. At least that's what my mother always said."

"Are you finished with your explorations for now? We really should be on our way. I'm feeling a bit guilty that Officer Bender is patiently waiting for us to move on. I'm not sure the kids are ready to go, but we really need to head back to Ocean City."

"I think you're right. But this sure has been fun." Calling to the children, "Come on, kids. Time to go. We're heading back to the shore." As the children gathered around her, she continued. "We can stop at the MacDonald's drive-thru on the way. And when we get back to our cottage, *after* we clean up some pretty dirty children, we can go to the boardwalk for soft ice cream."

That seemed to sweeten the deal for the kids. And amid many happy squeals, one loud cheer, and a handful of quiet groans, the Whyte family headed back to their van, satisfied that they'd just had a full day of discovery, almost got arrested, and that even more fun lay ahead.

With final words of appreciation to Officer Bender, the Whyte family loaded up their van and headed southeast for fast food, baths, and ice cream. Yum! What more could anyone want?

Chapter 2

Getting Ready for Sunday

During breakfast, between mouthfuls of yummy donuts, the five children were still talking about yesterday's adventure at Grace Church. That would forever be referred to as "the day Mom and Dad almost got arrested."

Jack had gotten up early. He was a morning person. He'd gone down to Bachmann's Bakery on Haven Avenue, just a block from their vacation house. Bachmann's was one of the favorite spots they all looked forward to when they went to Ocean City. The sweet aroma of delicious baked goods always filled the small store and the nostrils of all who entered there. Jack came back with a dozen of their sinfully delicious donuts, and everyone was enjoying the spoils of his efforts while recounting yesterday's fun.

"Boy, Mom," said Johnny, "you should have seen the look on your face when you turned around and saw that cop standing there."

"Yeah," chimed in Paul, "your eyes were so big, we thought they might pop out." A chorus of "yeahs" and a lot of giggles bubbled up around the big, green kitchen table.

Connie just smiled and said, "He was a big one, wasn't he?" She knew everyone had had a great time in Weaverton. Her only question was if they would all have a lot more good times in that little community in the future.

Jack was certainly thinking about that even while enjoying the conversation and one Bavarian cream donut, his favorite. While the chatter continued, he was distracted by thoughts of the upcoming Sunday morning worship service in Overland, Pennsylvania. To be honest, he was more concerned that he would be able to bless the worshipers than with the opinion of one or more pulpit committees who might come to hear him preach.

He and Connie had long ago turned this next move of their life in Christian ministry over to the Lord. He knew for sure they would be moving on to a new area of ministry. And they just trusted that wherever God wanted them to go next, He would make that clear. They liked to say they lived by the eleventh commandment: "Thou shalt not sweat it." But it sure would be nice to know sooner rather than later what the future held for them and their family.

Pastor Jack knew later that day he was going to have to take time to finish his sermon preparation. But for now, he was just going to enjoy being at the Jersey shore with his family. Swallowing another bite of his Bavarian cream, he said, "So, who wants to go to the beach?" His question was greeted with cheers from everyone around the table. "I guess that's a 'go' for beach fun."

"Let's take our time," instructed Connie. "Everyone get your rooms cleaned up before getting your swimsuits on. You have plenty of time. We won't leave till around ten o'clock. If anyone wants to help, I'm going to pack some goodies to take along to the beach. And don't forget to put on sunscreen. We don't want anyone looking like a cooked lobster when the day is done."

Amid more laughter, the children headed to their bedrooms. Sarah lingered a moment to tell her mother she'd be happy to help get goodies ready and packed. Then she ran off to her room as well. *My eleven-year-old is growing up*, thought Connie.

"What are your plans for the day?" she asked her husband. "I can tell sermon prep is on your mind."

"How could you know that?" he responded.

"I just know my hubby. And I love him."

"Well, I definitely want to spend time with you and the kids on the beach. But then I need some quiet time to go over my notes for Sunday."

"I'll plan something for the children and me to do so we can go off and let you alone for a while," offered Connie.

"Thanks. That would be a big help."

Time in the sand and by the ocean was as much fun as always. There was the building of sandcastles with buckets and assorted plastic containers as molds for various parts of the castle structure. Of course, everyone got wet

18

in the Atlantic Ocean, being buffeted about by some rather strong waves breaking on the shore.

Suzy and Paul had a great time digging up little sand fleas before they burrowed back into the sand as each wave receded once again. And everyone got involved in burying Dad in the sand until only his head was uncovered.

"And people wonder why I don't get a suntan when we go on vacation," he joked.

"You do look a little silly," laughed Connie. "You'd better be careful. Some of these college boys may come by and mistake your head for a soccer ball."

"Thanks for the warning," said Dad. "But I don't think they've ever kicked a soccer ball with so much hair on it."

Just then, nine-year-old Megan asked if they could have some of the snacks that Connie and Sarah had prepared for them. "Of course," said Connie. And then to all the kids, "Anyone hungry or thirsty? We've got a Styrofoam cooler full of goodies here. And we have more than just snacks, thanks to Sarah's help. Since it's almost noontime, I figure this will be lunch for today."

"Come and get it," called Sarah. "We made plenty for everyone."

"Hold on there," said Connie. "There is a price to pay. We've been out here in the sun for almost two hours, and most of us have been in and out of the ocean. Just to be safe, you all need another coating of sunscreen. Then you can have lunch." Only a few groans accompanied this announcement. They knew Mom was right. Wasn't she always right?

Then came a real loud groan from Dad. "Hey guys, I'm hungry too, but I don't think I can dig my way out of this sand grave all by myself." Immediately, five laughing children attacked the sand mound and rescued their hungry and very sandy father. Connie had to laugh. They looked like five curious dogs digging for treasure.

An hour later, the Whyte family packed up all their toys and towels and collapsible chairs, put leftovers in the cooler, sunscreen and other goodies in the backpack, and trudged the two short blocks back to their rented vacation home like a loaded-down, bedraggled caravan. Everyone helped carry the burdens, Dad carrying the beach umbrella under one arm and the larger beach chair under the other. These were the things about going to the beach with five children that Jack didn't think were so much fun. But being with the family was worth it, he thought.

Taking turns rinsing off and cleaning up in the outside shower stall, everyone got dressed and headed either for the partly-finished 5,000-piece jigsaw puzzle of Mount St. Helens on the rickety grey card table, the Xbox controls in the living room by the large, flat-screen TV, or a glass of Mom's famous homemade lemonade around the kitchen table.

Later, Connie got the attention of the whole clan. "Listen, kids. Dad has some work to do on his sermon for Sunday. So how about we head out to the city park down the street? We can watch the planes take off and land at the airport. We might even get a chance to play some miniature golf on the way back if anyone wants to risk losing to their mother." Some jeers and guffaws erupted in the living room. "Okay then. Let's get a move on. Last chance for a bathroom stop before we head out for the afternoon."

"Thanks, guys," said Dad. "Have fun. And be nice to your mother," he called after the departing children. "She really needs to win." Ducking a decorator pillow thrown in his direction, Jack went off to gather his files and finish his sermon preparation.

In the quiet of a house where he was now the only resident, Jack began to think about the task ahead of him as he spread out his notes on the dining room table. No one was more amazed than Pastor Jack when he preached a sermon each week that touched the hearts and minds of the congregation.

He loved to preach. To him, it was clear evidence, inwardly and outwardly, that God was real and speaking through him. To know that God would breathe His Word through the pastor every Sunday by the work of the Holy Spirit was truly awe-inspiring. Jack thought back over the years that he'd had the privilege of preaching the Word of God and challenging people to apply its principles in their daily lives. Countless pictures of changed lives filtered through his mind.

"Oh, boy," he said aloud to himself after a long time of traveling down the road of many memories, "enough reminiscing. Connie and the kids have given me this precious alone time to get my message finalized. I need to get to it."

Jack opened the file with his notes and began to pray for this unique preaching opportunity. Sometime later, as he wrapped up his preparation, he once again trusted that God would speak through him this Sunday and touch hearts once again, all to His glory.

The only question would be if any pulpit committees would attend. And if they did, would they think this was the kind of preaching they wanted for the people of their seeking congregation?

Chapter 3

THE NEUTRAL PULPIT

It was a common practice that was very familiar to Jack. When a pastor sensed that God wanted him to move on to another area of ministry, arrangements could be made for him to preach in a nearby "neutral pulpit." This was a congregation where the local minister would allow a seeking pastor to preach in his pulpit so that committees from congregations in the area who were seeking a pastor could come and hear him.

They were called "pulpit committees" because they were representing their church in trying to find a new pastor. If they were so inclined, these committees could make arrangements following the worship service to interview the prospective pastor in the near future.

The entire Whyte family was up very early in preparation for Sunday morning worship, looking forward to the drive from New Jersey to Pastor Jack's neutral pulpit at Trinity Church in Overland, Pennsylvania. Connie, in her amazingly efficient way, had everyone dressed and ready to go following a substantial breakfast of scrambled eggs, toast, bacon, and orange juice.

Almost all of the children were looking forward to another new adventure, a new worship experience, and a taste of different Sunday school classes. The only holdout seemed to be five-year-old Suzy. She was a bit hesitant about going into a new Sunday school class with people she didn't know.

After some tender conversations between Suzy and her parents, it was decided to play it by ear. When the children were allowed to leave the worship service for Sunday school, if Suzy was still a bit skittish, she could stay in the service by her mother's side and listen to her dad preach the sermon. But she would not be allowed to be "fidgety." This seemed to please everybody, so all seemed ready for the trip to Overland.

Everyone piled into the van, and Dad started the car for the three-hour drive to Trinity Church on the corner of 4th and Main. Jack asked Connie to pray for their safe travel and the Lord's hand upon all they did that day. Almost immediately after moving out of the driveway, the children began to sing their favorite Sunday school songs and choruses. This made the trip go much faster, although the children had fun joking with their dad and taking turns asking, "Are we there yet?" followed by lots of giggles.

It was a beautiful, early summer day. The traffic was not bad. The scenery was awesome. As they entered the hills and valleys of the southeast Pennsylvania countryside, kids and adults all pointed out the wonder of so many shades of green that seemed to be painted across the fields...corn stalks just tasseling and cabbage plants and bushes of green beans.

The apple orchards were beyond the pretty flower bud stage, and fruit was beginning to appear where the buds used to be. There were early-bird families, apparently skipping church, taking advantage of farms where they could pick sweet and tart cherries. A sign announced strawberries could also be harvested.

The Whyte children began to imagine how good strawberry shortcake might taste with some fresh pickings from the fields and cold milk poured over fresh-baked and aromatic biscuits. When Megan asked if they could have such a tasty treat for dinner, Connie said, "Let's see how things unfold this afternoon. Maybe we'll come across a good Pennsylvania Dutch restaurant where they're sure to have strawberry shortcake."

Dad and all five children cheered at the mention of such a wonderful possibility. That sounded even better than sugarplums dancing in your head at Christmas time...whatever sugarplums are.

With good traffic and a trusty GPS, the van pulled into the parking lot of Trinity Church fifteen minutes earlier than expected. And they only had to make one "potty stop" along the way, evidence that a day of miracles was developing before them.

Dad called out as the van came to a stop, "God is good." And the rest of the family shouted back, "All the time!" That prompted Dad to repeat, "All the time," which was followed by six enthusiastic voices, "God is good!"

"Okay, gang," he continued. "Let's find out where we're supposed to go. They're expecting us, so I'm sure someone will come to greet us."

Just then, a distinguished-looking gentleman approached them with a welcoming smile on his weathered face. He was dressed in a stylish suit, white shirt, and paisley tie and walked with an air of authority, his wavy head of gray hair shining in the summer sun.

"Good morning," he said with a booming voice, sounding almost like a news anchor on TV. "Welcome to Trinity Church. You must be the Whyte family. I noticed the Connecticut license plate on your van."

Reaching out a warm hand to Pastor Jack and then Connie, he continued, "I'm Stan Winfield, the senior pastor of Trinity. We're so happy you're here. I'm looking forward to getting to know you and also to hearing your message, Pastor Whyte. My, what a good-looking family!"

"Thank you," said Jack. "We're all looking forward to our time with you and your people this morning."

"The feeling is mutual," responded Pastor Winfield. "So let me tell you what the schedule is for the day. Would that be okay?"

"Yes, please," said Connie. "The children are looking forward to Sunday school classes."

"Well, that's going to be a problem," said the pastor, "because Sunday school began fifteen minutes ago."

Disappointment appeared on the faces of all the children...except Suzy.

"Oh dear," replied Connie, "I thought Sunday school took place at the same time as the worship service."

"I guess we didn't get the right information to you folks, and I'm truly sorry about that. But the news isn't all bad. Although Sunday school is in progress right now, we do have what we call 'children's church.' After an opening time of singing, reading Scripture, and sharing announcements, we excuse the younger children for a time of Bible stories, arts and crafts, and snacks while we remain in the sanctuary for the morning message. Does that sound like a good plan?"

Positive nods and smiles were the reactions to this new information.

"Okay then, let me show you around and introduce you to a few key people." As they moved up the elegant marble steps, through two towering oak doors, and into the huge brick edifice called Trinity Church, seven Whytes in tow, Pastor Winfield continued to chat with them. "My wife, Joan, is looking forward to meeting all of you, and she will be able to do that as soon as she finishes teaching her third and fourth-grade classes."

His informative commentary continued as this eight-person entourage moved through the hallways of the church building. Along the way, the pastor would point out items of interest and occasionally introduce a key person they met.

The tour ended in Pastor Winfield's sprawling office. A large mahogany desk was situated on the far wall in front of a picture window that offered a view of a well-kept, tree-lined cemetery yard situated behind the church building on a slightly raised hill. Built-in shelves lining two of the office walls overflowed with hundreds of tomes in various sizes and colors. Two office chairs faced the front of the pastor's desk. A small, upholstered sofa and matching chairs gathered comfortably around a rectangular table to the right of the door through which the wide-eyed family had entered.

"Make yourselves comfortable," offered the pastor and tour guide. "If you would like something to drink, we have a kitchenette next door for water or juice or a cup of coffee."

"Thank you. That would be very nice," said Pastor Jack. And then to his wife, "Connie, would you mind taking care of that for the children while Pastor Winfield and I go over the details of the service?"

"Not a problem," smiled Connie as she began quietly taking orders from the children for refreshments.

Sometime later, everyone had consumed some tasty fruit juice and made one more essential use of the pastor's private restroom. Things were ready for the transition from the ornate but warm office to the glorious sanctuary on the second floor of Trinity Church.

Connie and the children sat together near the front of the worship center but not all the way up front. They wanted to situate themselves where they could watch members of the church in the pews in front of them to know when to stand and when to sit down during the service.

Twenty-five minutes into the service, instructions were given for children eleven and younger to head off to children's church. To no one's surprise, Suzy chose to stay with her mother to hear the message her father had prepared for the morning.

Connie made a swift but careful visual sweep of the congregation. She took in the faces of the hundreds in attendance, ranging in age from young teens to those who appeared to be in their seventies or eighties. She wondered if, indeed, there were among them one or more pulpit committees waiting to hear her husband preach his sermon. More than that, she wondered if any of them would ask to interview him as a candidate for pastor of their congregation.

She might be biased, but Connie couldn't imagine any people who would not be impressed with the content and style of her husband's sermons. Connie, Suzy, and Johnny all bowed in prayer as the patriarch of their family stepped into the pulpit to share God's Word with the people.

After the service concluded, the two pastors left the sanctuary to greet folks at the big oak doors that opened onto Main Street. Connie took Johnny and Suzy to help round up their three siblings and join their father at the front door. The children always enjoyed hearing how much people liked their father and the way he preached. They were proud of him.

When the hubbub had died down, and only the Whyte family and Stan and Joan Winfield were left in the doorway, Jack thanked his gracious hosts for their help and hospitality.

Going down the steps and out onto the sidewalk, Jack and Connie looked at one another with question marks written on their faces. "No pulpit committees came to talk to you or asked about you while you were shaking hands?" asked Connie.

"Nope, no one."

"Oh, dear. That's odd, isn't it?"

"Very odd. Maybe they didn't like what they saw and heard."

"I can't believe that, Jack. Your message was powerful."

Just then, they noticed a group of five nicely-dressed people making their way up the sidewalk toward the family. Jack and Connie glanced and smiled at one another. Maybe this was the pulpit committee that wanted to talk to them. But, as they approached, they made no eye contact with the Whytes and moved on quickly to their car in the church parking lot. An empty feeling came over Jack and Connie as the group passed them by. Hope was replaced by disappointment.

Then, out of the corner of his eye, Jack saw a couple standing in the shade of a large maple tree to his right. When he turned and caught their eye, the couple, probably in their thirties and dressed nicely, came walking up to the Whytes.

The man said with a slight Pennsylvania Dutch accent, "Hi. My name is Pete Geisinger. My wife and I liked what we saw. We were pleased with what you said and the way you presented yourself and your message. We're interested in you. We're from Grace Church in Weaverton, and if you're interested in us, we would like you to meet with our committee for an interview."

A big grin spread across Pastor Jack's face as he glanced at Connie and marveled at how quiet his five children had remained. "Mr. Geisinger, I am very much interested in having an interview with your committee. How about I give you my cell phone number? We're presently on vacation in Ocean City and will be there for two more weeks before returning to Connecticut. If you can arrange a time for an interview in the next two weeks, I would be happy to drive to Weaverton and meet with your committee."

"Sounds good," said Pete. "I'm sure we can work something out. There is one thing you can do to help speed up the process. Does your church have a website with an archive of your previous sermons? I want our committee to see why I think you're an excellent preacher and a good candidate for Grace Church."

Handing him a business card, Pastor Jack said with a smile, "Thank you for your encouraging words, Mr. Geisinger. You can find my cell phone number and our website listed on this card. We look forward to hearing from you."

"Yes, thank you very much," added Connie.

With a warm handshake and smiles all around, the Geisingers and the Whytes headed for their cars with the possibility of new relationships and many future adventures racing through their minds.

When his family was all settled and buckled up in the van, Jack said, "Lord, we thank You for what You have in mind for our family and our future with You. Thank You that only one committee spoke to us. That sure makes the decision a lot easier. Lord, we trust You to take care of all the details. If You want us at Grace Church in Weaverton, that is where we want to be. We trust You to make the way clear. We pray in the name of Jesus. Amen." And the whole family said, "Amen."

"Soooo," began Jack, "I remember passing a Pennsylvania Dutch restaurant on the way this morning. Anyone interested in Sunday dinner with strawberry shortcake for dessert?" The cheers of one wife and five children reverberated in the old van. "Okay, let's go, then. Lord, lead the way."

Chapter 4

GRANDMA AND GRANDDAD ARRIVE

After a great dinner served family-style and delicious strawberry shortcake, the Whytes piled into the van and headed down the road for the long return trip to Ocean City, New Jersey. Most of the children slept on the way.

Jack and Connie rehearsed all the events of the day in quiet tones as the little ones zonked out in the comfort of the van's rear bucket seats. Those who were occasionally awake watched cartoons on the video screen that extended down from the ceiling of the van and listened with headsets so they wouldn't wake their siblings.

A major topic of conversation for Jack and Connie was the next adventure on their agenda. Connie's parents were scheduled to arrive at the Ocean City house shortly before sunset. They figured on their arrival about an hour after the Whyte van entered the driveway of their vacation home. Tight scheduling, but they could make it work.

If tradition could be counted on, Grandma and Granddad Wycliff would very generously treat all nine of them to a seafood dinner at their favorite restaurant, Shells and Such. It wasn't fancy, but the food was plentiful and delicious.

The plan was for Connie's parents to join them for the next seven days. Then, during the last week of their four-week vacation at the shore, Jack's parents would share the sun and fun and games with the children.

Of course, this meant some adjustments with sleeping quarters to make room for grandparents. And that meant Connie, the unrivaled queen of all things domestic, had some work to do for the hour between the family's arrival and the entry of Grandma and Granddad. The children loved both sets of grandparents and were happy to help in the preparation process. It became just one more wonderful adventure for everyone.

Bill and Marilyn Wycliff live in Willowbank, just outside of Salter's Glen in eastern Pennsylvania. You know quickly they are native Pennsylvanians because, when you ask them where they're from, they will say, "Penn-sa-van-ya." They claim only people from outside their home state pronounce the "l."

Bill is a pharmacist and manager of the pharmacy about halfway between Salter's Glen and Willowbank. He has worked there faithfully for more than thirty years. He is a pleasant man with a round face and very little hair. He says his mother was prematurely grey, and his father lost most of his hair early on. He always wondered who would win the race in his own life, grey hair or no hair. Apparently, it was baldness.

He is a big man with a real love for people. Many who have a choice like to go to Bill's pharmacy just because of his personality.

Marilyn and Bill paint an interesting picture as a couple. While Bill is big-boned and tall, Marilyn is five-foot-two with eyes of blue, just like in that old song. They'd been married almost forty years. She has been an emergency room nurse off and on when not tied down while raising three children—Connie and her two older brothers, Tim and Alex.

Bill and Marilyn are very active members of Willowbank Community Church, where Marilyn plays the piano for the opening worship service in the elementary grade Sunday school classes. Bill has been on the governing board of the congregation for the last seven years. In Willowbank, everyone knows the Wycliff family. And the Wycliffs know most of the residents of their small town. In fact, they're related to many of them.

Bill and Marilyn, Grandma and Granddad to the Whyte children, left for Ocean City after their church's late service and a scrumptious Sunday dinner miraculously created by Marilyn and also enjoyed by Tim and Alex and Tim's wife, Julie, who joined them for Sunday school and church. This was a Sunday tradition that had gone on for many, many years. Yes, they had a long drive to Ocean City, but that was not going to get in the way of this treasured Wycliff tradition.

Bill was the travel planner, and he assured everyone that if they stuck to his timeline, they would arrive in Ocean City right on time, as he predicted. Marilyn, the faithful navigator and keeper of the GPS, would do what she could to make sure Bill's prediction became a reality. They loved their grandchildren and were looking forward to seven wonderful days with the Whyte family at the Jersey shore.

It was right around 7 p.m. when Google Maps delivered Bill and Marilyn to the driveway of the Whyte family's July residence. This was the third year Jack and Connie had rented this same old Jersey shore house. The rental cost was shared with both sets of grandparents.

It was a two-story, wood-siding home painted off-white with light blue trim. It had a roomy screened-in porch the family loved to gather on each evening to watch people walk by while they enjoyed soft ice cream from the Kohr's storefront on the boardwalk.

Connie had done her magic with the rearranging of rooms in the big vacation home. That meant all five grandchildren were free to go racing out to the driveway to greet the new arrivals. Amid many squeals and hugs and kisses, the nine family members walked and skipped and jumped into the house, where everyone collapsed on the comfy sofas and chairs in the huge living room.

"We can take your luggage to your rooms after we have a chance to sit and relax for a few minutes," decided Jack.

"What about our regular annual trip to Shells and Such for dinner?" asked Bill.

"To tell you the truth," said Connie, "we all had a really late and very big dinner this afternoon, topped off with strawberry shortcake." This was accompanied by big smiles and the nodding of many heads in agreement. "We'd be happy to postpone Shells and Such until tomorrow evening if that's okay with you guys," suggested Connie.

"That would be more than okay," said Bill. "Your mother outdid herself with an amazing dinner after church today. We'd probably be better off avoiding another big meal this evening."

"I agree," piped in Marilyn. "Who would like to go to MacDonald's instead? It's getting rather late."

This suggestion was greeted with many versions of "yeah!" from all five children.

"How about this," proposed Connie. "Let's put together an order for MacDonald's. Then Daddy can bring back our order, and we can eat here while filling you guys in with a recap of today's adventure at Trinity Church in Overland."

"Sounds good to me," said Bill. "Jack and I can go on a food run while Marilyn and Connie get us settled in. How does that sound to everyone?"

———————•———————

It was in the middle of sharing the events of the day and the French fries of the evening that quite suddenly, without explanation, Bill got up from the big dining room table and went into the living room to lie down on the big over-stuffed and slightly worn sofa. Everyone but Marilyn was quite surprised.

"What's wrong, Dad?" said a very concerned Connie while every member of the Whyte family had a quizzical expression on their faces.

"Oh, he does this regularly, maybe five or six times a year," interjected Marilyn with surprising calm.

"Does what?" asked Connie a bit loudly, her forehead scrunched together with obvious concern. She noticed that her father had said not a word but just lay down on the sofa and proceeded to apparently go to sleep immediately. Or was he unconscious?

"Just let him alone for a few minutes," requested Marilyn. "For some unknown reason, about a half dozen times a year, he feels light-headed and has to lie down. And as you may have thought, he actually passes out and wakes up after a few minutes, rather tired but no worse for the wear."

"Isn't there something we can do?" asked Jack, feeling rather helpless.

"Have you seen a doctor about this?" added Connie.

34

"Of course we have," said Marilyn. "But after many tests, we still are not sure what the problem is. It doesn't seem to be a seizure. You can see he's very peaceful through it all. We tried changing his diet to see if he was having problems with low blood sugar. We just continue to pray that we'll find an answer soon. In the meantime, we're praying for God to heal Bill."

"But what if this happens while he's driving the car on the interstate with all kinds of traffic around? He could be hurt if he passes out, or even worse," questioned Connie, obviously not yet comforted by her mother's explanation of her father's medical condition. "As a nurse, you may not be concerned about this situation. But I am very concerned."

"I'm *very much* concerned too, but also trying to adjust to this mystery. You see, Dad is 'prodromal.'"

"What in the world is prodromal?"

"It's a unique condition in such events as these that allows the patient to know ahead of time when an event is about to take place. Just now, your dad knew he was about to pass out, so he had plenty of time to get up from the table, walk to the sofa, and lie down so he wouldn't fall and be hurt or harm anyone else. If this were to happen on the highway, he would have plenty of time to pull to the side of the road, park the car, and wait for the event to pass by. Afterward, he would be just slightly tired but in full control of his faculties. These events have never occurred without a few minutes' warning. It's almost like God is protecting him from harm until we get the answers we're looking for."

"Do you think it's his heart?" asked Connie.

"We don't know for sure. You see, since this only happens rarely, it does no good to wire him for a monitor because it could be months before it happens again, and those devices are designed for short-term monitoring."

Jack asked, "How long has this been going on? Why haven't you told us about this before?"

"Bill didn't want to worry you. There was nothing you could have done anyway."

"Well, we could have been praying," corrected Connie.

"That's true," said a quiet voice from the living room sofa, "but I just didn't want to worry you. Now, I hope no one ate my French fries while I was away for a few minutes," bantered Granddad as he rose from the sofa and made his way back to the dining room table, apparently ready to continue on as though nothing had happened.

"Well, I must say you have certainly seemed to adjust to something I still have a lot of questions about," noted Connie with continuing concern.

"We can talk more about this as the week moves on. But for now, I would like to finish my fries and get ready for bed. I'm a little tired," quipped Granddad.

Throughout this grown-up conversation, the grandchildren had been looking back and forth between their parents and their grandmother and glancing with deep concern at the grandfather they loved so much. There was a lot of whispering, but they seemed to sense that being quiet was the best thing to do.

After a few sighs of relief, accompanied by more unspoken and unanswered questions, everyone committed themselves to the bedtime transition...after Granddad finished his cold French fries.

After the children had all brushed their teeth and said evening prayers with their dad, particularly talking to the Lord on behalf of Granddad, and were tucked in for the night, Jack and Connie sat on the king-sized bed in the master bedroom and spoke quietly to one another. "Are you as upset as I am?" asked Connie.

"Absolutely," answered Jack, "but all we can do right now is pray about this, put it in the Lord's hands, and ask a lot more questions tomorrow."

"I guess you're right," said Connie, wiping a few tears from her eyes as she chose to pray herself to sleep.

Chapter 5

MORE QUESTIONS, MORE SUN, MORE FUN

Connie woke up praying. *Hmm*, she thought, *I fell asleep praying, and now I wake up praying. I wonder if the Lord was helping me pray through the whole night. Hmm. Something to think about. Is that even possible? I'll have to ask Jack what he thinks about that.*

She rolled over to look at her husband. His eyes were closed, but she was sure he was awake. Over all these years together, she was confident by listening to his breathing that she knew whether he was asleep or just resting. She reached out to Jack, put her arm around his waist, and rested her head on his chest. She always felt a sense of peace in this position, even protected.

When Jack put his arm around her shoulder, she felt free to talk to him, particularly about the conversation with her father that had been cut short the night before. "I'm really upset about my dad's condition, Jack. I really don't know what to do about it."

She loved talking to her husband with her head on his chest. In her mind, she liked to call this her head-to-heart chat because she could actually hear his heart beating while listening to his voice.

"I'm concerned, too," he replied, "but I'm not sure we can do more than pray about it at this point. Besides that, praying is the most important thing we can do anyway."

"I know. I just wish I could do something more. I need to have more information about this whole thing before it drives me crazy."

"Listen," counseled Jack. "I can smell coffee brewing right now. That means your mother is probably in the kitchen doing her usual thing and getting everything together for breakfast. Why don't you throw on your robe and join her? If she's alone, maybe you can get more information from her before the rest of the family gets up.

"If some of the kids are already there, you can at least make arrangements

37

to have a one-on-one conversation with her after breakfast. If that's the case, I'll keep your dad and the kids busy so you can have some private time with your mother. How does that sound?"

"I love you, Jack Whyte. You always have a way of making things simple. One more reason I love you. Okay, I'm heading for the bathroom and then to the kitchen."

"Don't forget your bathrobe," joked Jack with a grin on his face. He was quickly struck with a bed pillow. "Why do I always get hit with pillows these days? Is that any way to treat someone you said you loved?" At that moment, he felt a wet washcloth land on his face.

"Is that better?" laughed Connie as she scurried out to the kitchen before Jack could retaliate.

Well, at least her spirits are lifting a little. A definite improvement. Then he smiled and headed for the bathroom to get ready for a new day with the family, praying that things would go well for everyone. He was sure they would. *If I could arrange for a round of golf with my father-in-law,* he thought, *maybe I could make some headway about this whole medical thing. Something to pray about. The Lord is good about making things work out for the good of everyone who sincerely loves Him. Hmm. I guess I'm preaching to myself. I think that's better than talking to yourself. Or is it? Hmm.*

Downstairs in the big kitchen, Connie was chatting with her mother while looking for an opening to talk about her dad. *Good, there's no one else around. Maybe I can make some inroads into this whole thing with Dad,* thought Connie. But just then, the three girls came squealing into the kitchen, still in their PJs but ready for breakfast and chatting about some more fun at the beach.

Well, there goes Plan A, thought Connie. *I'll just take Jack up on his offer to give me some alone time with Mom while we clean up after breakfast. We should have plenty of time before getting ready to head off to the beach.*

"Okay, girls, I can see you're looking forward to some goodies, and right now, Grandma is getting things ready for breakfast. So, could you go and make sure your brothers are up and moving? As much as they like to eat, I'm surprised they haven't already beat us into the kitchen." Giggles erupted from the girls. "Grandma said Granddad is up and getting dressed right now, so we should be ready to eat in about a half hour."

"We'll make sure they're awake," tittered Sarah, "one way or another." And with that and more giggles, they ran up the stairs to the boys' bedroom.

"I hope the boys are awake," Connie said to her mother. "If they're not, I can only imagine what the girls will do. I think some tickling may be on the agenda."

"That sounds like something I remember you did to your brothers when you were the girls' age." Connie just smiled and went back to the refrigerator to help round up some things for the breakfast prep.

Marilyn had already put the ingredients in a greased 9x13-inch glass baking dish for her famous bacon, egg, and cheese breakfast casserole. Placing the treat in a 325-degree oven, it was already one-third of the way to serving time. She was cleaning up measuring cups and spoons, mixing bowls, a cutting board, and a few necessary knives, forks, and spoons. They would be washed in the double sink, dried, and out of the way in no time at all.

Grandma did not like any evidence that preparation had taken place in her kitchen. There would only be the finished product in sight when the family sat down to enjoy her culinary efforts. Just one of her wonderful idiosyncrasies.

Meanwhile, Connie got out her favorite cutting board and placed it on the kitchen counter. She used the sharpest paring knife she could find to fix the family's most-often-requested Hatfield smoked sausage. Having carefully unwrapped the packaging from the meat, she sliced it into quarter-inch segments to *sauté* in a large no-stick fry pan. When the sausage circles began to sizzle, and the delicious aroma wafted throughout the house, happy olfactories and busy salivary glands announced privately to each family member that it was almost time to eat.

When everything was served along with orange juice and buttered toast, followed by a prayer of gratitude by Granddad, the dining room became very quiet. At first, all one could hear was the clinking and scraping of silverware on dishes and the grateful utterances of very satisfied diners. Soon, however, a conversation began between breakfast bites. The main subject of the conversation centered on the upcoming events of the day.

When tummies were patted with happy satisfaction and words of gratitude bubbled across the dining room table, Connie made an important announcement. "Okay, everyone. Now that you have all had your fill, you know the routine. You have over an hour now to read or play or just chat contentedly before we go to the beach around ten o'clock. Make sure during that time that you have washed up, brushed your teeth, put your rooms in order, and put on your bathing suits. That means everyone."

A comical groan was heard coming from the lips of Bill Wycliff. "Ahhh, do I really have to?" he whined.

Everyone laughed, and Connie assured him, "Yes, Granddad, 'everyone' even includes honored grandfathers."

"Oh, Okay," responded her father with mock disappointment.

Amid the sound of titters and cheers, Connie went on, "Grandma and I will give all the children a vacation from cleaning up the dishes on this one day, and we'll take care of that ourselves."

At this announcement, laughter turned to joyful cheers as the children congratulated each other for Mommy's grace being poured out upon them. Of course, they didn't know it was not all grace. Connie was setting things up for her anticipated private chat with her mother about her dad's medical situation.

Jack and Connie quietly shared a knowing nod. Anyone who caught that glance would interpret it as Dad simply agreeing with Mom. Only Jack and

Connie knew they were acknowledging that the plans laid while in bed this morning would soon come to fruition.

Plan B was operational. So that Connie could spend uninterrupted time with her mother in the kitchen, Jack accepted the responsibility of keeping everyone else out of that room and busy with some fun things. That assignment proved to be one of the easiest ever given to him.

Suzy was the Whyte family's wonderful surprise, arriving after four planned children. She teamed up with her nine-year-old sister Megan in their bedroom on the second floor. They wanted to finish a game of Chutes and Ladders they were working on.

When given the opportunity to choose an activity for the morning before heading off to the beach, Paul, their seven-year-old, opted for playing video games. Mom and Dad thought some occasional video activity was okay but were definitely against any long-term involvement with Xbox.

So when Paul said he wanted to do just that, and Dad gave his approval, the boy was thrilled. Of course, Jack was thinking, *Good, that will keep him occupied and out of earshot of the kitchen conversation while he's busy in the boys' bedroom.*

That left Granddad and the two oldest children. Jack handled that easily enough when he challenged all three to a game of tossing beanbags at the cornhole boards in the backyard. Who would be better? The kids' team of Johnny and Sarah, or the adult team of Dad and Granddad? They all jumped at the opportunity and took up the challenge.

Meanwhile, Connie and her mother rounded up the dirty dishes and put them in the double sink. They cleaned up the serving bowls, scooping and scraping the leftovers into refrigerator dishes, and tried to find space in the crowded refrigerator for all those leftover goodies. They wiped off the big oak dining room table into which they had inserted two expansion sections to accommodate all nine family members and lots of food.

Now they were washing the empty serving dishes and the few dirty cooking pots and pans that Grandma had not already cleaned and put away when she finished her part of the breakfast preparation. In this relaxed atmosphere at the big farmhouse double sink, hands in soapy water and dish towel ready for drying, it was natural for Connie to ask her mother some important questions.

"So, tell me, Mom, what is really going on with Dad? How bad is this thing he's dealing with? I've been really stressed out ever since he went to lie down and apparently passed out on the sofa last night. What's going on? What are you doing about it? As a nurse, I would think you would be on top of this."

"I am on top of it," Marilyn calmly responded. "You don't think I would just let this slip on by, do you?"

"Well, you seemed so nonchalant about it last night. I was beginning to wonder what was going on. What doctors have you gone to? Who did you consult with? What kind of treatment have you started?"

"We've met with three different specialists about your father," responded Marilyn patiently. "But we haven't begun any treatment yet because they're not sure what's going on. None of the tests have shown them what's causing him to pass out about a half dozen times a year. And I'm not being nonchalant about this. I'm probably more distressed about it than you and your father combined. This is the man I've loved for so many wonderful years, and the thought of losing him so young scares the daylights out of me."

She paused to wipe away some quiet tears from her cheeks with the dish towel. "I have lost sleep over this, especially because the doctors don't seem to know what to do about it. We've existed on prayer and words of encouragement for one another for many months now. If it were not for our faith in God, I don't know what we would do."

"I'm sorry, Mom. I didn't mean to doubt you or your commitment to Dad. It's just that I'm scared too. And the whole incident last night has me really upset." Then the tears that had started in bed last night began to flow again. At this, mother and daughter hugged one another with a love that can only be felt in such a long and caring relationship.

When the sobs quieted down, Marilyn stepped back and said, "I will tell you about something we just learned last week. We were contacted by the medical team at Johns Hopkins Medical Center in Baltimore. They're leaning toward Dad's problem being related to the heart. But, as we said last night, since these events happen so randomly and so rarely, the usual heart monitor is not a practical way to get to the crux of the problem. They told us about another piece of technology that they believe will help uncover the hidden causes that have so far evaded them."

"Oh, good. A little light to shine on this whole mess," sighed Connie.

"That's what we think, too. It's called an 'event monitor.' With all the wireless technology that's available today, especially in small packages, they believe this event monitor will do the trick. It's a small electronic package about the size of an iPhone. On its back are four electrodes to receive information from the heart. Once they deliver this device to us, scheduled for next week, Dad will have to carry this with him wherever he goes. It will fit easily in his shirt or pants packet."

"So, how does it work?"

"It's called an event monitor because you only use it when an event takes place. And it only works for people who are prodromal because you have to know ahead of time that an event is imminent. It's almost as though it were created just for your dad. What your father will do when he feels this light-headedness coming on is to sit or lie down, preferably lie down, if possible, take the monitor out of his pocket, and reach inside his shirt to place it on his bare chest.

"The electrodes will pick up the signals from his heart. When he regains consciousness, he will call the phone number on the front of the monitor and send the info that was just recorded to a special receiver at the hospital. Hopefully, then we will know better and maybe definitively what exactly is the root of Dad's condition."

With a flicker of hope reflected on her face, Connie said, "That does sound promising. It gives me a little peace, anyway."

"Don't forget, this will not mean we'll have an answer next week. Remember how rarely these events take place. It could be months till it happens again. Or he could have another spell in a week or two. We just never know. Let's just keep praying for his protection until we have some real answers. Okay?"

"Okay, Mom. Thanks for taking the time to talk to me about this. It means a lot."

"Hey," said Marilyn, changing the subject, "isn't it about time to get ready for the daily trek to the beach? And by the way, I have never experienced such a quiet house in my life. Where is everybody?"

"To be honest, that's the result of Jack's plan."

"His plan? What plan?"

"The plan of keeping everybody busy with some activity somewhere else in the house so you and I could have this dedicated time for an uninterrupted conversation about Dad. And the kids were happy to avoid doing breakfast clean up anyway."

"Well, he certainly did a good job of carrying out his plan, I must say. So, do you think we can tear everyone away from whatever Jack has them doing so we can head to the beach? I can't wait to dip my feet into the Atlantic Ocean. It's been a year since I last did that."

"I don't think that will be a problem at all," smiled Connie, the first contented smile on her face since yesterday. "Thanks again, Mom." And they hugged once more.

While everyone got ready to head to the beach, in the privacy of their bedroom, Connie had a chance to review with Jack the conversation she'd had with her mother. With happy hugs and encouraging words, they held hands to thank God for good news and prayed for good reports and even the healing touch of the Lord.

Things at the beach followed their usual routine. There was fun in the ocean and in the sand. There was the usual ritual of spraying and spreading sun protection. There was the usual fly-by of an old airplane towing a banner advertising the latest sale at some shop or other. And when the cart filled with tasty popsicles worked its way up the shore, everyone was treated to their favorite confection.

Much of the conversation seemed to swirl around the evening meal to take place at Shells and Such. Each family member had his or her usual order. And having this celebration deferred since last night made each child and adult look forward to this repast even more than usual.

Besides, there was not a member of the family, from Grandma to little Suzy, who wasn't happy that Granddad seemed to be doing so well. In fact, he appeared to be his usual lively self. There was a lot of praising God in addition to the swimming and relaxation that morning.

Chapter 6

How They Got Together

The rest of the week was busy with fun, sun, and wonderful family time. Even the torrential rain on Thursday and Friday did not dampen their spirits. Hurricane Horace had worked its way out of the South Atlantic and up the Eastern Coast of the United States. It never made landfall, but some of the spaghetti models from the weather bureau warned that it was always a possibility.

All that rain meant that very few efforts were made to leave the summer house except for Jack's regular roundtrips to the grocery store. Picking up needed items from the store was an easy task for him because he went to the store almost every day for something...and not just while on vacation. This practice seemed to be a regular responsibility at least three times a week at home. But Jack never complained about it.

First of all, he thought it was cheaper for him to food shop by himself. He claimed it always cost more when Connie went along. She usually found a number of items to buy that were not on the store list they created.

Jack also liked to joke that these forays into the world of mass consumption were the closest thing to going out into the woods with a bow and arrow to bring home wild game for his wife to cook for the family. Of course, Jack had never gone wild game hunting in his entire life, nor would he ever want to, but it was fun to tease everyone with this delightful image.

Even hurricanes could not stop those necessary jaunts to the produce aisles of the local Acme Market. For Jack, it seemed like going food shopping was a way of life. *What would I do*, he wondered, *if those forays ever ceased?* Oh my. Sad to consider.

All the rain brought something no one expected. Although it was the third week of July, usually a fairly hot month in New Jersey, the rain and clouds so effectively hid the sun that it became quite chilly. What a wonderful excuse to light a fire in the functioning wood fireplace in their cozy Ocean City living room.

So that's what they did on Friday evening. This would be Grandma and Granddad's last evening before returning to Willowbank on Saturday afternoon.

That day, part of Jack's store order included hot dogs and rolls. He also bought marshmallows, graham crackers, and Hershey's milk chocolate squares in anticipation of making s'mores as they gathered around the fireplace. Fortunately, the owner of the rental property had a well-stocked garage, including all that was needed to roast hotdogs and melt marshmallows...or burn them in the case of the younger children.

While s'mores were usually made on the grill in the backyard, this year, for obvious reasons, the marshmallow roasting would be attempted in the living room. What fun!

After four adults and five children finished wolfing down some delicious roasted hot dogs as well as Grandma's special New York potato salad, but before the creation of sweet and fattening s'mores, Connie said something that gave a whole new direction to the evening's conversation.

"Jack, do you remember what week this is?" she asked.

"Sure, it's the third week of July."

"And do you remember what happened the third week of July, sixteen years ago?"

It was obvious that Jack was struggling to bring to mind something he was expected to know. In fact, he had the feeling, glancing up at the expectant look on his wife's face, that it would not be good if he did not remember what happened so many years ago. *It isn't her birthday*, he thought.

"Uh oh," said Granddad. "I think it's time for everyone to pray. Someone might be in trouble."

Everyone smiled. Some laughed. Jack thought deeply, and Connie sat mischievously and wide-eyed, enjoying the discomfort evident on her husband's face.

"Let's see," muttered Jack quietly, "sixteen years ago. What happened sixteen...of course. The third week of July, sixteen years ago," he said with obvious relief and even a little bit of pride, "I met the woman I would marry at Fernmill Christian Bible Camp."

"Very good, dear," smiled Connie. "That was the year that my life changed for the better."

"Mine too," laughed Jack. "Mine too."

He reached over to his wife and gave her a warm kiss while all the kids groaned, "Eww."

"Hey, Mom," asked Sarah. "How come you never told us about how you and Dad met?"

"I don't know. Probably because I didn't think you'd be interested in such an old, old story."

"Well, I'm definitely interested."

"Me too," came a chorus of young and old voices.

"Sounds to me," offered Granddad, "like you had better tell us all about it."

"Dad, you already know all the details."

"Well, probably not all the details. But methinks there are five children here who don't know and need to know at least some of those details. What do you think, kids?"

"Yeah, let's hear all about it."

"C'mon, Mom, tell us the story."

"I think there's a unanimous vote here," said Jack. "Why don't you share our story? I'll throw in some details as you talk about that fateful and wonderful week."

"Oh, okay," agreed Connie. "You asked for it." Everyone cheered.

"Just don't give us too many details," teased her father. "We still want to make s'mores before bedtime."

And so began Connie and Jack's favorite story told while the faces of eager children looked with expectancy in their mother's direction. *Boy*, thought

Connie, *I don't often get such undivided attention from my children. I may have to mark this day on my calendar.*

Focusing her attention on the children, Connie began, "Sixteen years ago, I had just graduated from Kutztown University. That's not too far from the church where your dad preached a few days ago. My roommate for all four years of college was Allison Cooper. We became best friends. I guess today some would say she's my BFF."

Sarah and Megan nodded their heads knowingly.

"The summer after we graduated," continued Connie, "Allison invited me to spend a few weeks with her family in Connecticut. It was our way of postponing a difficult goodbye after four years of friendship.

"Part of the deal had to do with summer camp in a beautiful country setting called Fernmill Christian Bible Camp. Allison had signed up for two weeks at camp, the third and fourth weeks of July. She had volunteered to be a cabin counselor, and she knew they could use more help. So if I spent a few weeks with her, I would have to agree to be a cabin counselor as well. And that was fine with me. I loved summer camp when I was a kid."

"You sure did," commented Grandma. "But the first year you attended summer camp, we had to almost bribe you to go because we knew you would love it."

"And after that first year," added her father, "you loved summer camp so much it almost seemed like we had to twist your arm each year to get you to come home."

"And that's why I was happy to agree with Allison. Staying with her sounded like fun. And helping out at summer camp would just be icing on the cake. It was the first day of the first of two weeks at Fernmill that I met this young pastor who was camp director for all of June, July, and August. And I thought he was gorgeous."

"Awwww, Connie," protested a blushing Jack Whyte.

"Well, I did. I still think you're the best-looking guy I know. And sixteen years ago, at that moment, that was all I knew about you. Oh, and that you

50

were a pastor. As Grandma and Granddad know, I always wanted to marry a pastor. So there he was, and I was smitten by him from the get-go. I always enjoyed summer camp. Meeting this guy, I was convinced, was going to make the camping experience even more enjoyable. When Allison introduced me to the man who was to become your dad, she saw the look on my face. And later, she told me she knew something monumental was going to come out of that encounter."

Jack jumped in. "This might be a good time for me to tell my part of this first meeting. Being a young single pastor can be a troublesome thing. You always have a few mothers in the congregation trying to get you to marry their daughters. I was always on my guard when it came to young women. I wanted to be married someday and have a family, but I didn't want just any girl. I wanted the one God had in mind for me. After all, being a pastor's wife can be a difficult job, especially if you don't have the gifts to do that.

"Whenever I acted as director of a summer camp, I knew I would meet some very nice young Christian women. I would be friendly with them, but I was hesitant to get close to any of them. And then I met your mother. All I could say at that time, but not out loud, was 'Wow!' Outwardly, I was Mr. Cool. On the inside, I was jumping up and down and shouting 'Hallelujah!'"

"Did you know right away that you had met your future wife?" asked Johnny.

"Well, son," answered Jack, "I was pretty sure, and I could not wait to see if a relationship would come out of those next two weeks at Fernmill."

"I think we both had similar thoughts at that time," commented Connie. "And I think my friend Allison was picking up on this at the same time. As the weeks progressed, and we talked about it together, I think she was as convinced as I was that I had found the man God wanted me to marry. And he was a pastor! Yay!"

"For the next fourteen days," added Jack, "we got to know each other, our likes and dislikes, our relationship with God, and our hopes and dreams for the future. We just found ourselves feeling very comfortable with one another, even when Mom fell out of the canoe and into Fernmill Lake."

Cutting short lots of laughs and trying to avoid embarrassing questions for more details about the canoe fiasco, Connie quickly picked up her narrative. "My biggest concern was that after two weeks, I was going back to Allison's for a few days, and then I was going back home to Pennsylvania with my parents and my two brothers. It turns out this was a concern for both of us, and we talked about how we would keep in touch and keep this relationship going. Long-distance didn't look like something that would work well. Or at least not something we wanted."

"So what did you do?" asked Megan, totally enthralled with this unfolding story.

"We decided the best thing to do was to pray about it. If this was part of God's plan, we had to trust that we could make something lasting come out of it. If it wasn't in God's plan for us, we didn't want to make the mistake of trying to twist God's arm. But saying goodbye at the end of summer camp was definitely a tearful time."

"Yes," added Jack. "We exchanged addresses, phone numbers, and emails, and we were committed to doing what we could to get together again... somehow."

"Obviously, you worked something out, or we wouldn't be here," noted Sarah. "What happened?"

"Well, as I said," Connie continued. "I'd just graduated from college and had not yet made a decision on what work I would get into. I had a few job offers, thankfully, but I was still praying about that."

"Meanwhile," interjected Grandma, "we are hearing about this perfect young man and how she really thinks he may be the one for her. It was going a little fast for us, and we were trying to make sure she was handling this possible relationship properly and not moving too quickly."

"Well," Connie said, "to make this story a bit shorter, we continued to have long phone conversations. We met each other's parents during occasional Skype chats. And when a few months had passed, and we were more and more convinced this was to be a lasting relationship, with my friend Allison's help,

52

I got a position as a substitute teacher in a Christian school near her home in Connecticut. Conveniently, in God's unique way of making things happen, Allison's family lived less than ten miles from the Connecticut church where your dad was the youth pastor. And her parents invited me to stay with them. Does anyone still believe in coincidences?"

"What were you and Granddad thinking about this," Sarah asked Grandma.

"At first, we were very much concerned. We were also praying together about it. We had long conversations with your Nana and PopPop, who were also in prayer. As events unfolded, we all became more and more convinced that these two were indeed meant for each other. This was God's plan for them! And look at what wonderful things have come out of all of this," noted Grandma as she indicated the children in front of her.

"So that's the story. I hope you enjoyed it," Connie concluded. Cheers went up from the five children. "Looks like the embers in the fireplace are just right for melting marshmallows. Who wants to make s'mores?"

And eight happy people shouted, "Me!"

The next day Bill and Marilyn had to be on their way home. It had been an enjoyable week, and the children were sad to see them go. Yet they knew later that same day, Tom and Janet Whyte, Jack's parents who were known as Nana and PopPop, would be joining them for the last week of their shore vacation.

Grandma and Granddad's departure went smoothly, yet Connie was particularly concerned about her father's unknown health issue and the safety factor as he drove all the way back to Willowbank. All she could do was pray and trust God that they would not receive a distressing phone call.

Chapter 7

WE HAVE A PLAN

Nana and PopPop had settled in. Everyone was enjoying a peaceful time catching up on the latest events in their lives when all of a sudden, the trill of Jack's cell phone interrupted their evening. Everyone turned to the source of the ringing, wondering who it could be. Connie was hoping it was not her mother with bad news.

With quiet determination, Jack answered. "Hello.... Yes, this is Pastor Whyte.... Oh, yes, thank you so much for calling. Could you hold one minute, please? Thank you."

Holding his cell phone to the side, Jack said, "It's okay, everyone, nothing to worry about. It's someone calling from the church in Weaverton. I need to talk to them." An audible sigh could be heard by all.

As Jack continued his conversation on the phone, Connie herded the rest of the family into the living room. *Why would someone call from the church at Weaverton on a Saturday evening? Is this good news or bad news?*

Connie's mind went into high gear while everyone just collapsed on the old, over-stuffed furniture in the living room and chose to relax, wondering what the head of the Whyte family would soon report to them. Quiet conversation was clearly centered around the questions on everyone's minds.

When Jack re-entered the room, every family member stopped where they were, in gameplay or conversation, and looked to him to ask, yet without saying a word, "Okay, what was that all about?"

"That was Pete Geisinger from Grace Church." To his parents, he explained that the family had met Pete and Lucy Geisinger following his preaching opportunity at the church in Overland.

"Pete heads up the pulpit committee. They want us to come to Weaverton for a formal interview about the possibility of becoming their pastor.

Apparently, after interviews with more than a dozen candidates, they were not convinced that any of them was God's candidate for their congregation. They have canvassed all the committee members and their spouses, and the night when most of them could meet with us would be Tuesday, preferably around 6 p.m. in the church parlor."

"What do you think, honey?" asked Connie. "Do you think you should meet with them?"

"No, I think you and I should both meet with them. And I know, Nana and PopPop, you could take charge of the children if we both go, but I don't want to put any kind of workload on you. After all, this is vacation time for you. You didn't come here to do this."

"Don't be silly," said Nana. "Of course, we'll watch the children. Won't we, Tom?"

"You bet! Don't even think about it. We could have a lot of fun together while you're gone. That'll just give us more concentrated time to fulfill our God-given responsibility to spoil our grandchildren rotten." PopPop was always joking about something, and, as usual, everyone had a good laugh about it.

"Well, if this is going to work, we'll have to figure out what food supplies to get in and how we're going to work out the details." Connie, as usual, was already in planning mode.

"Don't you worry about that, Connie. I'm sure we can get all those details worked out with no difficulty," Nana told her.

PopPop chimed in, his eyes lighting up with mischievous excitement. "Hey, I have an idea. How about if Nana and I get together with the kids for a family meeting tomorrow? The subjects on the agenda will be, first, what fun things to do with Mom and Dad out of the way." More laughs from everyone. "And second, what favorite foods do we want to eat when Mom and Dad are not looking." Those laughs turned into cheers.

"You really do plan to step up this grandchild-spoiling mission, don't you?" joked Connie with a smile on her face but also looking to Jack for some kind of support or reaction to his dad's plan.

"Sounds good to me," said Jack. "How many kids are in favor of PopPop's idea?" Of course, all hands went high in the air, accompanied by cheers and giggles.

"Well, okay then, it looks like we have a plan," concluded Connie. And the children began to murmur among themselves about the possibilities they might raise at PopPop's family meeting.

Now the problem is going to be, thought Connie, *how to quiet the children down enough to shift into bedtime mode.* But deep down, she was really happy about this plan. Her first thought, when Jack suggested they both attend the interview in Weaverton, was how the children would react about them leaving for so long. *Of course, it's only going to be an afternoon and evening. And now look at this. God is so good. What I was looking at as being a possible negative has turned into another adventure for the children with Jack's parents. Maybe I worry too much. Ya think?*

Then Jack, the problem-solver, spoke up. "Okay, kids. It's getting kind of late, and I know you have all kinds of things you want to bring up at your special family meeting. But you don't have time to do that tonight. So how about you each take a sheet of paper from the guest tablet on the mantle? Write down two or three things you have in mind to suggest at your meeting with Nana and PopPop.

"Megan, you can help Suzy with writing her suggestions. Put them in that empty cookie jar in the kitchen. By the way, why is that cookie jar empty? Someone needs to do something about that," he said with wide eyes directed toward Nana. "Anyway, take care of that simple project, put your ideas in the cookie jar, and get ready for bed. Sound like a plan?"

"I like the plan except for the going to bed part," groaned seven-year-old Paul.

"Well, it's the only plan we have right now, so let's all do our part. Pens and pencils are in the junk drawer in the kitchen to the right side of the sink. Megan, help out Suzy, please. Go!" And the children scattered.

"You handled that well," Connie told him. "I couldn't have done it better myself!"

"Oh boy, I hope PopPop didn't cause any problems with his idea," said Janet.

"No, the kids will love it! And it has certainly lifted a burden off our shoulders. Don't you think so, Jack?"

"Absolutely! This is going to be fine. I hope the interview goes as well as I think things are going to work out here in our absence."

"Well," said Nana, "I'm sure you're both going to do well. You can be sure the children and we will do our part by praying for you at dinnertime. I have very positive feelings about this, Jack. I would not be surprised if the Lord called you to Grace Church."

"We would like that. Let's see if your feelings become a reality, Mom."

Janet just looked to Tom, who added with a smile, "Son, you know your mother is usually right about these things."

"Yeah, I know. It's almost scary sometimes."

And then the phone rang again. "Oh, no," said Connie. "What now? Lord, please make this another good call."

"Hello," answered Jack. "This is Pastor Whyte.... Oh, hi, Grandma. How was your trip back home...? Glad to hear that. And Granddad is doing well...? Wait just a minute. Your daughter is hitting me on the shoulder and grabbing the phone. I'm turning the phone over to Connie now before she beats me to a pulp," teased Jack. And with that, a long, long, long conversation took place, as can only happen between a mother and her daughter.

—————————•—————————

When all the children had written their requests on tablet paper, they folded them and tucked them into the empty cookie jar on the kitchen counter, returning the pens and pencils to the junk drawer. The adults were having fun watching all the whispering among the children, apparently asking one another what they had written for the family meeting scheduled for tomorrow.

Then it was time to head off to bed. Fortunately, their summer house had two and a half bathrooms. There was almost no shoving among siblings to get to the sink for teeth-brushing and face-washing. When all were in their PJs in their respective rooms, the children spent time reading and whispering, waiting their turn for Dad to come into their rooms for the regular-as-clockwork goodnight tradition.

After Connie said good night to each of the children with a hug and a kiss, Jack made his fatherly rounds. Without fail, unless he was away and Connie had to take on this responsibility, Jack came to each child individually. After a brief, quiet chat about the events of the day, he would have a simple prayer with each child, give them a hug and a kiss, lay his hand on each child's head, and speak a blessing over them.

The children came to expect this tradition, and they loved it. Jack loved it too. The big surprise for him came last year. It was the night Sarah, his eleven-year-old, reached out, placed her little hand on Jack's head, and gave him a blessing as well. Grateful tears ran down his rough cheeks that night as he left the room to tell Connie their kids were growing up rather fast.

Lying in bed later and chatting about everything that was going on in the Whyte family, Connie turned to Jack and said, "I think we have the best kids in the world."

"Me too," said Jack.

"Do you think we're going to have such good kids forever, or should we brace ourselves and be concerned about a time when they're going to cause us trouble?"

"I think we just keep loving them and expecting good things from them and not worry about thoughts like that," suggested Jack. "Let's not question the extravagance of God."

"Sounds good to me, Pastor Jack," whispered Connie with the biggest smile on her face. "You always know what to say to me. Now, what do you have to say to me about Tuesday's meeting at Grace Church? Something that will make it possible for me to sleep tonight."

"I'm not sure I can help you with that. I will probably be awake off and on the whole night as well. I guess the best thing we can do is what we usually do. Apply the eleventh commandment."

"You always say that, Jack. But you're right. We can't worry about this. We've turned it over to the Lord, and we shouldn't try to take it back. We want to go to Grace if that is God's will for us. And if it's not His will, we certainly don't want to go there. I don't want to go anywhere outside of His plan for us."

"Well, then," agreed Jack, "let's turn it over to the Lord one more time. And let's commit ourselves to keeping the eleventh commandment. Say it with me, Connie." And together, they quietly and confidently declared, "Thou shalt not sweat it."

"Now," said Jack, "I would like to snuggle with my wife a little bit while I prepare for a night of as much sleep as the Lord wants to give me."

"I like the way you think, Jack Whyte."

Chapter 8

THE FAMILY MEETING

Every annual vacation in Ocean City included weekly Sunday worship at Chapel By The Sea. It was a small congregation with very few regular, year-round resident members. During the summer, vacationing guest preachers from various states would lead worship for one month at a time. Their remuneration for this preaching ministry was a free vacation at the beautiful church parsonage. The generous offerings received from vacationers made it possible for this little congregation to meet its annual budget.

This month's guest preacher was Pastor Gus Mellon from Akron, Ohio. He was in his late sixties and officially retired from active ministry. But he had been coming to this seaside church for more than two decades and was always invited to return to the pulpit. And that was significant. There was a long line of pastors on a waiting list who would love to take advantage of this opportunity offered each summer.

All nine Whyte family members left Sunday morning worship at Chapel By The Sea with their focus in two directions. It was sort of like the Greek mythological god called Janus with two faces, one looking forward and one looking back (which is where the month of January got its name). They were reveling in the sense of peace they had from a rich time of worship. Pastor Mellon shared an uplifting and challenging message.

The children, each year, had a kind of mini-reunion with other children they knew at the church...those who were Ocean City residents and those who, like the Whytes, came to this same location every year. So, while looking back at the morning church encounters, they were looking forward to PopPop's promised family meeting after lunch and before heading to the beach for some more fun.

Outside the church, with all nine of them squeezed tightly into the extended-body minivan, Jack managed to get everyone's attention. "Okay, everybody. I have an idea. What do you all think about giving the cooks a break today? Instead of eating at our house, how about heading down to the pizza parlor for lunch?" He asked this question with both index fingers poised to protect his ears from the loud screams of agreement he knew would follow his question and bounce around the inside of the van like a mini sonic boom.

Sure enough, there was unanimous agreement with his wonderful idea. Some of the younger children wanted to know if they could go to Chuck E. Cheese instead. Connie informed them there was no Chuck E. Cheese nearby, so that was not an option. Overall, the kids were thrilled about the pizza parlor. They hadn't eaten pizza since their arrival in Ocean City. How could that possibly happen? The cooks were happy to have a break while PopPop sat there wondering to himself, *Who in the world is Chuck E. Cheese?*

———————

Arriving back at the house, with tummies pleasantly sated, everyone went to their rooms to change out of their Sunday best and into their grungies. It was time to shift gears, goof off, and maybe even take a nap (like PopPop usually did) before the family meeting scheduled for around two o'clock.

As two o'clock began to approach, Nana gently nudged PopPop awake and counseled him, "Tom, it's almost time. You'd better get yourself ready for this family meeting you're in charge of. I hope you know what you're doing because the kids are really excited about it."

"Oh, I'm ready," he assured her. "I just have to get this yucky taste out of my mouth. I wasn't snoring, was I? Say, have you got a mint in your purse?"

Janet just smiled, rummaged through her purse, and presented him with a spearmint-flavored Life Saver.

After a quick potty stop, PopPop called all the children together to start their important meeting. Banning Mom and Dad from attending, they gathered on the chairs and sofa in the big living room to get started.

PopPop stood at the fireplace to conduct this special event. Nana was designated as secretary. She was expected to keep a record of the decisions made by the children. Johnny was asked to bring the cookie jar that was stuffed with ideas for Tuesday evening's meal. He placed it on the fireplace mantel where it was easily accessible.

"Well," began PopPop, "how shall we come up with the menu for our special meal?"

"Yes," added Nana, "I'm sure there are a lot of good ideas in this cookie jar. How do we decide which ones to choose? We certainly won't be able to have all of them."

"That's easy," answered Johnny. "We vote. In the Whyte family, each of us kids gets one vote."

"Yeah, we have a mocracy," Suzy proudly announced.

"She means democracy," corrected Sarah with an understanding smile.

"Yeah, that," added Suzy.

With interest and a bit of curiosity, Nana asked, "So when you make family decisions, each person gets one vote?"

"No, just the five kids," answered Johnny. "When just the five of us make a decision, we have a democracy. We each get one vote. When we make family decisions, Mom gets six votes."

"And your father?" asked an intrigued grandfather.

"Oh, he gets twelve votes," responded Paul with a smile.

"Twelve?" said a surprised PopPop.

"Yeah, we have a benevolent doctorship," a proud Suzy explained.

"She means benevolent dictatorship," added Sarah.

"Yeah, that," smiled Suzy.

"We call it the 'Whyte House Rules' for voting," continued Sarah. "Mom and Dad always listen to our opinions. And lots of times we all agree about what to do. But if not, Mom can outvote us, and Dad can outvote all of us and make the final decision."

"Dad says it's one way we can learn that, in life, our heavenly Father always has the final answer," Megan added. "You can't gang up on God and make Him do something that's not right."

"So," responded Nana, "if you five children and your mother get together and agree with your eleven votes on what you want to do, your father's twelve votes always win, right?"

"Right," answered Johnny. But that almost never happens. The Whyte House Rules probably wouldn't work for every family," he added wisely. "But they work for us."

"So if you're really smart," interjected Megan, "you learn to agree with Dad from the very beginning. And he's usually right," she added with a smile.

"And when you agree with God, you know He is always right because He's never selfish," concluded Sarah. All the children knowingly nodded their heads.

"Well, I certainly learned a lesson today. So let's get this 'mocracy' meeting started," PopPop teased.

"That's democracy," corrected Suzy with a smile.

"Right. That's what I meant. Democracy." And with stentorian tones, he bellowed, "Okay, thank you for coming to this significant event in the history of the Whyte family. We are about to experience democracy. Each one will have the opportunity to share ideas about the evening meal and festivities on Tuesday. When we have read all the ideas that are now hidden in this lovely cookie jar, we will vote. The idea with the most votes wins." And then, in his normal voice, he asked, "Are you sure you don't want me to come up with a menu on my own, choose my favorite meal?"

"I don't think so, PopPop," answered Paul.

"You know I was joking about that, don't you?"

"Yeah," they all agreed and giggled a little bit. Well, Johnny didn't giggle. He figured he was too old for that sort of thing. After all, he was thirteen. Almost fourteen. But everyone else giggled. Johnny just smiled knowingly.

"Okay, then," said PopPop. "Let's get started. Nana, why don't you pull out of the cookie jar, one at a time, the ideas that these wonderful citizens have presented? After you read the suggestions, we will have a discussion. And finally, in good democratic fashion, we will vote. Once we've decided on a menu for dinner, we'll have to work together to figure out who is going to do the shopping, who will be involved in food preparation, who will set the table, who will serve the food, and who will be designated to eat the food."

"PopPop!" came shouts from all five children.

"Did I say something wrong?" he asked.

"Yes," said Paul with conviction. "We're all going to eat the food."

"Oh, of course. How could I have made that mistake?" joked PopPop. And so the presentation of possibilities ensued, followed by enthusiastic discussion and concluding with clear decisions. Democracy worked once again. A rather yummy menu for dinner was the result.

Janet had to confess that the meal they came up with was the most bland-looking menu she could imagine. Every item was virtually the same color, with the exception of the beverage. There was a choice of Coke, orange soda, root beer, or 7 Up. The main course was to be chicken nuggets, corn on the cob, and mac and cheese.

It actually wasn't that bad a collection of ingredients. There was meat, although it was breaded and deep-fried. There was a vegetable, and Janet happened to be a fan of New Jersey's famous Silver Queen corn. And who didn't like Kraft Macaroni & Cheese? It's just that it all looked so boring.

Not one child even suggested maybe a pretty, bright green vegetable to add some color to the array. Or maybe some lovely red beets. And a nice green salad was obviously out of the question. But all the children, without exception, were enthusiastic about the menu they had created on their own. Goal accomplished!

PopPop could not have been happier with the whole exercise. He loved it. When all the planning was completed and assignments were made about which child was going to do what in preparation for the Tuesday meal, he was heard to say, "Wow, guys, look at what we have accomplished!" Everyone smiled and cheered. And they still had time to get themselves changed and organized for the short trek to the beach.

When the four adults had a moment together, Janet said, "Your children have been educating us this afternoon."

"What do you mean?" asked Connie.

"They introduced us to the Whyte House Rules for voting."

"Yeah, Jack and I came up with that idea a few years ago. We find it works for us because our 'dictator' is so benevolent," she laughed.

"And the children love it," added Jack. "It's one of the ways we try to bring a kind of order to our family life. We believe children thrive when they know what to expect and what the boundaries are."

"Jack has taught for a long time now that the most important responsibility of parents is to wean their children from them to God," explained his wife. "We want our children to see it as a natural transition to move on from agreeing with and obeying us to doing the same thing with God."

"I must say it's a unique and creative way to live as a family. And your children seem to be quite comfortable with it," commented Tom. "It sure looks like it works for you."

"Yes, it does," agreed Jack. "You know, before we established the Whyte House Rules, and by the way they cover more than just voting, the children didn't seem as sure of themselves. It's kind of hard to explain. Just something we sensed. When Connie and I came up with the rules and announced them to the children, they actually cheered."

"And do you remember, Jack, the comment Sarah made when she came back from visiting her friend Julie?" mentioned Connie. "She said she felt sorry for her friend because they had no rules in their home."

"We're happy to say our special meeting went well," explained Tom, "and we have a plan for Tuesday's meal while you're off on your trip to Weaverton."

"Thanks again for doing that. It's always good to see the children work together on such a project. And we have to admit, having a nice slot of time to ourselves on a Sunday afternoon with no interruptions or responsibilities was a nice bonus. When was the last time that happened?" asked Connie.

As things began to wind down in the evening, thoughts began moving on to the events to come on Monday. What was on the agenda, the children wanted to know. At that point, Nana spoke up. She was always great with the children. Not only was she a caring mother and grandmother, but she was also a fifth-grade teacher at the Bethlehem Christian School for many years.

She started a tradition with her grandchildren that was always highly anticipated every summer vacation. Much research went into what she liked to call The Great Summer Tour that she would plan for the family. They would travel to some unknown location to see something they had never seen before. Apparently, tomorrow was that day.

"Well," said Nana, "I thought tomorrow would be the best time to go on The Great Summer Tour. And let me tell you why. Tomorrow there is going to be a birthday party for a really big elephant. And there are special events at the party for all the children who attend. Does that sound like a good idea to everyone?"

Everyone agreed that it sounded like a great idea, especially nine-year-old Megan, who loved elephants. A tour of her bedroom would reveal lots of pictures of elephants, books on elephants, and a really fluffy, cuddly, cute stuffed elephant who had taken up residence on her bed.

As one might imagine, her favorite movie was the Disney classic, *Dumbo, the Flying Elephant*. Of course, the first time she watched it, she cried a lot at the sad moments of the story. But once she had seen the happy ending, watching subsequent showings of the film was pretty much tears-free.

"So then, are we going to a zoo tomorrow?" asked Megan.

"Oh, no," smiled Nana, "this elephant is much too big to fit in a zoo."

A skeptical Johnny responded, "How is it possible for an elephant not to fit in a zoo? Elephants are big but not that big, Nana."

"I'll tell you all about it tomorrow on the way to the birthday party. You will just have to wait until then."

Some pleading and groaning only caused Nana to grow an even bigger grin on her face. "All I can say is that you will really love this adventure. Until then, my lips are sealed." And she made believe she was inserting a key in her mouth and locking it shut for the night.

"It looks like we're all going to have to wait until tomorrow for this mystery to be solved. When does this grand tour begin, Nana?" asked Connie.

"PopPop and I think we should leave around ten o'clock. Is that okay?"

"Absolutely!" said Jack and Connie together.

"And we can have lunch at the party," PopPop added.

"That settles it, then. Tomorrow we're going to an elephant's birthday party!" concluded Connie. "Now you still have almost an hour until bedtime. That gives you all kinds of time to try and squeeze information out of Nana. But you need to know you will probably have better luck with PopPop. He's a pushover," she laughed. And with that, all five children surrounded Tom on the cushy sofa.

There he sat with his smiling lips sealed tightly and shaking his head from side to side. All the sweet smiles and hugs and kisses used to bribe and convince him to break his silence did absolutely no good. A resolute PopPop kept the mystery intact until tomorrow. And the other adults just sat back and laughed at the scene.

Chapter 9

LUCY'S BIG BIRTHDAY PARTY

As dawn was breaking and the sun was shining brightly on the blue and white house on 5th Street in Ocean City, New Jersey, the only one up and raring to go ahead of the Whyte family children was Janet Whyte. She had already made coffee and was in the process of preparing the batter for buttermilk pancakes with blueberry sauce and syrup. She was sure the smell of coffee would bring the other adults in the house back to consciousness. If that didn't do it, surely the smell of bacon would wake everyone up. And she was right.

The children got up and dressed, quickly washing their faces and brushing their teeth without complaint. They were excited about The Great Summer Tour that Nana had planted in their minds the night before. What was this business about an elephant that was too big to fit into a zoo? And why would there be a birthday party for this gigantic pachyderm? To say the least, the children were intrigued. The adults, not so much.

Of course, Tom already knew what the plans of the day were all about. And because Jack and Connie were familiar with the area and knew about the big attraction in Margate just fifteen minutes up the Atlantic coast on Route 629, they were familiar with this tourist site. But even they didn't know anything about a birthday party for the elephant. So in that sense, maybe they, too, were a bit intrigued.

Once the family had gathered around the big dining room table where Nana had things ready for breakfast, and once Tom thanked the Lord for the generous way He always provides, the hungry children and adults dug into the wonders of Nana's creativity in the culinary front. But they really wanted to know even more about the excursion she had planned for the day. And so, between mouthfuls of pancakes and bacon, the questions began again, almost a continuation of the grilling they had given Tom and Janet the night before.

"What is this great elephant we're going to see?" asked eleven-year-old Sarah. "And how big is it anyway?"

"Yeah," added seven-year-old Paul, "how big is it, Nana?"

Nana gave in. "Okay. I guess I've kept you in the dark long enough. More than a hundred years ago, a man named Lafferty got the unique idea to create a building in the shape of an elephant."

"So, it's not a real elephant?" asked a bit disappointed, elephant-loving Megan.

"No," said Nana, "but it really looks like one. It is grey, has two bright, white tusks, and on top of it is a huge howdah."

"What's a howdah?" Johnny wanted to know.

"It's kind of like a big seat or throne that the rider sits on, sort of like the saddle on a horse, except a whole lot bigger. It even has a canvas roof on top to protect the rider from the sun and the weather. If you lived in India many years ago, this is the kind of sight you might have seen, the ruler of the nation riding on such a glorious pachyderm."

"What is a pakky, uh pakky..." Suzy tried to ask.

"What is a pachyderm? Is that what you wanted to know, Suzy?"

"Yeah, that," she replied.

"Pachyderm means 'thick skin,' so any animal with thick skin is a pachyderm."

"So, an elephant, a rhinoceros, and a hippo would all be pachyderms?" Johnny wanted to know.

"Very good, Johnny," said Nana, now in children-teaching mode. "That's absolutely right."

"So why did this laughing guy make a building look like an elephant?" Megan asked.

"Not laughing guy," smiled Nana. "Lafferty. He was a real estate salesman, a person who sells houses. He wanted to create something that would bring attention to his business. Once he got people talking to him about his elephant building, he figured he had an open door to talk to them about the houses he had for sale. In fact, he could take them up the spiral stairs inside the elephant's one leg to the howdah. There they would have a bird's-eye view of the surrounding houses, many of which he had for sale. Basically, it was a publicity stunt. And it worked."

"So, how big is this elephant? Is it really the biggest elephant in the world?" asked an inquisitive Megan.

"It certainly is," responded Nana.

"How big is 'really big'?" Johnny asked.

"It is six stories high."

"That is a big elephant," proclaimed Sarah.

Suzy wanted to know how tall six stories were.

Nana explained, "If you go outside this house we're in, you can see it's two stories high or about twenty feet. Now imagine two more houses just as tall placed on top of our vacation home, one on top of the other. That's how tall Lucy is."

"Lucy?" asked Paul. "Who's Lucy?"

"That's the name the elephant's owner called her some years ago. You see, after a while, people stopped using the elephant building, and it began to fall apart. Finally, about fifty years ago, a family bought it, decided to rebuild it, and went door-to-door in the town of Margate to get donations to reinforce the wood and tin structure with steel beams.

"In 1970, they carefully put the building on trailers and moved it a few blocks down the street to where it stands today. Since then, to celebrate the rebirth of this huge pachyderm now called Lucy, they have a birthday party with all kinds of fun things for kids to do. It happens each year on July 20th. Does anybody know what day today is?"

"July 20th," proclaimed Johnny.

"Right. And because your four-week vacation is in July this year, this fourth week of July begins with Monday being the 20th. Isn't that great? One of those surprise blessings from God."

"God is good!" proclaimed Jack.

"All the time!" yelled the others.

"All the time," prompted Jack.

"God is good," came the response.

"Who's ready to go celebrate Lucy's birthday?" asked Connie.

"Me!" shouted all the children.

"Well, then, go clean up. Nana, PopPop, and I are going to quickly clean up the breakfast dishes. Jack, if you will get the van ready for our journey to Margate, we'll be ready to go in no time."

"Consider it done," he replied and headed out to the garage to make sure the van was cleaned out and things were in order.

"Do we need to take snacks with us?" Connie asked Nana.

"Oh, no. There'll be plenty of vendors near Lucy to take care of that."

Traffic north on 629 was not bad, but it was almost never good during tourist season. When the travelers approached their destination, they began the adventure of finding a parking place not too far from Lucy. Margate is almost all residential. There are basically no tourist attractions except for Lucy, the elephant. That meant there were no big parking lots and certainly no parking garages. Looking for a parking place was often a bit tricky.

Jack solved that problem in his mind by asking God for a convenient parking place. He would say that he almost always got one that way. When he did, he rejoiced and thanked God. And even when he didn't get a close parking place, he thanked God for the opportunity to get some needed exercise.

The loaded van was still a few blocks away from their destination on Atlantic Avenue when one of the children called out, "Look! There's Lucy!" Everyone maneuvered to get a vantage point to see this amazing sight.

When they were parked not too far from Lucy, Jack had some instructions to share. "Before we hop out and explore," he said, "let's determine that we are going to stick together. Look around you. We're far from the only ones here for the party. If anyone ever happens to get separated from the rest of the family because of the crowds, do not go looking for us. The one thing you will always be able to see is Lucy. Head straight for the big elephant and wait at her trunk. We'll be there quickly to find you. Got it?"

"Got it!" they all shouted.

"Now, once we get near the elephant, we'll see what's available. What should we expect, Nana?" Jack asked.

"Well, we'll be able to climb the stairs up into the elephant, but there will be a long line for that, so we'll have to time that well. Then there are games to play, a miniature golf course to enjoy, and of course, snacks too. But we don't want to spoil our lunch, so we'll have to keep that part under control. We may want to split up into two or more groups, depending on what we all want to do. We have plenty of adults to take charge of a group as we check out the venues. Okay? Let's do it!" And the gang tumbled out of the van and headed in Lucy's direction for her birthday celebration.

After scouting out the area as a group, some decisions were made about who was going to do what. Jack and PopPop took Johnny and Paul for a challenge match of miniature golf. Connie, Nana, and the three girls went to the craft booths to find some handmade souvenirs. On the way back for their prearranged time for lunch, they stopped to watch a clown create funny creatures out of long, skinny, colorful balloons. Suzy was thrilled.

Suzy, the wonderful family surprise, was always full of awe as she took in and seemed to savor all that she saw around her. While Sarah was so much like her good-looking father with his dark brown hair and brown, sparkling eyes, Megan was the perfect image of her mother. She had Connie's dirty-blond hair with natural streaks and bright blue eyes that seemed to penetrate when she was deeply interested in what she was doing or what you were talking to her about.

Sarah was the artistic, creative one, while Megan was the animal lover of the family. If it were up to her, they would have scads of cats and dogs in the house and maybe some goats in the backyard. Her parents would say that, fortunately, it was not up to her.

Suzy was an intriguing combination of both her parents except for her hair which was fine and fly-away and almost white-blond in color. But she had those blue eyes like her mother and Megan and Grandma. You could see in her the seeds of a very aware person who was hungry for more information. Of all the children, she was already showing an ability to think creatively outside the box. Verbally, she was not up-to-speed with her older siblings, but somehow you just knew she would be soon.

The four men of the family had a great time playing miniature golf. PopPop loved sports, and he was good at almost anything that used a ball of any size. He was always in good physical condition, primarily from his work as the owner and full-time manager of his home construction company. He was respected by the six men who worked with him on the job. His most striking physical trait was a full head of wavy hair that was a beautiful color of white, something many older women would pay large amounts of money to have. And his contrasting dark, full eyebrows were kind of like two caterpillars looking at each other.

Jack liked to play most games, from football to Uno, but he didn't seem to have a competitive bone in his body. Connie always said it was frustrating to be on the same team as him. She discovered early in their relationship that while he was good, he wasn't really concerned about whether he won or not. He just enjoyed the fun of it all.

Then there were the two boys. Firstborn Johnny was proud to have his father's name. Like his dad, he was named John but called Johnny to distinguish him from his father. When Connie called either one of them, no one had to wonder who she wanted. Johnny was a good-looking guy with a square jawline, an aquiline nose, and a full head of dark brown hair like his father.

Many would say he was like his father in temperament as well as appearance, with one exception. He was the most competitive member of the family. Maybe it was being the firstborn. For two years, he was pretty much the top dog in the family. Then along came Sarah. He loved his sister very much, but he did not want things to get out of order. He would never be considered bossy, just confident in his position in the family.

Paul was seven years old. Connie and Jack thought he was going to be their last child. Surprise! If there was anyone in the family who was going to be the computer/math genius, it was certainly going to be Paul. From the age of two, he was already playing computer games, pulling down menus, selecting options, and usually winning everything he tried. In fact, he enjoyed winning so much that, if he thought he couldn't win, he would choose not to play. His long, light-colored hair and slim figure caused him to stand out in a crowd, just like his mother.

Almost without fail, you would find Paul smiling. Sometimes you had to wonder why he was smiling, but he was usually smiling. Maybe he knew more about what was going on than most people expected of a boy of seven.

When everyone gathered back at the trunk of the sixty-five-foot tall elephant, there was a noisy exchange of experiences about golf scores, craft items, and colorful balloons. Then the group moved on to the refreshment area to choose lunch from one of three food trucks assembled there. Anything from tacos to sausage sandwiches to Philly cheesesteaks and hot dogs was available. The most difficult task for some of the children was deciding what to choose.

Once everyone had their order along with their favorite beverage and lots of napkins for cleaning up after the messier items, they settled down around two outdoor tables and had a very relaxing lunch. The time was accentuated by more tales of morning fun and laughs about the silly things they had seen and done.

As lunchtime was wrapping up, PopPop was the first to notice that the waiting line to get into the elephant was relatively short. His announcement was followed by a quiet determination to get in line before it grew too long again. Quickly, lunch debris was carefully placed in recycling receptacles, and the whole family followed their patriarch to the ticket booth and then to Lucy's entry leg.

They discovered that, even though Lucy was big on the outside, she was rather cramped on the inside. *People with claustrophobia*, thought Connie, *would not do well inside Lucy*. They took time to look around, peek out through a few of the twenty windows on her sides, and climb up to the top to take a look out over the horizon.

When all were satisfied with their clambering inside an elephant, they descended the spiral steps and, as preplanned, headed to their van for the brief but picturesque ride south along the Atlantic coast and their warm and inviting Ocean City house.

When they arrived, before climbing out of the van, Jack asked, "So how did you like The Great Summer Tour that Nana put together for us this year?"

All kinds of words of praise exploded from the grateful children. And Nana, very pleased that everyone seemed to enjoy her efforts, said, "I'm glad you had a good time. Do you think we should do it again next year?"

Shouts of affirmation were shared with Nana. She was as pleased as all the children and adults were for the wonderful day they had shared together.

That night, after the children were all in bed and settled down with prayers, hugs, kisses, and blessings given freely, Jack asked the other three adults to join him in the living room. "Tomorrow is a very important day in all our lives. Connie and I are excited about what God might have in mind for us. I'd like it if we could all pray together about the interview at the church tomorrow and the meal and all the events that might take place here while we're gone. But most importantly, we want to pray that the will of God may be made clear tomorrow. Can we do that together?"

"Absolutely," said his father.

"Let's just stand together, hold hands, and pray in whatever way God leads us," suggested Connie. With that moment of unity among the adults, another day of adventure came to an end. And another was about to begin.

Chapter 10

The First Interview

The return to Weaverton was a pleasant trip for Jack and Connie. They enjoyed these rare moments when it was just the two of them. Somehow their conversation edged over into matters of the distant future when being alone with one another would be the norm. Although they were more than a dozen years from being empty-nesters, and they certainly didn't know anyone who loved their children more than they did, Jack and Connie were wondering why so many couples thought the transition to having grown-up children was so traumatic.

They were excited about the people their children would grow up to be. For them, it was an honor, a gift from God to mold and shape and love these five precious boys and girls into adults who they believed would accomplish great things in a beautiful but needy world. And while their grown-up children would be off on their individual journeys with and for the Lord, Connie and Jack would have wonderful times together, just the two of them, enjoying what new experiences God had in mind for them at that time.

What might God unfold for them in that new setting? Fun things to think about. But more important now, and more immediate for them, was what God had in mind for them concerning Grace Church in Weaverton, Pennsylvania.

Imaginative ruminations gave way to more practical questions, such as the interview about to take place within a beautiful church on the corner of Weaverton Road and Church Street. Jack knew what it was like to be interviewed by a pulpit committee, but this was new ground for Connie. Even for Jack, there was an unknown factor in these upcoming conversations.

He had never been interviewed by the members of a committee and their spouses. He kind of liked the idea. It said something to him about the character of this congregation. To Pastor Jack, this meant that family was very important to these people. He really liked that. And Connie agreed this was a very positive sign. She imagined that having husbands and wives meet together with them would give the experience a more informal setting. She liked that.

As they approached the church building, Jack and Connie once again admired the beautiful surroundings. It was "in the country" and yet only two blocks from the edge of the small community of Weaverton. There were open fields; some dotted with sheep. Another held a handful of white Charolais cattle lazily ruminating under shady trees.

Some fields were laden with high stalks of bountiful corn near the end of harvest season. There was that gentle pond behind the parsonage with a few dozen quiet geese being guarded by the chosen sentinel, standing tall and looking in all directions for the safety of the flock. Though presently quiet, soon they would take off and noisily honk to one another as they moved on to the next watery respite in their daily routine.

There were only a few houses scattered across the area, mostly red brick construction. Copious trees in various shades of green gave the promise of transforming into the rich reds, oranges, and yellows of autumn only a few weeks away. And there was Grace Church, perhaps another sentinel for the community, sharing the truth of God's Word and hopefully guarding the Christian culture and life of the area.

Standing in front of the white stucco-clad church building was a welcoming committee of two, Pete and Lucy Geisinger. For Jack and Connie, it was a caring and thoughtful way to make them feel at home without a word being spoken. Seeing these two familiar, smiling faces was like "breaking the ice" before any ice had a chance to form. The Geisingers would be their entre into the interview about to take place.

After warm handshakes and greetings, Pete held the door open for them (Connie saw that as almost a symbolic act) as Lucy led them into the interior. The four chatted their way across a nice-sized vestibule and fellowship area and on into the beautiful sanctuary Jack and Connie had only seen through a window a few days ago.

Connie almost gasped. It was sooo beautiful. "It just feels so warm and welcoming in here."

Pete and Lucy smiled in agreement. "We have that same feeling every time we enter this sanctuary. It is a sanctuary in the true sense of that word," Lucy replied.

Jack remembered the words he spoke to Connie the first time he peeked into this room. He said it again for the benefit of Pete and Lucy. "I could really worship here." They responded with knowing smiles.

"Come on," Pete said, "let us show you around before we head into the meeting room downstairs."

The brief tour began. They saw classrooms of various sizes, a well-appointed kitchen for church suppers, the secretary's office and workroom, and the pastor's office.

Hmm, thought Jack, *we'll have to change that if we come here.* The door to the pastor's office was solid oak with no window. Jack had a firm rule that he never met alone with anyone in his office unless his secretary or another person could peek in and see that nothing untoward was taking place. Nor could any person he might be counseling suggest he was engaged in unacceptable behavior when all exchanges took place behind a door with a small window.

In fact, if he were to accept a call from God to be pastor of this congregation, once he had a small window installed in this door, he would instruct his secretary to walk by that door occasionally to confirm all was in order between him and anyone in his office.

"Well," said Pete, "why don't we head down to the meeting room where you can meet some of our members?"

"Sounds good," agreed Jack. And off they went.

The meeting room was pleasant. The walls were a rich blue but not dark in color. There were three single-panel windows near the ceiling with burgundy paisley curtains. In this lower-level room, these windows allowed warm, natural light to come in. In addition, there were table lamps on four pine tables, one in each corner of the room, plus can lights on the ceiling.

There was a collection of leather-padded chairs augmented with tan folding chairs in a kind of semi-circle. Some of the committee members were already seated there, and others were standing in groups of three or four, chatting when the four new participants entered the meeting room.

Conversations quickly ended as Pete introduced the group to Pastor Jack Whyte and his wife, Connie. Following the introduction, chattering began again as each person, in turn, walked up to the pastoral couple to welcome them with warm handshakes and even warmer smiles. All wore nametags in large letters to help Jack and Connie get to know who was greeting them and perhaps remember some of the names.

When all had a chance to say "Hello" and welcome the Whytes, Pete took the initiative to encourage everyone to sit. "I think we should get things started here. Let's begin with a prayer. 'Thank You, Lord, for calling us here for this important meeting in the life of our congregation. Thank You for bringing Pastor and Mrs. Whyte here safely. We ask that You guide our conversation and direct our intentions. And may You be honored in all that takes place in this room this evening. In Jesus' name. Amen.'"

Pete continued, "Well, you have all met Pastor Whyte and Connie now. By the way, Pastor, there are bottles of water on that table next to you if you or Connie ever need to wet your whistle. I would like to turn things over to the head of our committee and president of the church council, Ron Young."

"Thank you, Pete. And welcome to the two of you. We appreciate you taking time out of your vacation to meet with us. Ocean City is a nice place. I'll bet you're enjoying your time there." Jack and Connie nodded their heads in agreement while Connie was thinking, *I love Ron's slight Pennsylvania Dutch accent.*

"We have all had a chance to listen to one or more of your sermons on the internet. We like what we've heard. For this evening, I think," Ron went on, "it would be good for us to get to know one another and get into specific questions about the pastorate here and your style of ministry. I asked my wife, Molly, if she would take a little time to tell you about Grace Church to let you know what you might be getting yourself into if we were to call you as our next pastor."

All eyes turned to Molly as she began a ten-minute review of the history of Grace from its founding in 1795, as well as a summary of the various ministries and events that are part of the congregation's ministry today. Connie noted to herself that Molly had that same Pennsylvania Dutch accent she liked, and it was even a little more pronounced than her husband's.

When she finished, Molly walked over to Pastor Jack and handed him a folder. "These include a lot of the stuff I just said and a lot more about Grace. I'm sure you'll want to look that over when you have time. I could have told you everything in there, but I didn't want to put you to sleep."

Everyone laughed at that remark as Pastor Jack thanked her for the material. "Are you suggesting, if I have trouble sleeping when we go back to Ocean City tonight, that I should consider this material a sleeping aid?" he asked.

More laughter followed, with Molly suggesting, "Well, it wouldn't hurt."

Ron took charge once again, thanking his wife for her part. Then he said, "We have asked a number of our members to be prepared to ask the two of you some questions, and we do want to hear from both of you. That's important to us. Not that we're thinking of hiring two pastors. We just are sure what Miss Connie thinks is very important to us, as well as your intentions, Pastor Whyte."

"I couldn't agree more," said Jack.

"By the way, now that I think about it, how do you want us to address you? Reverend? Pastor? Your holiness?" He laughed.

Laughing as well, Pastor Jack said, "I tell people to call me whatever they feel comfortable calling me. I get 'Pastor Whyte,' 'Pastor Jack,' 'Hey, you,' and anything else that comes to mind. I have one elderly lady at our church in Connecticut who calls me 'the Rev.' So, take your pick."

"And you can just call me Connie," added his wife.

"Hmm, 'the Rev.' I think I like that," responded Ron. "Well, as I was saying before I interrupted myself, we have some planned questions to ask you. Let's start with Butch Highland."

Butch was a short but "beefy" kind of a guy. They would learn later that he drives an eighteen-wheeler throughout the tri-state area. "Hi, folks. I'm really glad you're here. My name is Allan Highland, but everyone calls me Butch. Feel free to do that as well. My question is, what are the most important areas of ministry for you?"

"Good question," responded Pastor Jack. "There are really two areas that are most important to me and that direct everything I say and do. First and foremost is Scripture. I base my ministry on what I read and understand from the Bible. It directs my life and is essential to all that I preach. Its principles underline the counsel I give. So, very simply, it is foundational to my ministry.

"The second most important area is family. Connie and I have been married for almost fifteen years. We have five children from ages five through thirteen, two boys and three girls. Scripture tells me if I don't have my family in order, how can I possibly think I could give direction to a congregation of believers? So, briefly, those are the two most important areas of my ministry. Is that what you wanted to know, Butch?"

"Yes, very good. Thank you."

"Well done," interjected Ron. "Okay, let's see what Becky Westerly has to ask you. Becky?"

"Thanks, Ron. Yes, I want to direct this question to Connie. What role do you, as the pastor's wife, play in the ministry?"

"I appreciate you asking me that, Becky. My biggest job is twofold. One, I support my husband. To me, that means giving him the time he needs to carry out his ministry. It also means giving him my opinions and suggestions about areas of ministry we might talk about."

"Yes, and she's very good at giving me her opinions. I look to her for that," interjected Pastor Jack.

Smiling, Connie continued, "My second job is taking care of our children alongside my husband. It is teamwork for us. And third is involvement in the ministry of the congregation, which is what most people really want to know. If we were to come here as your pastoral family, we would pray about my gifts and the areas where I might serve and make a decision as time unfolds. You should not expect, just because I'm the pastor's wife, that I will be head of your women's organization. I don't know yet what that might be.

"I'm pretty sure, since we have five children, that I will be involved in Sunday school and other areas of children's ministry. I tell people what I do in the church is because I'm a Christian woman, not because I'm the pastor's wife. So I guess my view is that all of us women should be involved in the ministry of the church because we're Christian women, not because of who our husbands happen to be. Was that all right, honey?" she asked Jack.

"Perfect," he responded.

"Thank you," said Becky. "I never thought of it that way before, but I like it."

"Okay," continued Ron. "Moving along, let's hear from Burt Thompson. Burt?"

"Hi, folks. I want to thank you again for being here. I like what I'm hearing, and I'm interested in your answer to the question I have for you. What is your preaching style?"

At this point, Pete Geisinger spoke up. "Let me add to that question if I might. As you know, Lucy and I are the only ones who have heard you preach in person. And as I've told everyone, we were very impressed. And I would like to add to Burt's question, Pastor Jack. To Lucy and me, it was quite obvious that your sermon was clearly focused on the Bible. Second, you didn't seem to have any notes. You spoke directly to the congregation. Is that the way you always preach? Is that the style Burt is asking about?"

"That's pretty much it," answered Pastor Jack. "I think all sermons should be an exposition of the Word of God, that is, the Bible. God has directed me in many ways to prepare sermons based on the Bible. It may be a theme or a verse-by-verse explanation of a book of the Bible. But it's always starting with the Bible. I try to avoid sounding like a college professor, however. I try to explain what the original writers were saying and then get practical. How would God have us live because of what we see in this particular portion of the Bible? I want it to be simple but meaningful. As far as the use of notes, I always have an outline, but it's short."

"So, you don't have a manuscript of your sermon then," commented Burt. "What do you say to someone who accuses you of preaching something you didn't say?"

"Good question, Burt. The answer is simple. I make sure we always record my preaching. If such a question comes up, we would simply sit down and listen to the recording together and make sure what I preached is properly understood."

"Good answer. Good answer," responded Burt.

The meeting progressed with many more questions being asked and people being pretty much impressed with the answers they received. At the conclusion of the session, Ron once again thanked the pastoral couple for their participation and wished them a safe trip back to Ocean City.

To his committee members, he said, "We will hang around here for a few more minutes after Pastor Jack and Connie leave to talk about our next step." To Jack and Connie, he said, "We will be in touch with you in the next few days. Before you leave, would you close our meeting with prayer, please?"

After the prayer, everyone took time to once again shake hands with the departing couple, all saying very encouraging words. Pete and Lucy escorted them out to the parking lot, exchanged hugs, and sent them on their way.

"Soooo," Connie said as they headed down the road, "what do you think?"

"I really liked those people. I liked the way they talked. I thought their questions were well thought out. And I was pleased with the way they received our answers. And you, my dear, were superb. But I expected nothing less."

"You don't think I messed things up when I answered the question about the role of the pastor's wife?"

"Absolutely not. First of all, it was the right answer. You explained it well. And second, if that is not the kind of pastor's wife they want, then I am not the kind of pastor they want."

Their chatting, dissecting, and commentary continued most of the way back to their waiting family in Ocean City, where, hopefully, all the children were already in bed. Tom and Janet would get a brief summary of the meeting with more details to be shared in the morning.

Jack and Connie were pretty much exhausted by the time they arrived back in Ocean City.

Later that night, in bed, Jack prayed, "Thank You, Lord, for guiding our path and our conversations. Now help us and the committee members to hear You as You give us directions for the future."

Chapter 11

WINDING DOWN AND PACKING UP

Connie and Jack woke up at the same time Wednesday morning to the wonderful aroma of brewing coffee and crackling bacon wafting up the stairs from the kitchen. Janet was on the job early again.

Rolling over sleepily to her husband of fifteen years, Connie said with furrowed brow, "Do you realize we only have a few days left before we have to pack up and head back to Connecticut?"

"I do," whispered Jack, "and it went by so quickly. But it has been a good four weeks, don't you think?"

"Absolutely! I've loved every minute of it. Trips to the beach, early evenings eating soft serve ice cream on the boardwalk. Sundays with friends we only see once a year at church."

"Playing games together in the backyard, s'mores at the fireplace, eating that delicious Pennsylvania Dutch meal," Jack continued.

"With strawberry shortcake for dessert," added Connie.

"Yum," agreed Jack. "It's been another great vacation at our favorite summer getaway, especially having our parents with us again. But, you know, Connie," he paused, "I think I'm ready to go back home."

"Yeah. Me too."

They lay there for a while without saying a word, remembering and imagining, shuffling in their minds pleasant memories and plans they would have to make for the future, recalling and wondering what God had in mind for them. Would they stay in Connecticut, move on to Weaverton, or go to some other yet unknown location for new ministry opportunities and new adventures as a family?

Connie broke the silence. "I thought things went well last night."

"Yeah, me too. I really liked those people. I think I'd like working with them and growing together."

"Do you think we'll hear from them soon?" asked Connie.

"Well," Jack conjectured, "I don't imagine it will be until we're back home...unless they already know one way or another. Ron did say they were going to stay in their meeting for a while after we left. I have no doubts they talked about the possibility of us coming there. They said they had already interviewed quite a few potential pastors and hadn't yet found the right one. So I guess they know by now what kind of a leader they want for Grace."

"Maybe they already prayed about it and have made a decision," imagined Connie.

"Maybe," agreed Jack. "They *could* call us before we head home. I don't know."

"Me neither. One thing I do know. We'd better get moving before we have children running in here and jumping up and down on our bed. I'm sure they'll want to tell us about their afternoon and evening with Nana and PopPop."

"You are absolutely right, wifey. Let's get a move on."

And with that, they both hopped out of bed, took turns bumping elbows in the small bathroom, and used the full-length mirror in the bedroom to prepare for another full day at the shore. Weather-wise, it was looking like another beautiful day was about to unfold.

———————————

When they got downstairs to the kitchen, most of the other family members were already gathering. They were greeted with hugs and kisses and questions about the interview.

Janet poured Connie a cup of coffee. None for Jack. He liked the smell of coffee but couldn't deal with the bitter taste. He was a tea drinker. Of course, his mother knew that and had hot water in the tea kettle ready to give him his preferred morning beverage…Irish breakfast tea. No milk. No sugar. Just tea.

"I would love to hear more of the details from your interview, Jack," prompted his mother.

"We were just talking about that," he responded. "We think it went well. But let's wait until we're all here before we get into the details." At that moment, PopPop and Paul wandered into the kitchen, mostly awake and interested in coffee for PopPop and OJ for Paul.

"Well, since we're all kind of here," Jack joked, "if you're interested, I think we can try to give a full report on the interview we had last night. But then we want to hear what you guys did while we were gone. We want a full report on that too."

"I think we're all anxious to hear," said PopPop.

"First of all, we really liked the people," Connie began. "And they were very well organized. They had apparently been through this process with a few other candidates, and it went well."

"They very wisely not only asked me what I believed. They specifically asked Connie for her viewpoint as well," noted Jack.

"Yeah, I really appreciated that," Connie added.

"Smart people," commented PopPop.

The recap of the interview unfolded with questions back and forth, mostly between the four adults. The children were interested up to a point, but higher on their priority list was telling their parents about the fun day they'd had with their grandparents.

"So then, tell us about the special meal you guys had yesterday," prompted Connie.

Nana began the report by noting, "Well, you know PopPop, the contractor. No one organizes and plans better than this man."

"I just arranged for us to work on the meal in teams," he said. "We got everything done on time, and we had a lot of fun doing it. Didn't we, kids?"

Shouts of "Yes" and "Yeah" answered the question.

"What did you do, Suzy?" asked her mother. "What was your job?"

"Johnny and I went shopping at the market with PopPop. It was really fun," answered the enthusiastic five-year-old who loved doing anything she could with her big brother. "You should have seen PopPop and Johnny tossing food from the shelves into the shopping cart. They were really good."

"PopPop," scolded Connie. "What kind of an example is that?"

"A pretty good one, I thought. Johnny learned quickly how to make two points with each toss into the cart." All the children laughed, and Johnny couldn't keep a smile off his face.

"What about you, Sarah," asked her father. "What was your job?"

"Megan and I helped Nana cook the food."

"And Paul, what was your job?" asked Connie. "You didn't just sit around and look handsome, did you?"

A blushing seven-year-old smiled and proudly reported, "I was the head waiter. First, I helped PopPop set the table. Once everyone was seated, we served the food like in a real restaurant. It was really fun."

After more details and jokes about what went right and who made some silly goofs, the whole gang agreed this was a fun thing to do and to hopefully do again sometime. Johnny summed it all up with an interesting comment. "You know, Mom. We never realized how much work you put into getting meals ready for us."

A pleased and grateful Connie simply said quietly, "Thank you, Johnny. That was a very nice thing to say."

The last few days of the Whyte vacation raced by quickly. A couple of days on the beach, one more challenging game of miniature golf, some trivia games, one last effort to finish the 5,000-piece jigsaw puzzle, and the time to depart for home was almost upon them.

Friday evening, everyone was given a job assignment to make the house look as good, if not better, than it did when they arrived. Some creative food prep for Friday lunch and dinner and Saturday breakfast was required to clean out the refrigerator and not waste any food. Saturday, one last run through the house with the vacuum cleaner and dust cloth, along with one last kitchen clean-up, finished their commitment to leave a pleasant surprise for the owner.

After packing suitcases and loading them into the van along with beach toys, beach umbrellas, and boxes of board games, everyone was ready to head out onto the highway. Jack took time to thank his parents for sharing the cost of this vacation at the shore. Their generosity, as well as that of Connie's parents, made this annual vacation a reality. Hugs and kisses were enthusiastically shared with Nana and PopPop just before they got into their car and took off for home...happy, refreshed, and satisfied.

Connie directed the boarding of the family van while Jack made one last walk through the house and backyard to make sure everything looked good and nothing was accidentally left behind.

Climbing into the driver's seat, Jack turned to Connie and the children and asked, "Did everyone have a good time?" Everyone shouted out positive responses.

"Well, say goodbye to our lovely summer home," instructed Connie. "We may be back again next year unless God has a better idea for us. Who knows?"

As they drove off and the children began to chat with one another, Connie looked at Jack and said, "So, we haven't heard from the pulpit committee. What do you think that means?"

"I have no idea," answered her husband. "But I'm sure we'll hear from them shortly after we get back home."

"I hope so. Oh, honey, I can really see us in that parsonage in Weaverton. And those nice people we met on Tuesday night, wouldn't it be great to minister with them? I really think God's going to say 'yes' and call us to that lovely church."

"You may be right, Connie. You may be right. All we can do now is pray. Besides, there is nothing more powerful for us to do than pray."

And so they did.

Season II

---•---

Autumn

Chapter 12

BACK HOME IN CONNECTICUT

Only a few days remained in the month of July when the Whyte family returned to their home in Bradford, Connecticut. The temperature was only about five degrees cooler than in New Jersey. *I wonder*, thought Connie, *if we'll be here to see the wonderful hues of yellow, orange, and red that paint the trees in the Connecticut countryside each fall. Or will we encounter autumn in Pennsylvania?*

On Monday, Jack was already back in the swing of things at the church. The day after they returned from New Jersey, they played hooky from Sunday worship. Instead, Jack had devotions with the family after breakfast. While he'd been gone, retired Pastor Ned Swanson had filled in for him. This was Ned's last Sunday to preach for Jack.

Now that he was back in his office again, Jack discovered mounds of mail and packages piled high on his desk, placed there by his faithful secretary, Miss Mercy Summerfeld. Most of it was junk and would end up in the trash, but he had to sort his way through the debris anyway. Maybe he would discover some surprise treasure in the stacks. Probably not. Still, it didn't hurt to imagine and look.

The children had very quickly gotten back in touch with their friends in the neighborhood. Johnny was playing baseball with his junior high group. Sarah had invited her friends over to reconvene their little club that met in the treehouse Jack had built for them in that old maple tree in their backyard. The older girls had condescended to invite Megan to join them. Paul was into a new video game that had come in the mail while they were away. And Suzy was next door with her very best friend, Alice.

It seemed the children might have been industriously busy for two reasons. First, they had missed their friends while being away in New Jersey.

Second, in four weeks, just after Labor Day, school would begin, and they wanted to take advantage of as much free time as they had left before getting back into the busyness of scholastic endeavors. It wasn't that they didn't like school. Actually, they did. They had good friends and good teachers.

The only one who had some hesitation was Suzy. Their school district required full-time kindergarten for all children. This would be a first for Suzy since last year had only been half-day pre-school. She thought it would probably be all right. Her siblings assured her she would enjoy it. And pre-school was fun. But it was still the unknown factor that sneaked into her thoughts once in a while.

Of course, all this meant that Connie was quickly preparing to transition all of her children back into the academic world. There was so much to do. School supplies to shop for, clothing to buy, and new backpacks to purchase. Maybe this year they could recycle some of the old backpacks. She would ask each of her kids what they wanted to do about that. And, of course, she also had to answer the many phone calls that came in, like right now.

"Hello.... Oh, hi, Jack. How's it going at church...? That's a lot of mail, Jack! I didn't realize how popular you were," she laughed. "Is Mercy working today? If I know her, she's going to want information for the church bulletin already.... Big surprise."

Jack tossed a few more items of junk in a trash bag as he continued talking to Connie. "I assume you're busy getting back into gear. What are the children doing...? Sounds good. Make sure Paul remembers what we told him. He cannot play video games all day. Tell him to read something. I know. Tell him to call his friend Doug. I saw Doug's dad downtown this morning, and he said his son was looking forward to seeing Paul now that we're back home.... Yeah, do that. And I'll tell Mercy you said hi.... No, I have to clean up this accumulated mess in my office. I'll just grab a sandwich somewhere. Tell the kids I'll see them at dinner. I love you. Bye."

It was 4:15 p.m. Mercy had just left for home when Jack's cell phone rang. It was Pete Geisinger from Grace Church in Weaverton. After some chatting and catching up, Pete said he wanted to schedule another meeting with the pulpit committee by Zoom and wanted to know if tomorrow evening was a possibility. Apparently, the committee members were clearly impressed with Jack, his demeanor, his answers to their questions, and the way his wife expressed herself.

They wanted to take the next step in calling Jack to be their pastor if he was still interested. Jack assured Pete he was. They scheduled the Zoom meeting for the next evening at 7 p.m. After more conversation, which he could not wait to tell Connie about, the call ended.

Jack simply, quietly said, "Thank You, Lord. Thank You. And thank You that You had Pete wait until I was all alone in the office to call me. Good timing. Pete probably thinks that was his idea. But we know better. Thank You for whatever You are opening up for my family and me. And Lord, if it truly is Your plan for us to go to Grace, please prepare the congregation there to be open to the ministry You have in mind for us. And prepare the church here in Connecticut. Lord, please help Connie and me that we will be open as well."

And with that, Jack left a few more items on his desk to go through tomorrow so he could go home and talk to Connie about this latest development. He could talk to her about it on the phone, but that would not be as satisfying as face-to-face.

Jack rushed through the door and kissed his wife.

"Guess what! Pete Geisinger just called! We scheduled a pulpit committee meeting for tomorrow night on Zoom. You know, we haven't done much with anything like Zoom since we used Skype to keep in touch after camp and before we were married. Skype was in its infancy back in those days."

"I think we should do some investigating into Zoom before tomorrow night to see how it works. I don't want us to appear ignorant about it when we're talking to the committee."

"Of course," said Jack.

"So what do they want to talk about? Did they like us? Are they interested in us coming to Grace? Did he sound positive?"

"Whoa, there, Connie! Settle down and let me get a word in here or there," Jack laughed.

"Sorry. I'm too excited. Talk to me."

"First of all, he said they are definitely interested in us coming to Grace and want to work out some important details."

"Like what?" Connie asked.

"I think the biggie is finances. They want to know what we want for a salary. Of course, they provide the parsonage, pay all utilities, take care of all maintenance, plus the usual benefits. And since we will have no equity because we won't own a house, they will also put a specific amount in our retirement fund."

"That sounds good. Once we sell this house, we can probably add that amount to the retirement fund as well."

"That's a good possibility. What I would like you to do, Connie, is to check over our budget. If you come up with a figure that we can live on, that will help."

When Jack and Connie were first married, Jack took care of the finances because they thought he should. The problem was Jack had so little interest in financial matters they started getting late notices on bills he should have paid regularly. So, within that first year of marriage, they both agreed that Connie would do a much better job. And she had. They were in a good financial position now because of her diligence.

"Okay, I can do that. What else do they want to know about?"

"We didn't talk about youth ministry when we were there last week. They want to know my ideas for that. They have a woman who is a member of

Grace who's been running it for years, and they want to know how we might work with her."

"That won't be a problem," assured Connie. "What else?"

"We talked about the style of worship they have there. Pete wanted to know what my approach is and if we would have trouble fitting into their style."

"With the traditional style we have here and the contemporary style you've used at your youth retreats with your guitar, you probably won't have any trouble fitting in. What do you think, Jack?"

"Yeah, you're right. They have an ordered liturgical service with hymns like we're used to, so that's no problem. I think maybe we could offer an additional contemporary service somewhere in the future if there's any interest in that. We'll have to wait and see."

"You know," said Connie, "they might be ready for that sooner than you think."

"That's true," agreed Jack. "As Bob Dylan would say, 'The times they are a-changin.'"

"How many do they have at worship on Sundays?" Connie wanted to know.

"They only have around a hundred each week. But Pete said those people are very dedicated. I'm hoping we can build that up."

"How many people can they fit into that sanctuary? It's beautiful but not very big."

"I asked Pete that same question. He said they can fit about 200 shoulder-to-shoulder."

"That looks like one of your first challenges, Jack. How to grow a church when there's not much room for growth."

"Are you listening to our conversation, Connie? We're talking as though we've already been asked to go to Grace."

"True, but it's fun to imagine, isn't it?"

The conversation, the imaginings, the hopes, and even dreams continued on for another half hour before the first of their children came home. Connie had to get things ready for supper. She and Jack had a lot to pray about.

Chapter 13

Zoom Time

The Zoom meeting went very well. Jack and Connie enjoyed seeing the committee members again. This time though, the spouses weren't there. All the technical factors of doing a Zoom meeting were no problem. The system worked really well. While the chairman, Ron Young, conducted the meeting, Pete took the responsibility to turn the computer toward whoever was talking in the meeting room so Jack and Connie could see them.

They learned a lot about the church, which was very helpful. It had been the very first church in the Weaverton area. At one point, another church was established in the center of town, and a number of members of Grace moved their membership there because it was more convenient for them.

Jack learned there is presently a small staff at Grace. They have a secretary, a custodian, an organist/accompanist, and a music director. Everything else, including the youth director and a Sunday school superintendent, is done by church members who volunteer. That fact fit in with Jack's philosophy of ministry.

Rather than hire people to staff the church, Jack emphasized having members find their spiritual gifts and use them to carry out the church's ministry. He felt that the more people who were actively involved in the church's ministry, the more vital the church would be. But if the church began to grow and the ministries expanded, the possibility of adding another pastor might be a necessity.

Perhaps the two biggest issues raised during the Zoom meeting had to do with finances and Jack's style of ministry. The money issue came up when the treasurer, Tom Lightfoot, asked, "So what do you want for a salary?" They had already discussed the parsonage and the benefit package, but no one had come right out and asked this key question before. Jack's answer surprised them.

"I never ask for a specific salary. I ask you to pray about it. I expect you know the cost of living in your area better than I do. You know that we have five children to raise. And you know what people in the area earn who are in a similar level of work. If you call me to be your pastor, and Connie and I feel very much this is where God wants us to be, we will live on whatever salary you offer me. You just need to keep in mind that if it is not quite enough, I will not be as effective as your pastor if I'm worried about meeting our financial obligations."

"So, you don't have a salary figure in mind?" asked Tom.

"No, I leave that up to you."

Surprised looks passed from one committee member to another as Tom continued. "I am head of the finance committee of the church, as you might imagine. And we did come up with an amount that we thought was fair and that our budget would allow."

When he told Jack the amount they were offering, Jack and Connie looked at each other with a big smile. "I think you will find it interesting to know that I asked Connie yesterday to review our finances and our budget and come up with the amount she thought we would need. You may or may not be surprised that the salary you are offering is the exact amount Connie came up with."

Lots of smiles and sighs permeated the meeting room. Some who had been holding their breath just laughed. "That sounds like God to me," offered Ron.

"We agree," said Jack.

Another key issue addressed at the meeting came from a question that surprised Jack. And it came from a familiar voice.

"What would you say is your style of ministry?" asked Butch Highland.

Jack sat quietly for a moment and thought. Finally, he said, "I'm not sure how to answer that question."

Connie jumped in, "I can answer that."

"Oh good," laughed Jack. "I'd like to hear this too."

"Jack's style is very simple. He prays a lot." Many heads nodded their support of that. "He prays about everything," Connie went on. "Jack asks God what He wants the church to do. When he gets an answer, he presents it to the church's leadership. If they agree, they move ahead with it. If they don't approve, Jack just prays some more until God changes their minds…or his. As I said, it's really quite simple."

"I guess you're right, Connie," responded Jack, "that is what I do."

After a few more areas of discussion, Ron summed up the sense of the committee. "Before this meeting began, we were pretty sure you're the man we want to recommend to the congregation to be our pastor. Given the sense I have now of how we're all responding to your answers, I think we can move on to the next step in the process.

"Jack and Connie, we're going to continue meeting for a while after we close out this Zoom session. I want us to work out how we'll officially invite you, Jack, to come and preach a trial sermon here at Grace. Now, this is the protocol. This committee has to make a recommendation to the church council. If they approve—and I would be the most surprised person in this room if they didn't. If they approve, they, in turn, will announce to the congregation the date for you to come and preach that trial sermon.

"That day, after the service, we will hold a brief congregational meeting to vote on your candidacy. What we'll need from you, Jack, is a date when you could be away from your present pulpit to preach here. Does that make sense to everyone?"

There was verbal agreement and nods from the meeting room, and Jack and Connie both said, "Yes."

"Okay, we'll go with that, then," confirmed Ron. "We'll continue with Pete being your contact, Pastor Jack. He will call you after our council meeting. Meanwhile, you can begin the tricky business of letting your congregation know of your plans."

The meeting ended with words of thanks expressed enthusiastically by Jack and Connie.

"That went well," noted Connie.

"It sure did," said Jack. "But Ron was right. Now comes the difficult part. How do we tell this congregation of our plans? That is if the Grace council agrees with the pulpit committee."

"We just have to do some serious praying," counseled Connie. "The Lord has been in this all along. I'm sure He's already preparing the people here. I know they won't be happy about it. But they'll understand."

"It's only a little after nine o'clock," noted Jack. "I think we have time to call our parents and bring them up to speed on what's happening. They will definitely want to know."

"Right," said Connie. "Let's do that. We can put them on speaker phone and fill them in." And so they did.

Both sets of parents were almost as excited as Jack and Connie about the developments. They had some helpful suggestions to make concerning how to inform their present congregation and how to make the transition as smooth as possible.

With a warm hug and a kiss, Jack and Connie helped the children finish getting ready for bed. It had been a busy and momentous day for every member of the family. They were all tired and would sleep well tonight.

Chapter 14

A New Idea

It was while Connie was putting the dirty breakfast dishes into the dishwasher that the idea was planted in her brain like a quiet seed ready to germinate. It was one of those rare moments in her life. Jack was off to the office to finish cleaning up what had accumulated during four weeks away. All five children were occupied with friends and neighbors. It was completely quiet in the house.

Suzy was once again next door with her friend Alice. Alice's mother had promised to help them create a little playhouse by throwing a sheet over a card table where they could create cute domestic activities. Johnny and his friends were back to playing baseball. Paul and his friend Doug were competing against other friends on long-distance video games. Megan was now considered a real part of Sarah's group of friends, and they were all gathering once again in the backyard treehouse.

It was nice to have this quiet time, thought Connie, but she actually preferred to have the children bring friends home. Yes, it was noisy and sometimes chaotic when that happened, but under her sure hand, it was controlled chaos. It seemed the more children they had, the more organizational skills she was able to develop.

What was that old adage? Necessity was the mother of invention or something like that. At any rate, Connie was blessed with administrative skills that she would tell you were a gift from God. And you can be sure Jack gratefully took advantage of those abilities often, both at home and at the church. In many ways, they were a great team.

Wearing her "mommy" hat, Connie was concerned about the likely transition that would soon take place. Discovering a new home and scouting out a new area, designating who and what went into each of the many rooms of a rather large parsonage, packing up and moving all they had accumulated, and judiciously deciding what would be left behind, given away, or trashed. That last item might be the most difficult.

No. The most difficult transition would be uprooting the children from the places and friends and schools they had all known all their lives and finding new schools and friends and so much more. Yes, the family had talked about the likelihood of moving to a new location and even got excited about some of the possibilities on the horizon, but when it came right down to the actual move, there were bound to be tears and concerns.

For the children, Connie considered, it would not be just one transition. First would be getting used to their new grade in school here in Connecticut with new teachers, new subjects, and new classmates. And then, if Connie had it figured right, when they moved, they would have to leave all those things behind for a whole new array of schools, teachers, subjects, and classmates, but this time with no old friends by their sides.

This would be especially disruptive because it would happen in the middle of a semester. Connie wasn't sure how that would even work. That was when the seed was planted. A new idea for sure. But it just might work. She had to think and pray about this a little more, let her creative mind and organizational imagination get to work, and when she had the answers to a myriad of questions racing through her mind, she would approach Jack and get his reaction...and probably more questions.

She was actually getting excited about the possibilities. And even if he thought this idea was not workable, she would enjoy the mental adventure of it all. But she really liked this new idea. And the more she thought about it, the more she was convinced it really was workable.

Connie decided the best thing to do was to write down her thoughts, objections, and answers. Then she would call Jack to make sure he was coming home early for lunch. She wanted them to be able to talk about this before the children came home from their scattered events.

"So, what have you been up to?" asked Jack abruptly as he entered the kitchen where Connie was getting things ready for lunch.

"Hi, honey, it's nice to see you too," joked Connie with a hug and a kiss. "Let's go sit on the sofa. I'll tell you what I've been thinking about all morning."

After settling in on the sofa, she shared with Jack all the concerns she'd had about the difficult transitions this new move might bring for the children since it would be in the middle of a school year. And then came the big question. "So, I was wondering. What do you think about homeschooling the children?"

"Whoa, hold on there, my creative one. Homeschooling? Where did that come from?"

"I just think it would solve a number of potential problems with this possible new transition to Grace."

"Tell me about it," prompted Jack. He knew better than to shoot down any new ideas Connie came up with. More often than not, she was spot on. But this one seemed a bit radical to him. It may have been the planting of a seed for Connie. For him, it was more like the dropping of a bomb. But fifteen years of marriage had taught him to withhold judgment until all the details and ramifications were literally on the table, along with Connie's many notes.

"Okay, think about it. The children's lives would not be disrupted twice, once at the start of school here and then leaving that school and starting an entirely new school setting in the middle of a semester. Also, while we're homeschooling here in Connecticut, the children would have a gradual, rather than sudden, uprooting of their relationships with friends and classmates. For a couple of months, they could still see their friends occasionally, especially on weekends, before the actual move to Weaverton."

"You realize you're doing it again, creating detailed plans for a move that might not take place," noted Jack.

"I know. But you also know I love making plans. Besides, we really do have to look ahead and consider all the possibilities."

"But what if they don't actually vote for me to be their pastor?" asked Jack.

"I am not even considering that as a possibility," she said. "There is no doubt in my mind that once they meet you and hear you preach, they'll want you to be their pastor."

"Okay, optimistic one, how would we go about this?"

"We have a number of friends that already homeschool their kids. I'm sure they would be more than happy to help us set things up and make the transition. We would have to decide what things I would teach and how you would be involved. We already know we have to do some extensive shopping to get ready for the school year in a few weeks. This just means we change the items on our shopping list. For example, we won't need new backpacks."

"What are the kids going to say about this? Do you think they'll really go for it?" asked Jack.

"I think we might be surprised how open they might be to it. We'll just have to assume there would be a gradual acceptance of the idea for a couple of them."

"It never ceases to amaze me how you can take such a radical idea and, in a few minutes, make it sound so sensible," commented Jack.

Connie smiled and said, "It's a gift."

"Well," counseled Jack, "let's reserve judgment on this until we can pick the brains of some of our homeschooling friends. We're going to have to trust them to hold all this in confidence for two reasons. One, we don't know if we're actually leaving soon. And two, if we are leaving, the congregation needs to be told at the right time and in the right way."

"You're absolutely right. If you want me to, I'll contact the people whose brains we want to pick, and we can see where we go from there."

"So, if we are going to do this, do you see it as an ongoing thing or just for the first year we're in Weaverton? Oh boy, now I'm talking as though it's a sure thing."

With a laugh, Connie said, "I think that if we do this, we should try it for a year and see how the children respond. Then we can decide if we continue or not. We still have some research to do in Weaverton. I know there's a good Christian school there in addition to the public school. We need to keep our options open."

"I must say, Connie, when you called the office and said you had a new idea to discuss, this possibility was not even on my radar."

"It wasn't on mine either before this morning," she responded. "It just might be the Lord. We'll have to pray about it."

"I've already started," said Jack.

Just then, there was a knock on the front door and a gentle female voice saying, "Hello, is anyone there? It's Marge."

"Come on in, Marge," called Connie. "We're in the living room." To Jack, she said, "It's Marge Wadsworth from next door. Suzy is over there playing with her daughter Alice."

"Hi, Connie. Hi, Jack. The girls are having a great time together, and I just wanted to know if it's okay for Suzy to stay for lunch."

"Sure," said Connie. "As long as it's not a bother."

"No bother at all. I'm going to serve them lunch in their little house under the card table."

"I'm sure they'll like that," encouraged Connie.

"I really should get back there. I don't want to leave them alone for too long. But I wanted to ask. How was your vacation? We missed seeing you guys while you were gone."

"We all had a great time," piped in Jack. "Once again, the grandparents were able to join us for part of the time. And the weather was perfect. Well, except for a couple of days when that hurricane came by offshore. Other than that, it was great. Now all we need is a vacation to get things back in order after our vacation, especially at the office."

"I know what you mean," laughed Marge. "I think we all have that problem after being away for a while. Well, I want to get back to the girls and their lunch. Thanks for letting Suzy visit. Alice loves it."

"I'm sure Suzy will fill us in on all the fun she's having. Just send her home whenever it's best for you. I'll be here all afternoon," suggested Connie.

"Okay. Sounds good." And with that, Marge was off, out the front door and across the connected front porches of the duplex, ready to serve lunch to her minions for the day.

"That was nice," said Jack. "I'm glad things are going so well over there. I guess you'll have one less person for lunch today."

"I think so."

That's when they heard a young voice calling from the backdoor and coming into the kitchen. "Hey, Mom, can Doug have lunch with us?"

"Of course," said Connie, entering the kitchen. "Come on in, Doug. It's good to see you again."

"Hi, Mrs. Whyte. Thanks for letting me have lunch with you."

"Does your mother know you're staying?"

"No, but I'll call her right away."

"If she agrees, you're welcome to join us for lunch. Nothing fancy, just sandwiches," advised Connie.

"That sounds good to me. Hi, Pastor Jack," said Doug, seeing the pastor standing in the doorway.

"Hi, Doug. Look, why don't you call your mother right away, and then you and Paul can get washed up for lunch."

"Okay," said Doug with a high five.

After they went back into the living room, Jack said to Connie, "I guess you don't have one less mouth to feed for lunch after all."

"I guess not," she smiled.

"What about Sarah and Megan? Are they still in the treehouse?"

"Yes. I told them I'd give them lemonade and sandwiches if they came in and helped to make them."

"Good idea," said Jack. "I'll go tell them it's time to come in."

A few minutes later, Jack came in the back door amidst a flurry of five giggling girls. They headed for the kitchen and began chattering over each other as they reported to Connie on the fun they'd been having in the treehouse. Jack wisely chose to leave the kitchen and the babbling girls to enter the quiet and safety of his home office.

About fifteen minutes later, the five young ladies came to Pastor Jack's office, tapped gently on the door, and quietly entered at his invitation. As the speaker for the group, Melody, a friend of Sarah's, led them to his desk laden with lemonade, sandwiches, cookies, and a napkin on a tray. She said, "All of us wanted to thank you for building that great treehouse and letting us play in it. It's lots of fun. And here is your lunch." It was obviously a rehearsed speech but just as obviously heartfelt.

Jack was touched. "I'm glad you're enjoying it so much. And thank you for bringing me lunch. That's very nice of you." Accompanied by quiet giggles, the five girls headed back to the kitchen to get their own lunch and head back to the treehouse. Connie watched them from the backdoor with a smile on her face as they so carefully ascended the ladder to the treehouse without spilling anything. It was a valiant effort in teamwork, but they got it done.

A rather sweaty firstborn son came noisily through the front door and headed for the kitchen. "Hi, Mom. What's for lunch?"

Connie joined him in the kitchen. "Ham and Swiss cheese sandwiches, lemonade, and chocolate chip cookies. It looks like you might have worked up an appetite."

"Yeah, I did. We had a great time, but it's really getting hot out there."

"Why don't you go say hi to your dad while I make your lunch? He's in the office."

With that, Johnny headed off to talk to his father. When he entered the office, Jack looked up with wide eyes and said, "I suppose it's possible to be dirtier, but I'm not sure how. You must have been having a great time."

"Yeah, we were."

"So, where were you playing baseball?"

"It's part of the city summer league down at the park. They let you play even if you aren't there for the whole summer. I was on a team with some of the kids from school. The problem is that it's the city league, so you have to wear all this safety stuff."

"Safety stuff? Is this fastball or softball?"

"Fastball."

"And they make you wear safety stuff? Like what?"

"You know, Dad. Those hard baseball hats, and now they have a guard across the front of your face. And they want you to put on these arm pads to protect your arm and elbow that faces the pitcher. It's a real bother. We don't wear that stuff when we have a game on our own."

"No, I guess not. So let me understand this. Why don't you like wearing this stuff?"

"It's just a bother," said Johnny. "And no one ever gets hurt, so what's the big deal?"

"Well, son, let's reason this through. Do professional MLB players wear this safety stuff?"

"Yeah, I guess."

"All the time?"

"Yeah."

"Okay. Let's think about this then," Jack went on. "Who do you think are the better players? The pros or the guys in the city league?"

"The pros, of course."

"And between the pros and the city league players, who do you think has the most experience and knows better if it's smart to wear safety equipment?"

"Okay, Dad, I see what you're getting at. It might be a bother, but it's also smart."

"What an intelligent son I've raised," smiled Jack.

From the kitchen came welcome words. "Johnny, your lunch is ready. Go wash your hands."

"Coming, Mom."

And as he left the office, he turned, simply smiled, and said, "Thanks, Dad."

"You're welcome, son. Enjoy your lunch. I already had mine, and it's good."

Having sent everyone away with lunch and a smile on their faces, Connie continued to think about the issue of homeschooling. Who would be the best people to talk to about this fresh idea? Immediately, at the top of her list of possibilities, her mother's name came to mind. Who better to talk to than someone who loved her children and who would be open and honest with her? A phone call to Marilyn Wycliff, all of a sudden, became a top priority.

Chapter 15

DOING THE RESEARCH

Marilyn Wycliff's iPhone rang six times before she answered it. "Hello," she said, out of breath.

"Mom? Why are you huffing and puffing?" Connie wanted to know. "Is everything all right? Is Dad okay?"

"Oh, yes, dear," Marilyn replied, catching her breath. "Everything's fine. Your father is good. The fact is I just finished my cardio jog, and when I came in the backdoor, my phone was ringing."

"You didn't take your phone with you?" Connie asked.

"Of course I did. But it started ringing just as I was unlocking the backdoor. But that's really not important, Connie. What's on your mind? How are things developing with the possibility of a move? How are the children?"

"Hold on there, Mom. I'll answer one question at a time. But first, and most importantly, how is Dad doing? Any news on the medical front?"

"No, nothing new right now. He gets that event monitor soon. Hopefully, that will answer some questions for us. But he feels fine."

"That's good," Connie said with a sigh of relief. "The second reason I'm calling is that I am doing some research."

"Research?"

"Yes, and I wanted to talk to you about a new idea I believe the Lord dropped in my mind this week. I need some feedback, and I really trust your judgment."

"Okay. What are you researching?" asked Marilyn, now breathing normally again.

"We're thinking about homeschooling the children. If we go to Weaverton, like in November, I think homeschooling would make the transition a lot easier for them." With that, Connie went on to explain the ideas she and Jack had been bouncing around for a few days. "What do you think, Mom? Are we crazy to be thinking about this, or do you think it makes sense?"

"Well," said Marilyn, "you're talking about taking on a big job at the same time all seven of you will be making an important move. But I understand your reasoning behind such a project. And, to tell you the truth, honey, if anyone can pull off something like this, it's you. We have a handful of young families in our church who homeschool, and I must say it seems to be going very well for them. You know, you really should be talking to Jack's mother about this. As a seasoned teacher, I'm sure she could give you some better feedback about it than I can."

"I know, Mom. Janet is the next phone call on my list."

"Good. Who else is on your list to call?"

"Well, there's this young couple in our church. They're in their thirties and have boy and girl twins who are Megan's age and will be fourth graders this year. They just started homeschooling last year, and I want to pick their brains about this too."

"That's an excellent idea, Connie. Let me know how it goes."

"Yeah, Jack and I hope to stop by their home tomorrow and just interview all four of them."

"I don't like saying this, Connie, but I'm going to have to end this conversation. I really need to get out of this very wet jogging outfit. You know that old saying, 'Men perspire, women glow.' But to tell you the truth, dear, I sweat a lot, especially on a very warm day in August. And I can't stand being around myself. Before your dad gets home, I really need to get out of these wet clothes and take a refreshing shower."

"I understand, Mom. Go shower and give my love to Dad when he gets there."

"I will. Call again. We really appreciate you keeping us in the loop."

"Okay, I will. Bye for now."

"Goodbye, Connie." And with that, the call ended.

The conversation with Jack's mother went pretty much along the same lines as the one with her own mother. Janet did say that as a teacher for many years, she preferred public school to homeschooling but admitted she had very little contact with homeschooled children. She did note, however, that statistics showed that homeschooled children do very well academically in colleges and universities. And homeschooling was on the rise.

She encouraged Connie that if they went ahead with homeschooling, to make sure the children had good social contacts outside the family so they would develop those skills as well. She also offered to give Connie any ideas or advice on the teaching end of things, which Connie really appreciated.

———•———

It was on the way to visit with Marty and Fran Kaiser the next day that Jack and Connie came to the realization that they were very close to deciding to go the homeschool route. The more they thought about it, the more they liked it. They were going to be very interested in the conversation with the Kaiser twins, Jonathan and Carol. What did they like or dislike about their experience during this past year?

They were warmly greeted by all four of the Kaisers, and Fran offered coffee or tea. It was coffee for Connie and tea for Jack as they gathered together in the living room. Jack and Connie carefully placed their hot drinks on the blue and white ceramic coasters provided for them, and the interview began.

Speaking to the twins, Jack asked what they liked about homeschooling. "No homework!" they immediately called out together.

"I hadn't thought about that," said Connie. "But that makes sense. You mean you get all your work done in class time?"

"Yes," answered Carol, the more soft-spoken of the two. "Most of our class time is on the computer with videos and stuff."

"Yeah," blurted out Jonathan. "And we have all kinds of computer games to help us learn our lessons. I like that."

"Who does the teaching?" asked Connie.

"I guess you could say I'm sort of the superintendent," explained Fran. "And I do most of the teaching. Marty specializes in music, Phys. Ed., and math. I take care of the rest of the subjects."

"Where do you get your curriculum?" wondered Jack.

"We went to the school and got some of the books they use there. We don't know how long we'll continue in the homeschool mode, and we want Jonathan and Carol to be on track with their classmates if they do return to public school in a year or so. We're kinda just playing it by ear."

As the conversation continued, Marty explained some of the rules established for homeschoolers in the state of Connecticut—who to report to about beginning homeschooling, a minimum of 180 hours of class time each year, and other technical facts that the Whytes needed to know.

Fortunately, the Kaisers didn't ask why they were thinking about homeschooling, so Jack and Connie didn't need to ask them to keep their visit confidential. They did, however, mention that they hadn't talked to their children yet about the possibility. That was next on their list. So, if the Kaisers could keep this conversation to themselves, for the time being, that would be helpful. They said they fully understood and would cooperate with their wishes.

With many thanks for the insights, suggestions, and information, Jack and Connie left the Kaiser home with more details to help them in making a decision. Now, how would their children react to what would be to them an idea out of left field? That was on Jack and Connie's agenda for dinner conversation that evening.

———————————

Connie had time to whip up a tuna noodle casserole for supper. She added corn on the cob because that was a favorite of the children. Dessert would be fresh-made brownies and vanilla ice cream. By the time the five Whytes returned from their games and activities with their friends and got cleaned up for dinner, the meal was ready, with a little help from Sarah and Megan setting the dining room table.

It was between dinner and dessert that Jack and Connie planned to bring up the issue of homeschooling. Jack opened up the subject. "We have an important decision to make," he began, immediately gaining the attention of all five children. "You all remember our trip to Grace Church a few weeks ago."

"You mean where you and Mommy almost got arrested?" laughed Paul.

"Yes, that time," said Jack with a smile. "It looks like we might be moving there, but we don't really know that for sure yet."

"I'm pretty sure," added Connie. "But Daddy's very wisely being cautious."

"Right," said Jack. "But...if we go there, it might be pretty soon."

"We really liked that parsonage," noted Sarah.

"Yes, it was very nice," Jack responded. "And you've all known for a while now that it's very likely we'll be leaving our home here. What we don't know for sure is where God wants us to go and when. And that's obviously very important."

"But it's looking like that church in Weaverton might be the place. Right?" asked Johnny.

"That's what we're thinking right now. And we know when we do move, it's going to be hardest for the five of you because you will have to leave the friends you've made over the years. We feel bad about that, but that's something we can't avoid," Jack told them.

"If we move to Grace Church, it will probably be pretty soon, like maybe in November," added Connie. "And that means starting school here after Labor Day, leaving in November, and getting started again in a different school in Pennsylvania if we end up going there. Adding that kind of potential change to leaving your friends here is something we're really not happy about for you."

"That does sound sort of messy," agreed Megan.

"So, we've been praying about this whole move possibility, and your mother came up with a very interesting idea to make the move easier for everyone. Why don't you tell them about it, Connie?"

"Okay. Well, you all know what homeschooling is. That's what the Kaiser family from church and some others do."

"Yeah," commented Suzy. "They don't go to school, do they?"

"Well, they don't actually go to school, but they have school at home. Their parents are their teachers, and they have lots of subjects on the computer. Everyone does a lot of work online, using earphones, so they don't disturb each other during class time." Paul, their resident computer geek, really liked this idea already.

"The main reason I think this will work for us is this," continued Connie. "If we homeschool, we'll start that right away in September. You won't go to public school here for September and October. We'll have school at home. If we move in November, we'll just continue with homeschooling, and you won't have to start public school twice. We would continue this for the whole school year. And then decide next summer if we want to continue homeschooling or have you go back to public school or maybe to a Christian school."

"This would also give us a lot of time," added Jack, "to investigate what schools are like in the Weaverton area and which schools you might want to go to if we decide not to continue homeschooling. For example, there's a Christian school in the area that is one of the possibilities. Is all this making sense?"

"What's really weird about this idea is having school at home while all of our friends here are going to public school," noted Sarah.

"That's one of the things I thought of," Connie responded. "It will make the transition of having to leave your friends much more gradual. You'll still be able to see them, but not in school every day. Maybe on weekends until we actually leave."

"If we leave in November," added Jack.

"Yes, dear," said Connie. "If we leave in November."

After a few more minutes of comments, questions, and answers, Jack suggested, "Why don't the five of you go into the living room and talk about this? Your mother and I will clean up from supper and load the dishwasher. If you have any more questions, we'll be in the kitchen. After you have time to discuss this new idea with each other, we'll sit down around the table again and see where we go from here. So, head into the living room for a kid huddle, and let us know when you want to get back together with us again. Then we'll finish off the meal with the brownies Mommy made for us."

While cleaning up after dinner, occasionally, Jack or Connie would glance into the living room to see how things were progressing. The children seemed to be totally engrossed in their discussion. After about twenty minutes, everyone met around the dining room table again with the brownies.

"How did things go?" Jack asked.

"Well, we talked about it a lot," Johnny answered for all of them. "And we all agreed this seems like a good idea. We would at least like to try it and see how it works out. We figured we're the Whyte family, and we like adventures. This seems like a good adventure. Suzy especially liked it because she won't have to start all-day kindergarten this year." Suzy just nodded her head enthusiastically.

"And Paul likes the idea of the computers," Sarah added.

"We're happy you think this makes sense," commented Jack.

"We sort of talked in circles for a while before we actually got down to deciding what each one of us thought about the idea," Sarah continued.

"That's when Johnny took over, and we got somewhere," added Megan.

It was at times like this when it became obvious that Johnny was a natural leader. It wasn't that he tried to take charge or needed to run things. Rather, people around him just seemed to expect him to lead, whether at home, at school, or at play. Somehow, perhaps by the grace of God, this attitude manifested itself as confidence and not as being a bully. His siblings respected him for it, while his parents just marveled at the way he had with people from such an early age and wondered about his future.

"Oh, I see," said Connie. "Please continue, Johnny."

"First of all," he said, "you've taught us that when you believe God is telling you to do something, it would be really dumb to argue with Him. And we all agreed that we trust you, Dad, to know what God wants us to do as a family."

It did not escape Connie's attention that Johnny called his father Dad, and she just smiled. She wondered if all her children might eventually go from calling him Daddy to addressing him as Dad. Although from her own experience as a daughter, even in her thirties, her father was still Daddy to her. She imagined that might be the experience of her three girls. *We shall see*, she thought, *soon I may become Mom and not Mommy.*

"I agree with you, Johnny," responded Connie.

"We also thought," he continued, "that you and Dad have already let us know you think sometime soon God will want us to move to another church. So, we're kind of getting ready for that move anyway. If it's not to Grace in November, it will probably be another church soon. That would also make transitioning from school to school a bit messy, as Megan put it. So, deciding now to try homeschooling makes sense."

"Wow," said Connie. "Are you sure you're only thirteen?"

"Well, I'm going to be fourteen in January."

"Yes, you are," agreed Connie.

"One more thing. And this is very important," said their father. "Since we don't know for sure if we'll be moving in November, we need to ask all of you to keep this to yourselves for a few more weeks, just until school starts."

"We can do that, Daddy," assured Sarah.

"No problem, Dad," agreed Johnny.

And the three younger children each gave an enthusiastic thumbs up. "So, this is a go then?" asked Jack. All heads nodded in agreement.

"I must say that went more smoothly than I expected," he told them all. "But it's what I hoped would happen. So how about we keep praying and ask God to make this whole transition, whenever it takes place, go as smoothly as our conversations did today? Now let's have your mother's brownies with ice cream." And so they did.

Chapter 16

The Next Step

The phone call they had been expecting came early on Friday. The children were spending the morning at home with their parents, going over ideas for homeschooling plans. They were looking at a number of websites that gave suggestions for how to set up homeschooling, what resources and materials they would need, how to schedule class times, and so much more.

They also wanted to research homeschool curricula to see which one they liked best. There were a number of programs written from a Christian perspective. They would choose one of those, they were sure. Their preference was to have the education system reinforce their Christian perspective rather than fight against it.

It was Pete Geisinger from Grace Church calling again. After some friendly chit-chat, Pete reported that the pulpit committee had sent their recommendation to the church council, and they were inviting Pastor Jack to schedule a trial sermon.

Pete's purpose for the phone call was to update Jack on the council's approval and to tell him the next step was his to take. The church would want a date when he could come and preach. And, of course, Pastor Jack would have to notify the Bradford church council in Connecticut of his plans to make that trip.

"Connie and I have been talking about this possibility ever since we last met with you," Jack informed Pete. "And if it fits into your schedule, we would like to aim for the first Sunday in September. If that's not too soon for you guys, it will work best for us and our plans here in Connecticut...not only for the congregation here but also for the children and their education."

"I think that date would work for us," answered Pete with enthusiasm. "As Ron said at our last meeting on Zoom, after you preach, we'll excuse you while we have a brief congregational meeting to take a vote on your candidacy. Assuming they approve of you as our new pastor, we'll call you back into the sanctuary to make the official announcement. Quite frankly, and I hope we're not being too presumptuous, we would like to have a little social event in our Fellowship Hall afterward where you can informally meet and greet the people of Grace and get introduced to some tasty Pennsylvania Dutch refreshments."

That idea made Connie smile in approval.

"If things go that smoothly," Jack commented to Connie, "we could possibly be ready to move to Pennsylvania by the beginning of November."

"I think that would work out well," she agreed.

"That would give you time to get started here at Grace before the busy Christmas season," noted Pete, "and maybe to change any of those events."

"I don't plan to even suggest any changes until we've been there for some time and have developed good trust relationships with one another," assured Jack.

"Sounds good," said Pete.

"Arriving in early November would make it easier for an interim pastor to get things moving here as well," added Jack. "I have a retired pastor friend who fills in for me when I'm away, like when we were in New Jersey last month. I'm pretty sure he'd be open to being the interim pastor here or at least filling in until they get an official interim. The people know him and like him a lot. That would have to be agreed upon by him and our council, of course. But I feel very positive about it, actually, about all that we're talking about."

"Me too," said Pete.

"That makes me three," laughed Connie, almost giggling.

"I guess the next step then is for you, Pastor Jack, to clear this with your church council. Once they give you permission to be away on the first Sunday in September and you notify me, we'll set things up here," assured Pete.

"Are you sure this is not moving too quickly for you, Pete?" asked Connie. "We're talking only a few weeks from now."

"I don't think it will be a problem here. We've been searching for a long time for the right person to be our next pastor," he answered. "There is enthusiastic support for Pastor Jack to fill that position. If you believe, and we agree, that this is God making this happen, a short notice to schedule a trial sermon is just going to fall into place."

"I like the way you think, Pete," replied Jack. "In the words of Humphrey Bogart in *Casablanca*, 'I think this is the beginning of a beautiful friendship.'" All three of them laughed.

After ending the phone call, Jack and Connie looked at each other and let out sighs of relief, big smiles spreading across their faces. "I'm excited," said Connie.

"Yeah, me too," responded Jack. "I'm beginning to pick up on your positive attitude about this possible move."

"It's always good to be on the same page," she agreed.

"So now I have to talk to the church council."

"Yes, and you have to do that soon for everything to work out," agreed his wife.

Pastor Jack simply nodded as he began to think about the best way to handle that.

The children were just finishing breakfast in the kitchen when the phone call with Pete Geisinger ended. Jack and Connie filled them in on what looked like positive signs for them to be moving to Weaverton in the fall. That garnered many smiles and words of approval. The only children who gave any hint of concern about this move were Sarah and Megan. This was a new development. Connie was going to have to follow up on that.

She didn't want negative concerns to arise without dealing with them immediately. She would make it a point to talk with the two girls later today, maybe after lunch. She wondered if Jack had picked up on those subtle negative vibes. She would talk with him about that as well.

As planned, the family gathered around Jack's big twenty-seven-inch desktop computer to check out some of the websites that talked about homeschooling. At the beginning of this effort, there seemed to be much enthusiasm. However, after a while, each child's attention and interest seemed to waver. Connie picked up on this, which prompted her to say, "Are you guys really interested in all this research? Or do you want your father and me to take care of the rest of the details?"

Johnny seemed to catch the tone of the gathering when he said, "We really are interested, but yeah, we think you and Dad can probably handle this better than we can. Maybe it's a little much. What do you think, guys?"

There was a verbal agreement with Johnny's assessment of everyone's mood.

"We just want to make sure you're all on board and feel like you're a part of this important new adventure for our family," assured Connie.

"Thanks," interjected Paul. "But honestly, I think I would have more fun playing video games with Doug."

"That's okay with us if that's what you want. Tell you what," offered Jack, "why don't you have some fun for the rest of the morning with your friends? Let us know what you want to do. And if anyone wants to keep their nose in this planning session, you're welcome to join us. Sound like a plan?"

Affirmation followed, and all the children scattered.

When they were gone from the study, Connie turned to Jack and asked, "Did you pick up on Sarah and Megan's attitude this morning when we reported on our conversation with Pete Geisinger? I don't think there was the enthusiasm that we saw in them previously. I'm wondering if they're having second thoughts about this move."

"Sorry, Connie, I missed that completely. We certainly don't want them being upset about the move."

"Well, I think I should talk to them about it. What do you think?"

"I definitely agree, Connie. We don't want to let this slip on by without dealing with it if there is, in fact, something to be concerned about."

"Oh, I have no doubt about it, Jack. I think I'm going to go chat with them right now before they take off with their friends for the morning."

"Good idea," Jack agreed. "I'll continue on the computer and make some more notes."

"Okay, Jack. Make sure you pray for me while I'm talking to Sarah and Megan."

"You can be sure of that."

With that, Connie left Jack's study in search of two apparently concerned girls. As she headed to their bedrooms for her chat, Connie wondered, *Is this a male/female thing? On the one hand, Johnny and Paul don't seem to be stressed about this move at all. In fact, I think they're looking forward to the change. But Sarah and Megan are having second thoughts, I'm sure. It wasn't my imagination when I picked up on their concern earlier. But where does that leave Suzy? She seems to go with the flow no matter which way the river bends. Well, not completely. She definitely does not like to do new things on her own, like her hesitation to go to a new Sunday school class at Overland while Jack was preaching a few weeks ago. But she'll go anywhere with me. Now I'm thinking like some psychological counselor. Get it together, Connie. Time to talk to your daughters and see what's going on.*

With that, she knocked on the door of the bedroom shared by the two girls. "What's going on, girls?" she asked.

"Nothing, I was just talking to Melody earlier about some ideas for getting together," answered Sarah. And Megan just nodded.

"That's not what I meant," Connie went on. "You know Daddy and I are very much concerned that this apparent move should go as smoothly as possible for all of us. And it was obvious to me this morning that the two of you are feeling a bit concerned about it. That's not surprising. But talk to me. What's going on?"

Sarah and Megan looked at each other for a few moments, and then Megan spoke up. "Well, our tummies are kinda churning from time to time. Sometimes we're excited about the new church and seeing what will happen there.

I mean, it really is a nice place. And we really want to do what God wants us to do."

"But then," contributed Sarah, "we're having so much fun with the girls in our little club in the treehouse. And when we're with them, it makes us feel really bad about not being with them anymore. That's when our tummies start doing their dancing again."

"Sarah and her friends have been really nice to me. They've accepted me in their little group, and I've never had anything like that before. I don't like to think about missing out on that when we move."

"I understand all that, girls. And it makes all the sense in the world. I feel very bad that you're going to have to leave all that behind. But you know we're all going to lose something when we leave here. Your Daddy and I have lots of really close friends that we've been with over the years. It's going to be hard to leave them. But at the same time, we know the Lord has some new friends He's already preparing for us to meet when we move. And as much fun as we've been having here, I have no doubt we're going to have even more fun when we get to the new church. After all, we're the Whytes!"

That brought a chuckle from Sarah and Megan. "We understand all that, Mommy, but it still hurts sometimes when we think about it," said Sarah.

"I'm sure it does," agreed Connie. "But you know, you're comparing being in our new home with all the fun you're having together right now because of all the free time you have. But when school starts, the amount of time you'll have for your special club and the treehouse will be greatly limited. That may be God's way of giving you a transitional period to help get you more ready for the big move. What do you think?"

"That could be," said Sarah.

"I hadn't thought about it that way," added Megan.

"I'm sure you and your tummies will continue to have some ups and downs for a while, but I'm also sure it will gradually get better as we move into a new phase of life here before the big change to a new life in a new home with a new church and some new adventures," counseled Connie.

"I hope so," Megan said.

"Me too," added Sarah.

With that, Connie sensed it was a good time to shift gears. "Okay, so what are you doing for the rest of the day?"

Sarah reported on the plan that she and Melody had been working on a few minutes ago. As she left the bedroom, Connie reminded the girls that there was nothing wrong with the feelings they were having and, if they wanted to talk about it some more, to just let her know. They agreed.

As Connie entered Jack's study, he looked up expectantly and asked, "So, how did it go?"

"It went well," she said and reported on her conversation in the bedroom. "What have you been doing?"

"I think I've narrowed down the curriculum to two Christian publishers. I want your final decision on which one we choose because you will be carrying the heaviest load in this venture. I want you to feel really comfortable with our choice."

And that was how the pastor and his wife spent the rest of the morning, making key decisions about how best to educate their children now and in their new home and working out a budget for resources and supplies. They were sure the children would have been really bored with that part of the morning's discussions.

Chapter 17

REVEALING THE MOVE

It was certainly in the Lord's timing that the regular meeting of the Bradford Church council was the first Monday of the month, only a few days away. That was the time when Jack decided he would reveal to his leaders that it was clearly time for him to move on and accept the next call the Lord extended to him.

While trying to figure out how to approach the subject with the church council, he was praying for some kind of guidance from the Lord. That was when He sensed God telling him to simply share with the council what God had been revealing to him over the last year of his ministry with them. Boy, that made so much sense. Jack wrote down his thoughts.

Monday evening, near the end of the council meeting, Pastor Jack told these leaders that he had an item to share with them that was not on the agenda. "I have something I want to read to you. It's pretty important, and that's why I've written it down."

The president of the council assured him that he would have their undivided attention. So, Pastor Jack stood up and read what he felt God wanted him to share with his leadership team.

"I've been your pastor for more than fifteen years now, and I've enjoyed our time of ministry together." Jack saw the members glancing at one another. He was sure they knew what was coming. "I believe we've grown together as individuals and as a congregation. I also believe, by the grace of God and the cooperative efforts of so many people, that we're a better church now than we were fifteen years ago.

"During this time, our family has grown from two people to seven. And you have been more than supportive of us over these years. In fact, you've been very generous in many ways. And we are very grateful.

"When I came to this church as your pastor, I brought with me certain gifts, talents, and abilities that God has given me to share with you. And I can see how those gifts have been instrumental in helping our church to grow. It's been a joy to watch all of you discover your own special gifts and use them to serve the Lord. It has always been my understanding that the Lord wanted me to help you in this so that our church would become the vital congregation the Lord had in mind for it to be.

"The Lord has made it clear to me during the last year, and Connie and I have talked and prayed about this at great length, that the gifts the Lord has given me have been helpful for the growth of this church up to this point, but that now there's a need for another pastor with a different gift-mix to come and take you to new levels of ministry for which I'm not gifted. Therefore, I believe the Lord wants me to move on to another congregation where I can be useful in helping them seek and do the Lord's work in their area.

"I have been in conversation with Grace Church in Weaverton, Pennsylvania. They've been very supportive of my candidacy and have asked me to preach a trial sermon in their pulpit on the first Sunday in September, just a few weeks from now. Of course, there's no guarantee that they will vote in favor of me, but usually, when we get to this point in the process, it moves along rather quickly. You all know that from your experience in the past.

"I'm sharing this with you in confidence. I don't think any word should get out to the congregation about my moving on until it is certain that it will, in fact, happen. I'm also asking for your permission to be away from our pulpit on the first Sunday in September so that I can travel to Pennsylvania to preach this trial sermon.

"This has been very difficult for me to do because we have friendships and experiences that go very deep into our lives. It will not be easy to leave, but Connie and I are so sure this is God's will that I am trusting in God's grace to make this transition as easy as possible for all of us."

After ending his written statement, Pastor Jack continued, "I'm sorry that statement was so long, but I feel it will answer most of the questions you might have. Yet, I know there's more you might want to know, so what questions do you have?"

The council president was the first to speak. "To say I'm surprised is an understatement. But to be honest with you, I've felt for some time now that it was only a matter of time before God called you someplace else. You just have too many gifts and abilities for us to keep you to ourselves."

"Thank you, Ben, that is very kind of you," responded Pastor Jack.

The president added, "So if you are approved in September, how long will you continue with us?"

"Our bylaws call for a two-month notice to be given when the pastor leaves. That means I would finish up here at the end of October and begin in Pennsylvania the first week of November," explained Pastor Jack.

Elder Ray Laird asked, "What do we do about pastoral leadership in the meantime?"

"It's all pretty much mapped out in the bylaws. Simply put, you would need an interim pastor to give you leadership while you carry out the process of forming a pulpit committee, decide what kind of pastor you want next, and let it be known you are looking for candidates. That will be followed by lots of resumes and interviews. The process can take quite a few months."

"Where do we get an interim pastor?" asked Gerald Smithson.

"There are many organizations to help you with that. One option is to ask Pastor Ned Swanson, who always fills in for me when I'm on vacation. He knows you well, and everyone likes him. That's one possibility."

Not surprisingly, many more questions were asked and answered. Finally, the council took official action to keep this information in confidence and to grant Pastor Jack permission to be away from the pulpit to preach a trial sermon in September at Grace Church in Weaverton.

When Jack arrived home after the meeting, Connie could tell the emotions of having to announce their leaving had quite drained him of his usual energy. "So, how did it go?" she asked.

"They were very understanding. I don't think it could have gone any better. I'm glad the Lord prompted me to write down what I had to say, though. That made it a lot easier to express myself." Jack filled her in with a summary of the reactions and questions.

After a glass of Connie's special mint iced tea, Jack said very quietly, "Connie, I'm exhausted. Let's head off to bed. Tomorrow, we'll have to call Pete and let him know we have the go-ahead for the trial sermon."

"That sounds like a good plan, Jack. We can talk more tomorrow."

Chapter 18

Time Flies

Oh, the days dwindle down

To a precious few

September, November

—Kurt Weill & Maxwell Anderson

It appeared that September and November would be very important months for the Whyte family. The plans were already set up for preaching a trial sermon at Grace Church on the first Sunday in September. If all things went as well as Connie predicted, November would mark the beginning of a new era for their family and their ministry in a new location, their first new location in almost fifteen years. The children had all been born in Connecticut. They were now thirteen (soon to be fourteen), eleven (soon to be twelve), nine, seven, and five.

For the children, time seemed to go at an even pace. But for Jack and Connie, every year seemed to go faster and faster. Jack had a theory about this. For Sarah and Megan, his eleven and nine-year-olds, for example, one year was about one-tenth of their whole life, a truly long period of time in their minds. For Suzy, his five-year-old, one year was 20 percent of her life. Now that is a significant length of time from Suzy's limited perspective. But for Jack, one year is, give or take, about 1/40th of his life. In comparison to the time he had enjoyed so far, each year seemed to go by rather quickly.

Also passing by rapidly were the few weeks leading up to the first Sunday in September. So much to do and so little time to do it.

Distressing for him was the feeling in his heart that he had already moved to Pennsylvania. He knew he had to fight that. The people here at Bradford Church deserved all he had and all he was for as long as he was still their pastor. This took a conscious and intentional attitude adjustment on his part. He would trust the Lord to help him serve them well as long as he was given the honor of doing so.

That included advance planning for their traditional Thanksgiving Eve service even though Pastor Jack knew he might not be there to lead the celebration. They certainly couldn't wait until the last minute to put plans on the calendar for the busy season of Advent and Christmas, either. Obviously, his director of music would take care of most of those details, but Pastor Jack had to give oversight to all such events, even though he might not be present to carry them out.

He had already planned months ago to preach a series of sermons on the apostle Paul's letter to the Philippians during September and October. He would have to adjust the Sundays he would preach each of the messages already being planned in his mind and on his sermon worksheets. He would take advantage of experiences he'd had and insights God had given him and write them down in the advanced stages of his sermon preparation.

It might surprise many of his people to know that he did not write down the final outline of his sermon until the day before he preached it. Yet the preparation of each message was in the works for months before that day. He thought it was the theologian Karl Barth who said that if he wanted to teach a lesson, all he needed was a few days' notice. But a sermon took him nine months of preparation.

Sitting at his desk in the church office, Pastor Jack was thinking about his messages on Philippians. When he'd planned months ago to preach this series, he had no idea he might be leaving for a new ministry. He had to smile to himself. God knew. And that was why God had planted the idea in his mind to preach this series now. There were more reasons than he had known at the time. And that caused him to think it was more than likely God was working things out for him to move to Grace. How appropriate that the apostle Paul begins his letter to the Philippians (chapter 1, verses 3–7a) with these words:

I thank my God in all my remembrance of you, always offering prayer with joy in my every prayer for you all, in view of your participation in the gospel from the first day until now. For I am confident of this very thing, that He who began a good work in you will perfect it until the day of Christ Jesus. For it is only right for me to feel this way about you all, because I have you in my heart.

That might work out to be the text for his final sermon at Bradford. *Wow,* thought Pastor Jack, *I'm getting just like Connie, planning for things before they've even been decided. Let's get back to the present, Jack. You have a lot of work to do.*

That's when Mercy knocked on the door of his office. She needed his article for the next issue of the church's monthly newsletter and wanted to know when he would have it ready for her. Back to reality!

———————•———————

Meanwhile, Connie was busier than usual. In addition to her regular responsibilities as wife and mother of a busy clan, she was getting things ready for homeschooling. She and Jack had ordered a Christian homeschool curriculum. While waiting for it to arrive, they also made decisions about where to hold classes. Going on the assumption they might be leaving soon, they didn't want to do anything permanent in setting up the class area at home.

For supplies, the family took an excursion to the local mall. What they couldn't find there, they ordered online. They realized that, once the curriculum arrived, they would discover more supplies that needed to be purchased. Even though they were careful in their purchases, the cost was mounting up, but Connie was convinced it was worth the expense. Their goal remained to make the expected transition to a new home in the middle of the school year an easier one for the children.

Although Jack and Connie had discussed the best way to handle the trip to Weaverton for the trial sermon, Connie took on the responsibility of working out the final details. This included talking to her parents about hosting the children in Willowbank while they went on to Weaverton. They would be staying at a hotel near the church for the night (arrangements made by Lucy Geisinger), enjoy the hotel's lavish, complimentary breakfast, and meet the pulpit committee's members in the Grace Fellowship Hall in plenty of time for the 10:45 a.m. worship service.

Assuming the church members voted to ask Jack to be their pastor, there would be an informal fellowship time with goodies provided by church members before the couple headed back to pick up their children in Willowbank. It was shaping up to be a whirlwind kind of weekend. But they were still young. They figured they could all deal with the schedule with no difficulty.

Chapter 19

THE BIG WEEKEND

The first weekend in September seemed to arrive almost before they knew it. Thanks to Connie's organizational skills, everything was in place for the trip to Pennsylvania. Ned Swanson, Jack's friend and retired pastor, was set to fill in for him in his absence. The children were up bright and early, excited to spend Saturday and Sunday with Grandma and Granddad. It was always a positive adventure for everyone whenever such a visit could be arranged.

There was some questioning among the members of the Connecticut church about the reason for their pastor to be away again so soon after a four-week vacation. They were informed it was for a special occasion, and Pastor Jack would fill them in upon his return.

Speculation began to circulate among some members about the real reason for this absence. There was clearly suspicion that Pastor Jack was checking out a possible move to another church. Would he still be their pastor after this weekend? Inquiring minds wanted to know. But they would have to wait until he returned to get any answers.

After dropping off five very excited children at Grandma and Granddad's home, Jack and Connie were on the last leg of a possible life-changing journey. The subject of the vote to take place was an important part of their conversation.

"If they vote in favor of you being their pastor, is it automatic for you to say yes?" wondered Connie.

"Well, I will have a decision to make at that time," answered her husband.

"With all the signs that seem to point to God wanting you at Grace, could you really say no to them?"

"It would certainly be difficult to say no. But what if the vote is 55 percent in favor and 45 percent against? Could I really go there knowing that almost half of the congregation didn't want me to be their pastor? That would be difficult for me to do. I think I would be okay with a 75 percent vote in favor of them calling me to be the pastor. Not happy, but okay. But 90 percent or more would make me a lot more comfortable."

"Jack, I really can't believe we're even talking about this. I suppose it's a good thing, but I don't think you realize how good a person and a pastor you actually are and how excellent your preaching is. As I told you before, I'm convinced that once the people at Grace meet you and hear you preach, you're going to be a shoo-in."

"I appreciate your vote of confidence, but I think you might be a little bit prejudiced."

Connie just smiled and said, "We'll just have to wait and see if I'm right." And that was the end of that topic of conversation.

———————————•——————————

When Jack and Connie were about ten minutes away from Grace, they carried out the arrival protocol they'd agreed on. Connie used her cell phone to call Pete and let him and Lucy know they would be arriving in less than ten minutes. Sure enough, when they arrived in the church parking lot, just as they had done the night of their first interview, Pete and Lucy were waiting to greet them with hugs and handshakes. It seemed like they were already old friends.

As promised, the Geisingers took the Whytes on a tour of the big brick parsonage. Having tried to peek in the windows on their very first visit to the church property and having been prevented from seeing anything because the blinds were drawn shut, Connie was especially looking forward to seeing where they might be living and what room would be the best location to set up their homeschool.

———————————•——————————

While they were making this tour, Connie's parents and the five children were sitting down to an evening meal of meatloaf, mashed potatoes, and green beans.

"I wonder what your parents are doing right about now," said Grandma.

"They should be at the church soon if they're not already there," noted Granddad.

"Do you know what their schedule is?" Grandma asked the children.

"Yes," responded Sarah. "The first thing they're going to do is take a tour of the church parsonage. I can't wait to find out what it's like."

"I hope we each get our own bedrooms," added Megan. Everyone agreed that would be a good idea.

"Is the house really that big?" wondered Granddad.

"Oh, yeah," said Johnny. "And it's got this big yard with a really huge pond next to it."

"I skipped stones on the pond with Johnny," added Suzy with a sense of pride.

"Are you all hoping to move there?" asked Grandma. "Or are you worried about it?"

"I'm going to miss my friend Doug," said Paul. "But this looks like a really cool place to live."

"And we're the Whytes," proclaimed Johnny. "We can make it work." Heads nodded all around the dining room table.

"I'm sure you can," agreed Granddad as a pleasant smile spread across his face. "I'm sure you can."

When the tour of the parsonage was over, it was just about time to meet Ron and Molly Young for dinner. They all agreed that Jack and Connie should follow Pete and Lucy in their car. After dinner, they would be led to their hotel and given simple directions to get back to the church in time for the service the next morning. Of course, there was always GPS.

Dinner was at the Coat of Arms Restaurant on the highway near the edge of town. From there, it was only a short jaunt to get to their hotel for the night. Jack and Connie were pleased. Some wise and friendly planning had obviously gone into all the events of the weekend.

Allowing them to stay at a hotel rather than in the home of a church member also meant they could relax as much as possible for the evening. They wouldn't have to feel they had to engage in some kind of impressive conversation with their hosts before going to bed later than they wanted to.

The Coat of Arms Restaurant was a very nicely-appointed establishment. It was white stucco with forest green shutters at each window. In fact, all the trim was that same rich color of green. A coat of arms was emblazoned on the outside of the building, on the face of the rather large and broad chimney on its north side. Beneath this symbol was the number 1895, apparently the year the restaurant was established.

When Connie saw the character of this old building, she looked at Jack with concern. They were in their casual traveling clothes, and this place looked a bit upscale for such attire. Connie whispered her concern as they followed Pete and Lucy through the entrance. Just then, they both noticed that Pete and Lucy were also not dressed for a fancy meal. They breathed a sigh of relief. When they entered the restaurant, they immediately noticed that about half of the diners were "dressed up" and half were casual. All was well.

Jack and Connie were pleased to see Ron and Molly waiting for them in the foyer. They imagined a real friendship developing with them if they moved to Weaverton. Once seated, the conversation around the table among the six of them was relaxed and friendly.

At one point, getting down to business, Ron asked, "Are you comfortable with the arrangements we've made for the weekend?"

"Absolutely," said Jack.

"For the service, you only have three responsibilities," continued Ron. "I will be conducting the service. I'll welcome the people, announce the hymns, and lead in prayer. After the offering, I will introduce you, Pastor Jack. You can approach the pulpit, read your Scripture text, and share the message God has given you. Do you usually conclude your message with a prayer?"

"Yes, I do," answered Pastor Jack.

"Okay, after your prayer, I'll remind the people of the brief congregational meeting we will conduct. I will then point out where Connie is sitting and ask her to stand up. Pete and Lucy, that's when I want you to escort Pastor Jack and Connie to the church office while the meeting takes place."

"Sounds like a good plan," agreed Jack with a smile.

"After the meeting is over and the voting has taken place," continued Ron, "assuming the congregation has approved your candidacy as our pastor, I'll come to the church office to tell you the results of the vote. If you feel good about the numbers, we'll invite the two of you back into the sanctuary. At that point, Pastor Jack, it would be good for you to say whatever you feel is appropriate. And if you don't mind, I think you should dismiss us with a benediction. Do either of you have any questions?"

"No, it all makes sense to me," responded Jack.

"I just want to thank you for how well-organized and encouraging you've been to us. We're really looking forward to what God has in mind for all of us," added Connie.

"Okay, then, let's get you to your hotel so you can settle in for the night," concluded Ron.

"Just follow us," instructed Pete. "While Ron takes care of the check, Lucy and I will guide you to your hotel." After hugs and handshakes, they left the restaurant.

The hotel was one of the nicer hotel chains but certainly not ostentatious. Their room was what you might call a large one-room suite. Against one wall was a large king-size bed with two end tables and a radio/alarm clock. That would come in handy, although Connie had already planned on using the alarm on her cell phone to get them up on time. *Nice to have a backup, though,* she thought.

There was a desk with wifi connections along the right wall. Next to it was a small refrigerator. Located beneath the window that looked out on the highway was a small round table with two chairs. And in the opposite corner was a love seat. The only other door in the room led to the bathroom, which was a nice size and pristine. Jack noted the rain showerhead and smiled approvingly.

Having settled into their hotel room, the couple collapsed on the love seat, just looked at one another for a moment, and smiled. Connie took Jack's hand in hers and asked, "So, how are you feeling about all of this?"

"Actually, I'm feeling quite relaxed. I feel quite confident that Grace is where the Lord wants us to be; at least, all the signs seem to point in that direction. Tomorrow, we shall see if the congregation agrees. I'm willing to be proven wrong. If God wants us here, I want to be here. If that's not His plan for us, it's not my plan for us either."

"Do you need some time to go over your notes for tomorrow's message?" she asked.

"Yes, but that won't take long. You know what God does with me every weekend."

"Yes, I do," said Connie.

"Then you know that sometime in the middle of the night, He will wake me up and give me the final insights to emphasize in my message and what to change if anything needs altering. When that happens, I'll try not to wake you up. Maybe I'll just sneak into the bathroom and quietly go over my notes there. That way, I won't have to turn on any lights that might disturb you."

"Well, if you do happen to wake me up, I'll just pray for you in bed while you do your reviewing."

"You know, I think I have the best wife possible," smiled Jack.

"That's true," responded Connie, "and don't you forget it." With that, she began to get ready for a good night's rest.

About an hour later, Jack left the comfort of the love seat in the corner of their hotel room, placed his Bible and his notes on the small desk in the corner, set the alarm clock for 7:30 a.m., and joined Connie in the comfy king-size bed. In a short amount of time, it was lights out for a pleasant sleep, with hopes of discovering in the morning the next step God had for them on their journey with Him.

Chapter 20

THE CALL

Jack and Connie were both awake about fifteen minutes before their two alarms alerted them. Thanks to Connie's efficient packing, getting ready for the beginning of an exciting day went quite smoothly. Within an hour, they were dressed and headed to the hotel's dining room for a sumptuous breakfast that did not disappoint. They both had real scrambled eggs, bacon, and toast. The shoofly pie was sweet and delicious. Jack had his Irish breakfast tea while Connie enjoyed fresh-brewed Colombian roast coffee with just a touch of half-and-half.

Back in their room after breakfast, they sat together on the love seat. Holding hands, Jack and Connie prayed for God's guidance and strength and for His will to be revealed through the events of the morning. Then Jack took time to call his parents to catch them up on their experiences since yesterday and to ask them to pray as well. Tom and Janet assured Jack they would certainly be doing that throughout the morning. With a promise to call and let them know the results of the congregational meeting, Jack ended the conversation and turned to Connie.

"Are you ready? I think we should be going."

"One last stop in the bathroom, and I'll be set to go," she said.

Jack checked the drawers and the desktop to make sure they were leaving nothing behind and rolled their one suitcase to the door, ready to head out. After checking out, they headed to their car in the parking lot, put the luggage in the trunk, checked the gas gauge, and started the car. Jack reviewed his instructions to get to the church, confident he knew how to get there, and with that, they were off onto the highway to Grace. He was quite sure he wouldn't need the GPS this time.

They arrived at the church property just about the time Sunday school was starting. The parking lot was fairly full. That was a good sign, Jack thought. As promised, there was a space marked "Reserved for Pastor" available for them. As soon as they began to walk toward the church building, they looked up and saw Pete and Lucy's familiar and smiling faces. They felt welcome already and waved to their greeters.

The four of them headed to the Fellowship Hall, where preparations for a luncheon were already in progress. There was some whispering back and forth in the kitchen upon their arrival as Pete and Lucy led the way to a small delegation from the pulpit committee who were waiting for them. Not all committee members could be there because some of them had responsibilities in the various Sunday school classes now in session.

When they were seated around a table, Betty Pierce from the kitchen committee came over to offer them coffee or tea while they took care of business. The mood of the gathering was relaxed and friendly. Yet, under the surface, there was a sense of excitement. It was agreed that Jack and Connie would sit in the sanctuary with Pete and Lucy, with Pastor Jack on the center aisle so it would be convenient for him to move up to the pulpit at the appropriate time.

Ron entered the Fellowship Hall with final instructions and invited Pastor Jack to accompany him into the sanctuary so they could go over logistics for the service while Connie continued to visit with the committee members. Pastor Jack, with notes in Bible and Bible in hand, followed Ron's lead. As they entered the sanctuary, the choir was going over their special music for the service. Early arrivers had already begun to find seats in their usual pews.

As Ron and Pastor Jack worked their way down the center aisle to the chancel area in the front, heads turned, and mouths whispered. People wondered what God had in mind for them today. Was this good-looking man in his blue blazer and gray trousers going to be their new pastor? What kind of preacher was he? What does his wife look like? Did she pick out that beautiful tie he was wearing, or did he have a fashion sense of his own? Ron and Pastor Jack smiled at one another, imagining what was going on quietly around them.

The two of them talked about what would happen and where it would take place. Ron's desire was to make sure Pastor Jack was comfortable with the surroundings and at ease with the order of the service. He asked Pastor Jack if he wanted to put his notes and Bible on the pulpit. Jack chose to keep them with him. When Ron was sure the candidate was familiar with what was to take place, they rejoined Connie and the others in the Fellowship Hall and discussed when they would enter the sanctuary for the start of the service.

A few minutes before the 10:45 a.m. service was to begin, the growing Fellowship Hall group headed into the sanctuary. Jack, Connie, Pete, and Lucy went to the seats reserved for them near the front of the sanctuary while the other committee members dispersed to their usual seats for worship. On the way to their seats, Pastor Jack and Connie were greeted with many smiles, words of welcome, and many handshakes. *What a friendly group of people,* they thought.

Ron welcomed the people to this special service and invited them to focus their attention on the Lord, the one they had come to honor and worship. The congregation sang the hymns with enthusiasm, the choir's special music was quite good, and Ron conducted the service in a relaxed and informal manner.

Jack thought back to that first day they'd seen this church building. He remembered peering into the sanctuary through one of the windows, noting the beauty of the setting, and saying to his wife, "I could really worship here." At this moment in their first worship service in this beautiful setting with people praising God, he realized he had been right.

Then the time came for Pastor Jack to step into the pulpit. Ron introduced him and Connie and invited Pastor Jack to come forward. Standing in front of the congregation, a smile spread across Pastor Jack's face. He sensed that these people were open to hearing God's Word for them today.

His message was a simple one and basic to the faith of every Christian. He began by reading his text from the first letter of the apostle John, chapter 4, verses 7 through 11.

Beloved, let us love one another, for love is from God; and
everyone who loves is born of God and knows God. The one

who does not love does not know God, for God is love. By this
the love of God was manifested in us, as God has sent His only
begotten Son into the world so that we might live through
Him. In this is love, not that we loved God, but that He loved
us and sent his Son to be the propitiation for our sins. Beloved,
if God so loved us, we also ought to love one another.

If, at that moment, someone were to look over the preacher's shoulder, they would get a glimpse of his sermon notes.

God Loves You (1 John 4:7–11)

Tell the boat story.

I. Why does God love you?

    A. He made you.

    B. He bought you.

    C. He is love. It is His nature to love you.

        1. He doesn't love you because of what you've done.

        2. Often in spite of what you've done.

II. Therefore, we ought to love one another.

    A. Why?

        1. Because God made us all.

        2. Because God bought us all (precious in His sight).

        Sing: "Jesus Loves the Little Children."

3. Because He is our example and Lord.

"Just do it!"

B. How?

1. Listen to one another.

2. Observe one another.

See others through God's eyes.

3. Reach out to one another. Take time for them.

Pastor Jack began his message with a simple prayer. "Bless us, O Lord, and guide us by Your Word and by Your Holy Spirit. Amen." He had learned this opening prayer from a seminary professor whose tongue had been cut for preaching the gospel after the Russians invaded Hungary in 1956. The professor always began his classes with that verse. Since then, Jack has always used it to start his sermons.

He continued, "I would like to tell you a story about a young boy. He was given a piece of wood by his father and challenged to make something of it. Taking out his penknife, this young lad began to whittle away until, finally, he had carved a small boat. To check if it was seaworthy, he took it down to the local creek and put it in the water. That cute little boat got caught in a current and went rushing downstream so fast the little boy couldn't keep up with it. Very sad, he went home to tell his father about his great loss.

"Some weeks later, this same little boy was walking down Main Street when he noticed his very own little boat in a pawnshop window. It was his boat. He made it. He recognized it. And he loved it. When he approached the store clerk and asked to claim what was his, the man said, 'I'm sorry, son, but that boat is mine now. If you want it, you will have to pay for it.' Saddened but determined, that young lad decided to earn enough money to buy back his little boat. It wasn't a perfect boat, but it was his boat.

"After a few weeks of lawn mowing and doing chores around the house, the boy went back to the pawnshop and saw that his boat was still in the front window. With a smile and determination in his step, the lad entered the store and bought back his little boat. As he left the store, the boy held that boat to his chest and said, 'Oh, little boat, you are twice my boat now. You are mine because I made you, and you are mine because I bought you.'"

Based on this simple story, Pastor Jack proceeded through his sermon notes, encouraging the congregation to accept the fact that they were made, bought, and really loved by God at a great price. He challenged them to increase their ongoing efforts to love God and one another. After a brief prayer, he returned to his seat alongside his wife. She leaned over to him and whispered, "I love that boat story."

Ron thanked Pastor Jack for his message and excused him and Connie while the congregation conducted their brief meeting. The two of them left with Pete and Lucy and headed to the church office. On the way, the Geisingers told them how much they appreciated his message. "You helped me to finally accept the fact that God really does love me," exclaimed Lucy.

After less than ten minutes, Ron joined them in the church office. "I know you had some concern about the percentage of votes that would be cast for you. And I appreciate that. But I have no doubt you will be more than happy about the numbers. It was unanimous. I'll tell you more about that when we return to the sanctuary. That is if you accept."

"Do I accept? Absolutely! Connie, do you agree?"

"Absolutely. Praise God."

Pete and Lucy returned to their seats in the sanctuary while Pastor Jack and Connie happily remained up front with Ron.

"Pastor Jack, members, I have what I think is good news for all of us. Jack Whyte, we believe you are the man God is calling to be our next pastor. And we ask you to accept our invitation. Before you respond, I want everyone to know that for the first time in anyone's memory, you are the only candidate we've ever called to be our pastor who received a unanimous vote from the congregation."

Instantaneous applause erupted throughout the sanctuary. Jack stood there smiling broadly while Connie looked at her husband with an expression that communicated to him, "I told you so."

"The microphone is yours," said Ron.

After a few moments to gather his thoughts, Pastor Jack said, "Thank you so very much. Connie and I and our five children have been praying about this and praying for you for a few weeks now. We had a deep sense that God wanted us to come here as your pastor. We thank God that you agree. We're excited about the possibilities for years of ministry together. I'm impressed with who you are as a people and what you've done as a congregation. We look forward to what we will accomplish together as God leads us into the future. So, in a few words, I accept your invitation to be your new pastor with hope and gratitude."

More applause followed as he returned the microphone to Ron. When invited to do so, Connie declined the opportunity to make some remarks with the comment, "I'll leave the speaking to my husband."

Ron invited everyone to attend the celebratory luncheon in the Fellowship Hall following the benediction from Pastor Jack. Molly joined her husband, Ron, from the choir pews and the two of them led the procession down the center aisle to the Fellowship Hall.

The time celebrating in Fellowship Hall was enjoyable and uplifting. The food was delicious. The people were encouraging. But Jack and Connie couldn't wait to call their parents and the children to share the excitement. They finally knew the answer to the big question they had all been wondering about for so long.

The trip to Willowbank and then the long trek back to Connecticut were both filled with lots of chatting and singing and imagining. But underlying it all, buried in deep silence, was the unpleasant task of informing their present congregation that their time of ministry together was soon coming to an end.

It would be difficult to make that announcement. It would be uncomfortable for two months to deal with the impending loss of rich relationships nurtured over many years. But they had a God who would carry them through it all and bring blessings for those who would trust Him, a God who directs and heals and makes whole.

Chapter 21

MAKING THE TRANSITION

What a strange term that is! Receiving a "call" to pastor a church. It's something like responding to the ringing of your telephone, but certainly much more than that. It's a biblical term. It goes all the way back to Genesis when God called Abram out of Ur of the Chaldees and told him to leave where he had been living for so long and go to a place to be revealed later. It took a lot of faith to do that. Not knowing where you're going but believing that the God you love and trust, the God who loves you, will let you know what you need to know when you need to know it.

But a call from God is not always to another place. Sometimes it's a call to take on a new role with new challenges and responsibilities. The apostle Paul was one of many who experienced that. In Romans 1:1, Paul describes himself as someone "called as an apostle, set apart for the gospel of God."

This verse was running through Jack's mind as he prepared to tell the Bradford congregation what it meant that God was calling him and his family to leave where they had lived for so long to go to a place they were only now getting to know, a place He had assigned to them. They would be going with joy and expectation but also with sadness at leaving those they had loved for so long and who had been so supportive and loving to their family in so many ways.

The first thing Pastor Jack did after returning to Connecticut was to email all the council members. They deserved to be the first to know the results of his trial sermon. He again asked them to keep this in confidence until he could make the announcement to the congregation the next Sunday morning. In the meantime, he suggested they answer any question by saying: "Everyone will find out on Sunday" or "Pastor will tell us everything on Sunday."

Next on his list was to call a meeting of the staff. They needed to be in the loop from the beginning. They would need to talk about new responsibilities and new possibilities that would arise in the next few months while the search for a new pastor would be carried out.

Soon Pastor Jack would have to face his congregation to tell them about this new development. He was sure some of them expected it already. They were intelligent people. They could read the signs. But most were going to be shocked. Pastor Jack hurt for them. They were the ones most prominent in his prayers right now. After talking to Connie about the announcement to be made, they both agreed that reading a statement similar to the one he had read to the church council would be the best way to go.

This was going to be a difficult week coming to a head with the service on Sunday morning. But it was all being balanced out with dreams of the good that was soon to come to the family in a new location. And Pastor Jack also had to believe that God had new and exciting things in mind for the Connecticut church and the new leadership He already had in mind for them in the future.

Perhaps the one person Pastor Jack was most concerned about was Mercy, his secretary of almost ten years. She had grown so much in her job over the years. In the beginning, he used to say of her, "She's a lousy secretary but great with people." The fact is that from the very beginning of her employment as church secretary, Mercy probably did as much counseling as Pastor Jack. And what a great sense of humor. He remembered laughing so hard the first time she asked him about some new attendees, "Well, tell me, Pastor Jack, are they Spirit-filled, cream-filled, or jelly-filled?"

When Mercy began as his secretary, the bulletins she typed for Sunday morning services had so many mistakes it was hard to believe. And yet, they did have to laugh about it. But she had grown so much over the years as a secretary and as a child of God.

No pastor was ever protected as much as Pastor Jack was protected by Mercy Summerfeld. She guarded the access to his office, only allowing people in who really needed to see him. She graciously filtered all his emails. She could be trusted to forward to him only the ones that were important for him to handle. Others were either shuffled off to other responsible persons or quietly deleted.

This task of insolating Pastor Jack from unnecessary intrusions was granted to her gradually and carefully over the years. He was not looking forward to having to train another secretary to be as efficient as Mercy was. Who knows? His new secretary at Grace might already be that efficient. No, probably not.

Jack and Connie had been concerned all along about the need to ask their children to keep quiet about the possibility of them moving to a new church soon. They didn't like putting them under that kind of pressure. Yet they didn't know how to avoid it and still maintain some sense of unity and peace in the congregation.

Thank God for wonderful kids! The children had been so good about keeping this possible move to themselves. Now Jack and Connie were happy to give them the green light. After their father's announcement on Sunday morning, they were free to talk about the move to anyone, anywhere, anytime. And they could also explain this was the reason the Whyte children were having school at home.

Meanwhile, Connie was busy getting things set up for homeschooling. The curriculum had arrived. Honestly, it looked a bit overwhelming. But she and Jack were both convinced this was what the Lord wanted them to do, so they tried to be positive about it.

During the week before the trial sermon, there had been a bit of furniture moving and relocation of tables that could be utilized as desks. They already had four computers that were adaptable for homeschool use. Two more had been ordered from an online agency that specialized in low-cost computers for homeschoolers, and they had arrived the previous week. These were not designed with the memory needed for fancy video games, but that was not why they were being purchased.

Earplugs were necessary to make sure these students didn't distract one another while watching a video class. Connie continued to be thankful for the many homeschool websites with practical tips for getting started in this new adventure.

There was no doubt in Connie's mind that the first few days and weeks of homeschooling were going to be a bit rough, to put it mildly. Maybe even chaotic. Yet all seven members of the Whyte family were looking forward to trying something new, especially five-year-old Suzy. She had not been looking forward to starting full-day kindergarten. For her, homeschooling was the best idea ever.

Chapter 22

CLASSES BEGIN

Jack was usually in his office at the church no later than 8 a.m. He would heat up some water for his Irish breakfast tea in the tea kettle in the church kitchen and try not to destroy the teapot. One of the jokes going around the church and the family was to tease him about the offensive odor in the church office wing whenever he would forget that he was heating water for tea and allowed the aluminum pot to almost melt after all the water had evaporated. Over the years, Jack bought quite a few new tea kettles for the church kitchen. His excuse was that he could never do more than one thing at a time. He admitted he was not good at multitasking.

On this first morning of school at home, his plan was not to show up at the church office until 10 a.m. He wanted to help Connie get things started for their first effort at homeschooling. He sent an email to Mercy, letting her know of his plans.

Supplies had been put in place. Workbooks were selected for each child. Appropriate videos that accompanied the curriculum had been downloaded. Now, making it all happen without too many glitches was the challenge of the day.

They began with breakfast at 7:30 a.m. Connie had no trouble waking the children. Everyone seemed excited about this new challenge in education and family life. This was followed by breakfast together around the kitchen table. Then Jack led them in devotions and Bible reading for the morning.

They decided this would be a good time to have everyone memorize a Bible verse each week. For the older children, the challenge would be greater. They were using an online program designed to help families memorize Scripture in an organized and fun way. Creatively dealing with the curriculum for five different ages was the real challenge, but Connie was up to the task.

She was encouraged by suggestions from homeschooling parents who had "how-to" blogs on the internet for first-time homeschoolers.

The four younger children gathered around the large, rectangular dining room table, using it for their desks. Jack had created some custom-sized booster seats for the children who needed them. He had also reworked an end table for Johnny to use as his work desk.

Connie began with story time for Suzy while Jack introduced Paul and Megan to their first experience with workbooks, answering any questions they had about how to proceed, including how much time to spend on their first assignment. Sarah was a self-starter and had no trouble at all beginning her first lesson as a sixth grader in language arts.

Meanwhile, Johnny settled himself in an upholstered chair, laptop in hand, to take on the challenge of eighth-grade math. Fortunately for him, his father had been a whiz at math and science in high school and college, so questions that might come up about those subjects would likely be referred to him.

At the end of the time allotted for the first two classes of the morning, during which Jack and Connie moved from child to child to review their progress and answer any questions they had, there was a break for a mid-morning snack. This is when Jack said goodbye to the children, instructed them to cooperate completely with their mother, and turned over the reins to Connie. He headed off to the church office, bracing himself for any curious parishioners with questions about the previous weekend away.

Mercy had developed into such an efficient church secretary by this time that things ran smoothly with or without Pastor Jack. Add to this the fact that he was a great delegator and had long ago developed an effective leadership team.

When the pastor went away for four weeks of vacation, everyone just wished him well. But when Mercy took a vacation, there was almost a sense of panic. "Oh, dear, what are we going to do while Mercy is away from the office?"

Pastor Jack had organized the church into twelve groups of families with an assigned and trained "shepherd" to generally oversee each "flock." These lay shepherds dealt with a number of issues. Were their "sheep" in church services? Did they have any needs? Should the pastor step in to provide counsel or resolve an issue?

It was this awareness of the teamwork they had developed over the years that caused Pastor Jack to know that he and Mercy needed to sit down and talk about the best way to make this transition happen. How could they make this move the least disruptive possible, from his pastorate through an interim period and leading on to a new pastor arriving?

Pastor Jack's practice was to have a one-day fall staff retreat at a nearby camp for the purpose of scheduling programs and dates for the entire upcoming year. Normally held in October, his plan now was to have a modified three-hour retreat in the church building whenever they could schedule it, preferably in the next week or two. This process would be a big help for an interim pastor and a good potential roadmap for the permanent pastor when he is chosen.

Having worked on this project for over an hour, Jack took a break to call Connie to see how things were going at home with her students. He was encouraged to learn that she did not have to pull out even one hair during the morning session. Things were going fairly smoothly. She was convinced they would all be in a groove once a few weeks were under their belts.

No. Jack didn't need to come home if he was busy with his work at the church, but if he wanted a BLT sandwich with pickles and chips for lunch, he was invited. So, Jack told Mercy he was going home for lunch, and they would take care of any loose ends in their planning process when he returned.

Lunch was a noisy affair. Well, it was never a quiet event, but the chattering around the kitchen table today was a few decibels above normal. When Jack entered the house through the backdoor and came into the kitchen, shouts of welcome rang out from all five children. The children and Connie were all in a good mood.

"It looks like everyone enjoyed the first morning of school," commented Jack.

"Yeah, it was great," agreed Suzy. Depending on the amount of food in their mouths, the other children affirmed her opinion.

"And how is the teacher doing?" asked Jack.

"Mommy was really cool," said Sarah.

"Cool?" questioned Jack. "You called your mother cool? Do kids still use that term today?"

"Well, no," clarified Sarah. "I just wanted to use a vocabulary your generation would understand." Everyone, including the cool mother, guffawed.

"So, Mommy," asked Jack. "Did you think the morning was cool?

"I thought things went well, considering I didn't know what I was doing. There were a few times when one or the other of the children had to wait for an answer from me because I was tied up with a brother or sister. But all in all, I think it went well. I'm sure once we get a routine worked out, each one will be able to move on to the next project and leave a note on the calendar about what was done and when it was finished so we can keep an accurate record."

"That sounds good to me. By the way, I heard a rumor that there might be a BLT available for me if I came home. Is there any truth in that?"

"Of course, dear," said Connie. "Just have a seat, and I'll get that ready for you. While you're waiting, how did things go at the office today? Were you bombarded by church members wanting to know what reason you had for taking another Sunday off?"

Jack had to laugh at that. "Actually, we had a morning free of interruptions. Mercy and I had a chance to come up with a process to get things ready for the congregation after we leave. I'm sure that whoever the interim pastor is, he will be pleased with what we hand to him."

Turning to his oldest child, he said, "Hey, Johnny, would you pass the chips, please."

"Here's your sandwich, Jack," offered Connie. "So, what's your schedule for the rest of the day?"

"If you don't need me here, I want to check back with Mercy to see how she may have finalized our efforts of the morning. Then I need to make two hospital visits. Erma Spotts and Hank Crane are both in Memorial Hospital with some sort of bug and, sad to say, not doing well. I am concerned about them. So are their families. Erma has a problem with dehydration, and I'm not sure at this point what Hank is dealing with. But I want to find out."

Connie nodded her head. "Okay, then. I'll see you when? In time for dinner?"

"Absolutely," Jack assured her. "Do you think the cook is going to have time to prepare a meal?"

"I don't think that will be a problem," answered Connie. "We'll be finished with our first day of classes between two and three o'clock. I'll have plenty of time to get things done in the kitchen. And look around you at all the sous chefs I have available right here in the kitchen."

Their youngest child made sure there was no mistake about her identity. "My name is not Sue; it's Suzy. But I can help you in the kitchen."

"Thank you for reminding us, Suzy," said Connie. "I should probably explain that 'sous' is a French word. And no, you won't be studying a foreign language for a few years. But in French, 'sous' means 'under.' A sous chef is someone who works under the chef. And the chef would be me. So, I would be very happy for the help. And that goes for the rest of you as well."

"Okay, I'm off to the office and the hospital. Thanks for lunch. Bye, guys." Everyone waved to him as he headed for his car.

"Time to get back to class," said Connie. "Let's clean up the kitchen and get started." And with the sliding of chairs and the noise of dishes being rounded up, that is just what they did.

Chapter 23

FINAL DAYS IN CONNECTICUT

The months of September and October were going by so quickly and yet so slowly. There didn't seem to be enough time to do all that was necessary for the transition. Yet it also seemed like the move was never going to take place. So much to do, so many plans to be made, and so many people to talk to. Add to that the fact that there were the usual ongoing responsibilities at the church for Pastor Jack and the oversight of the family and homeschooling for Connie.

An early item on the checklist was contacting a moving company. Having asked for recommendations from friends and church members, there were five companies suggested. Connie volunteered to take care of this matter. *It's fortunate*, thought Connie, *that there are five companies on my list because it took phone calls to all of them to find one that had a moving van available the last week of October to pack up our belongings and cart them to the parsonage in Pennsylvania.*

Now all they had to do was come up with a schedule for packing and labeling everything they had accumulated over almost fifteen years of family living. One option to help with the cost of the move was to give away a lot of items of clothing and numerous incidentals that were currently stored in the attic and had not seen the light of day for months and, in some cases, years. Yes, Grace Church was going to pay for their move, but that was no reason to make them pay more than was necessary. Connie felt they should be as cost-effective as though they were paying the bill themselves. Her mind was made up. A lot of things had to go!

Meanwhile, Pastor Jack was committed to making the transition for the Connecticut church's new pastor as easy as possible. This meant putting together a packet of material that included the names of key people in the church and their responsibilities. There was contact information for local hospitals and funeral directories to help with pastoral duties.

Names of the dentists and family doctors the Whytes had used over the years, as well as the most convenient and economical grocery stores, were included. Very significant were the names, addresses, phone numbers, and emails of the twelve laymen who were shepherds of the church's flocks. Pastor Jack would also provide his own personal cell phone number in case the new interim or permanent pastor had questions.

Other than that, however, it was his conviction that he should keep his nose out of the business of the Connecticut church and its members once he left for Pennsylvania. It would not be fair to the new pastor to act otherwise.

At the regular meeting of the lay shepherds, Pastor Jack followed his usual schedule, which included opening devotions and prayer by one of the shepherds, followed by Pastor Jack's teaching on a portion of Scripture. Currently, they were studying the apostle Paul's first letter to the Corinthians.

Jack had to smile when he considered the timing of it all. Months ago, when they began this study of 1 Corinthians, he did not know he would be moving to Pennsylvania at this time. Yet here they were studying in 1 Corinthians 12:12–27 the importance of each member of the church being an essential part of the body of Christ. No one was more important than any other, yet all were important in God's plan. What a great lesson to leave with these dedicated shepherds upon his departure.

One important thing, he believed, had to be said. "Your lay ministry has been one of the most important things I've done since I came here as pastor. As we've grown, we've been able to avoid the high cost of adding more pastors to the staff while expanding very personal, loving, and meaningful pastoral care for all our members. I'm extremely grateful for your ministry help over the years, both to the congregation and to me. Next to my wife, you are the ones I go to for advice and counsel. You need to understand, however, that when the new pastor arrives on the scene, he may have an entirely different approach to ministry.

"You need to go with the flow in that matter. If he continues with the lay shepherd program, I believe he and the congregation will benefit. If he doesn't see the value in doing so, I know you will continue informally and personally to be of assistance to those who need it in the church, just because you are brothers and sisters in the family of God."

Pastor Jack closed the meeting with prayer after inviting any of the shepherds to pray as well. This was followed by some rich conversations, warm hugs, and firm handshakes. Pastor Jack would miss these leaders. That was evident in the tears beginning to well up in his eyes.

"We need to make some decisions about the actual move itself," said Connie one evening after dinner. "Our house will be emptied by the movers. It will be a few days before their schedule allows them to arrive at the parsonage. We're going to need a place to stay during that time. Any thoughts?"

Jack responded, "Yes, I've been thinking about that. Since my parents live not too far from Weaverton, and Dad has been able to purchase a few furnished rental properties over time through his contracting business, I thought it might be good to check and see if he had anything available during the time we're talking about. What do you think? If he has anything, and that's a big if...but God is good at handling big ifs...if Dad has something, I'm sure it won't cost us anything."

"Wouldn't that be great!" said Connie. "Do you really think that's a possibility?"

"I guess we won't know until we ask. I can call him right now and see about it."

"Okay," encouraged Connie. "You call, and I'll pray. Meanwhile, I'll see how things are going with the children. They're being very quiet, and I hope that's good."

After making sure all was well in the family room, only having to referee one contested dispute about whose turn it was to control the TV remote, Connie went to Jack's study. "So, how did it go?" she asked.

With a big smile on his face, Jack looked at Connie and said, "You are not going to believe this. Well, yes, you probably will. One of Dad's tenants contacted him yesterday with good news and bad news. The good news was he got a promotion. The bad news was that the company was moving him to Virginia. Guess when he will be moving." Not giving her time to respond, Jack continued, "He asked to get out of his contract with Dad because he has to move the last week of October and start his new job in November. Hallelujah!"

"And your dad says we can stay there during the move?"

"Yep, no problem."

"You know," speculated Connie, "this would make a good story for a novel. Isn't it sad that so many people miss out on such amazing interventions by God in their lives because they don't expect them?"

"Do you remember how I used to sign all of my letters to you?" asked Jack.

"You would write 'Love, and expect a miracle,'" answered Connie. "I wish more people would live like that. If they did, I'm convinced they would see more miracles in their lives."

"You're absolutely right," agreed Jack. "Absolutely right."

"So...God and your dad came through for us. Wow, I never cease to be amazed at God's perfect timing."

"Well, there is one complicating factor."

"Oh, no. Now what?"

"Dad is very happy to have us stay in this soon-to-be vacated home. But... they really want us to stay with them. You know how big their house is. There would be room for all of us to stay comfortably for five days. And it would be familiar territory for the children, so one less adjustment for them to make. Mom and Dad would love to have fun with the children while we're there."

"I don't know what to say, Jack. I guess we should be thankful that our generous God has given us more than we asked for...two possible places for us to stay. Take your choice."

"As the apostle Paul told the Ephesians in 3:20, God 'is able to do exceeding abundantly beyond all that we ask or think.' Another plus for staying with my parents is that the home Dad said is available is very nice but certainly not as spacious."

"You know how I hate to make decisions. Which home do you think the kids would prefer?"

"Why don't we ask them?" And with that, Jack called the children to join them for a little powwow.

Amid a little hubbub and jostling, Connie got the children settled. "We have a decision to make," she said, "and we would like your opinion." Five pairs of young eyes opened wide in anticipation.

"We need to find a place to stay while the moving van people clean out our house and deliver our stuff to the parsonage in Pennsylvania. That's going to mean five days without a home."

"Gee, we've never been homeless before," said Paul.

"That's true," continued Connie. "But we actually have found a place to stay during those five days. In fact, we have two places where we can stay."

"Yes," interjected Jack, "I called Nana and PopPop about this. They own a few homes that they rent to people. So PopPop said we could stay in one of those homes for the five days, or we could move in with them while the movers do their thing. What do you think? Any preferences?"

After a brief huddle and some animated conversation, Johnny said, "We want to stay at Nana and PopPop's house."

"Yeah!" the other four children agreed.

"Well, that was easy," said Connie. "What do you think, honey?"

"I guess we're going to stay with Nana and PopPop for a few days. I'll call and let them know our decision," offered Jack. "They're going to be pleased." And the children cheered.

At the southern end of the geographical move, Pastor Jack had some key conversations with the leadership of Grace Church. Of central importance was working out details with council president Ron Young. It was agreed, because of the timing of the moving company's schedule, they would ask the interim pastor at Grace to continue on through the first Sunday in November.

Meanwhile, Pastor Jack had been in contact with the church's music director, Sally Erb. She wanted to know what his preferences were musically. Did he want her to select all the music for Sunday morning services or only the special music each week by the choir? They agreed that for the first month or more, Sally would prayerfully select the hymns based on the sermon titles and Scripture text for the message of the morning. Pastor Jack would make that information available to her in an email in plenty of time for her to make those decisions. Jack was impressed with the music director and her attitude.

Sally had much praise for the organist/pianist, who was also on staff and had been a part of the church for the past two years. Her name was Anita Garcia. Anita had three children, all boys, while Sally was single and in her forties.

Another key conversation for Pastor Jack was with the church secretary. Admittedly, he has been spoiled by Mercy Summerfeld, who he had personally trained. How would things work out with the new one, Linda Hartman? She certainly seemed personable. Before she came to the church, she'd had a dozen years of experience working in a high-level business office. Based on her well-documented experience and his conversation with her, Jack was feeling very positive about them working well together as a team.

He assured her he would send her the same email that would go to Sally Erb, including his sermon titles and Scripture texts, so she would have more than enough time to include the pertinent information in the church's Sunday bulletin. She seemed quite happy about that.

───────────·───────────

Connie surveyed the homeschool setup once more. They had been in operation for more than four weeks at this point. As expected, they were now in a kind of groove. They had a good rhythm going but not a schedule so rigid that there was no room for variety. Connie felt good about the progress the children were making in their studies. Sometimes questions came up for which she had no answers, but she always knew where to find them.

At lunchtime, Jack joined them in the kitchen. "How did things go today, guys and gals?" he asked. "Is your teacher still doing well?"

"Yeah," said Sarah laughingly. "She's still cool."

Before going back to work, Jack asked the children what they thought at this point about schoolwork.

Johnny spoke for all of them. "First of all, Dad, it doesn't seem like work. It's really fun. Not always easy, but fun." His sisters and brothers voiced their agreement.

"But the best part," added Paul, "is that there's no homework! Who wouldn't be happy about that?" Cheers went up from the kids around the table.

"That sounds good to me, too. Okay, gang, I'm off to work. I'll see you at dinner. But Connie, remember I have a meeting of the Sunday school teachers tonight at seven."

"I won't forget," she said, giving her husband a hug and kiss goodbye.

"Bye, Daddy," chimed in the children.

"Goodbye. Make sure you get your schoolwork done. Oh, I forgot. It's not work; it's fun." Out the door he went.

Chapter 24

THE LAST SUNDAY

The last Sunday in October was Pastor Jack's last day as the Bradford Church pastor. There were quite a few tears shed during the service, as well as some relief when Pastor Jack was able to add some levity to his message.

The people loved it when he began his sermon with the old story of the man who said to his wife on Sunday morning, "I'm not going to church today." His wife said, "Give me three good reasons why you shouldn't go." "One," he said, "because I don't feel like it. Two, because I had a bad night last night and I'm tired. And three, because I don't think the people there like me."

His wife said to him, "Okay, I'll give you three good reasons why you should go to church today. One, because it's Sunday and we always go to church on Sunday. Two, because the children and I are going, and it will look bad if you don't go with us. And three, you should be going to church today because you're the pastor."

The day before, when Pastor Jack had made the final outline for his message of the morning, it was confirmation of what he'd been thinking just a few months before. He was able to conclude his ongoing sermon series from Paul's letter to the Philippians on this special day. He used as his sermon text Philippians 1:3–7.

I thank my God in all my remembrance of you, always offering prayer with joy in my every prayer for you all, in view of your participation in the gospel from the first day until now. For I am confident of this very thing, that He who began a good work in you will perfect it until the day of Christ Jesus. For it is only right for me to feel this way about you all, because I have you in my heart.

171

That passage in Philippians 1, assuring the readers of Paul's love for them, was the exact passage Pastor Jack could use to express his love for this congregation. He said, "The apostle Paul knew that he might never again see this fellowship of people that he loved so much, a congregation he may have loved more than any other church he established.

"As I conclude this message and this time of shared ministry with you, I can't help feeling the same way Paul must have felt. You need to know that I love you, and it has been an honor to serve you during these years we've had together. As Paul said, I will be thinking of you often, even though I'm not in your presence. And I will be praying for you as well. Please pray for us."

More tears, both in joy and in sadness, were shared at the special farewell luncheon following the morning service. This was particularly true when people were given the opportunity to share memories and words of gratitude for Pastor Jack's service.

Carol, a mother of two teenage boys, said, "I just want to thank you for the guidance you gave me and the time you spent with my sons. Since their father died, they have not had a male figure to look up to and respect. Pastor Jack, you provided that for them, and I will never forget your kindness."

A man in his fifties stood up next. "Most of you know me," he began. "My name is Gene Cressman. More than five years ago, I found myself walking by this church. My marriage had ended in divorce. I felt like a failure. I wasn't really sure anyone cared about me. I don't know why I came into the church building.... Well, I didn't know then. Now I know it was God prompting me to enter the church. I felt I had to come in and talk to the pastor or anyone who would take time for me. I'm happy to say that Pastor Jack was in the office and invited me to sit down and talk to him. Poor guy.

"I really unloaded on him all the negative things that were going on in my life. He never interrupted me. He just let me talk. And somehow, I could tell he really cared about what I was saying. At that time, I knew I was the most important person in the world to him.

"Well, to make a very long story shorter, Pastor Jack asked about my relationship with God. When he told me there was a God who loved me no matter what I'd done in the past and who sent His only Son to take on Himself all the punishment that should have been mine, I just started to cry. He told me how to talk to God about it, and then he led me in a prayer for salvation. After a big hug and a few more tears, we left his office, and he introduced me to Mercy.

"Pastor asked me to tell her what I had prayed in his office. When I told her, she had this really big smile on her face. She gave me a big hug and said, 'Welcome to the family.' I found out later that was something Pastor and Mercy always did when someone accepted Christ. He said it was based on the passage in Romans 10:9, where Paul tells us salvation comes to those who believe in their hearts and confess with their mouths that Jesus is Lord and that He was raised from the dead.

"After that, Pastor Jack arranged for me to meet with him once a week to study a book together on the Christian life." Looking at Pastor Jack, he continued, "Pastor, I want you to know the most important thing you ever shared with me might surprise you. When I told you some of the things I'd done wrong, and you said you made a bunch of errors too, it just made me realize there was hope for me."

Looking again around the room, Gene said, "Who would have thought that two years ago, three years after I met this man, he would train me to be one of the church's lay shepherds? Thank you, Pastor, for not giving up on me."

Noticing how often Pastor Jack was wiping tears from his eyes, someone called out, "Does he always cry this much?" Laughter rippled through the room.

That prompted Connie to get to her feet. She laughed and said, "One of the many things Jack is good at is crying at the drop of a hat. If you were to sit with him watching a movie, you would definitely catch him weeping at the happy ending. If you were to stand with him at a funeral in respect for a veteran, when the surviving spouse receives a carefully folded American flag and is told it is presented in gratitude for the spouse's service, Jack would have trouble holding back the tears.

"Jack told me his father is even worse than him. He said his father could walk down the street when a bride and groom were coming out of a church, and even if he didn't know the couple, he would cry happy tears for them. So, to tell you the truth, I expected my husband would be shedding some tears on this special day."

After some applause and a few more stories, Mary Olson stood to speak. "Okay, we've had enough talk about this wonderful man. Let's not forget the wife who helped make him what he is today. Connie, you have been such a wonderful blessing to all of us, particularly the women of the church. You've been such an example of what it means to be a godly woman. Those of us who attended your Bible studies over the years have learned so much from you. To be in one of your classes, it was just like we were sitting across the kitchen table and having a chat with you over a cup of coffee. You made the Bible so real and so understandable. We want to thank you for all you've taught us in so many ways."

A few more stories were told before Pastor Jack finally stood to speak. "You people have been so kind to share these words of encouragement with us. But you should know there are some non-spiritual but very practical things I have done for people that almost no one knows about. For example, one Sunday morning, I was sitting in my office behind my desk when I happened to glance up to see something surprising.

"One of our ladies, who shall remain nameless, had just left the restroom and was walking across the lobby when I noticed that the back hem of her skirt was tucked up in the waistband of her pantyhose." Gasps went through the room. "Knowing there was no way I could approach her about this, I quickly called out to one of her friends and sent her off to rescue the lady from certain embarrassment. The things a pastor has to do for his people!" At that, laughter filled the room.

Pastor Jack told that story to lighten the mood while wrapping things up. "Thank you so much for your kind words and your support over the years. We've enjoyed growing with you. You know this is a special privilege you have given me today. Most of us don't get a chance to hear people say nice things about us like this because, usually, it happens only after we're dead at our memorial service." After the nodding of heads and some quiet laughter, Pastor Jack simply said, "Thank you for this special time together. We love you all very much."

Season III

Winter

Chapter 25

AN INTERIM HOME

Jack's parents lived in Cedar Street, Pennsylvania, a small community in the heart of Lancaster County with an unusual name, surrounded by bountiful farmland and lots of Amish communities. There were a few street names in the little town that also used the word Cedar, but none were actually named Cedar Street.

Tom and Janet Whyte were in their sixties, married for more than forty years, and better known as Nana and PopPop to their grandchildren. Janet had been a fifth-grade teacher in a small Christian school for most of their married life. She had retired only three years ago. Three times she was singled out and honored as teacher of the year by her county association of Christian schools. She was loved by her students and known for her creativity in the classroom.

Tom had a thriving construction business. Janet would tell you that it grew and became successful because he was a good carpenter, a sensible businessman, and always fair to his many customers. People sought him out to build their homes because of his reputation and workmanship. He was sensitive to the fact that whenever he built a home, some open land would be lost. He avoided the practice of destroying farmland to build housing developments. Yes, there was a lot of money to be made with that approach, but he just felt uncomfortable being a part of it.

The house Tom built for his family was large but not ostentatious. It was a traditional, two-story brick home with four bedrooms and three-and-a-half bathrooms. Tom and Janet enjoyed having company and made sure the house was big enough to meet their needs in that area. A shaker-style detached garage accommodated two cars and was wide enough for a workshop on the outside wall. It was connected to the house by a covered walkway. There was a large, fenced-in backyard but no swimming pool.

It was during the last week of October that Tom and Janet welcomed their son and his family into their home for what was expected to be a five-day encampment while the moving van was en route from Bradford to Weaverton. Three of the upstairs bedrooms and the finished basement with its own bathroom easily accommodated the invasion of seven Whyte family members.

Jack, Connie, and the three girls moved in upstairs with the two boys in the basement. Connie had engineered the packing of bags for this event. To her, it was just like taking a five-day vacation, and she packed accordingly. Once they were pretty much settled in their home-away-from-home, they collapsed in the spacious living room to finally relax after their long trip from Connecticut.

"What are your plans for this week?" asked Tom. "And what can we do to make things work?"

"We will definitely see that you're well-fed while you're here," added Janet.

That caused some cheers to rise up from the children. They always loved Nana's cooking.

"And we will all help with that," added Connie, "with the cooking and the cost of the food."

"I'm sure we can work all that out somehow," assured Nana. "Nothing to be concerned about," she said with a smile.

"To answer your question, Dad, we will probably make at least two day trips to the church and the parsonage while we're here. I want to have one day on my own where I just meet with the staff so we can get to know each other. We need to talk about how things have been done and how I like to approach ministry. It may or may not be different from how the previous pastor did it, but one way or another, this will be the beginning of a new era for the church. And while I'm there, I want to visit the school district office to let them know we're moving in and that we'll be homeschooling for at least the first year."

"Also," explained Connie, "we want to take one day for all of us to make a tour of the parsonage at our leisure. The children haven't seen the inside of our new home yet. Jack and I already have some preliminary thoughts about what will go where. But we want the children to be involved in who will be in what bedrooms, for example. And we can only do that by walking through the house together."

Whispers and interested looks passed between the children at their mother's remark. This was evidence they had already been thinking about bedrooms and who might be where.

"And I want to see where I might be able to have a study in the parsonage," explained Jack. "I'm used to doing a lot of work at home, not just at the church office, and I'd like to continue working that way. There's one small room just inside the side entrance to the parsonage with quite a few bookshelves on the walls. That might work well for a study. And a likely room for our homeschool is just across the hall from it. It's a good-sized room, and it would be so convenient for me to do my part of that job if I'm already in the house rather than next door at the church."

"That's one thing we need to decide when our whole family drives to Weaverton," noted Connie.

"Actually, I have a little surprise for you that might help you make that decision," said PopPop. "Why don't you all come with me into my workshop in the garage."

Looks of wonder and excited questions bubbled up from the children as they followed PopPop out of the house, across the covered walkway, and into the garage. What could this be? When he turned on the lights in the workshop, the children were shocked to see five brand-new desks shining in the glow from the overhead fluorescents. Each of the five students now had a desk with their own name etched on each one.

"I've been working on this little project—"

"Little project!" interjected Jack.

"Well, okay, this big project," admitted PopPop. "I built these over the past two months during my spare time. Nana was a big help with the design of the desks and chairs because of her years of experience in the school system.

What do you think? Do you like them?"

All seven of the guests burst forth with words of thanks and expressions of amazement at what PopPop had accomplished for them.

"This is really great, PopPop. Thank you so much," said Connie. "We never expected anything like this."

Jack added, "Thanks, Dad. This is over and above anything you could have done for us. I am absolutely in shock."

"You want to try them out?" asked Nana.

With that, all five children moved to their individual desks and tested for size and comfort.

"Okay, Mommy," said Paul. "We're ready for our first lesson." And everyone laughed.

Being the very practical one, Connie asked, "How will we get them to Weaverton?"

"Don't you worry about that," answered Tom. "I have a truck we can use for that."

"Thank you again," said Connie. "This is amazing."

"I think it's about time we head back to the house," prompted Janet. "Anybody interested in hot chocolate and cookies before getting ready for bed?"

Gleeful shouts answered her question. What a great way to wrap up the day's activities and get ready to enjoy their temporary home.

Chapter 26

THE FIRST STAFF MEETING

The Whytes were all settled in at Nana and PopPop's house. The first day trip to Grace Church occurred the next day. It was a beautiful October morning with a fresh autumn breeze scattering brightly colored leaves across the front lawn.

Jack had made arrangements earlier with his new secretary, Linda Hartman, to contact the music director, the organist/pianist, and the custodian to schedule a time to meet with them. If possible, the volunteers in charge of Sunday school and youth ministry were also invited to attend this first official staff meeting with their new pastor.

Part of his agenda for that meeting was to schedule private meetings later in the week with each leader. He wanted to hear from them what the church had been doing in their area of interest but also to imagine and dream about possibilities for new directions in the ministry's future.

During breakfast, before leaving for this first forage into his new ministry, Jack heard the disappointments of his children about not going with him. They were eager to check out the new parsonage and the possibilities it offered in this new adventure.

"I'm sorry to put your visit off until tomorrow," Jack said, "but I want to make sure we have enough time to investigate the parsonage and all its potential. And I don't want to be distracted by anything else today. So...let's plan to make that trip with you tomorrow. We'll make a full day out of it.

"I hope to learn some things today about the town we'll be living in. Then I'll be able to take us all on a tour tomorrow as a family. That means you have today to just have fun and maybe do some imagining about what we might discover tomorrow. Okay?" There was reluctant agreement from the breakfast group.

"Good. Then I'm going to go brush my teeth and get myself ready for today's work trip. Tomorrow, we'll have our fun excursion."

In their bedroom, Jack consulted with Connie concerning proper attire for his first meeting with his staff. "What do you think, Connie? Shirt, tie, and a sports coat? Jeans and open collar shirt? Something in between?"

"Well, I don't think you should be too dressy. Let's think about this. It's a beautiful day, but the high temperature is only going to be in the low to mid-sixties. You won't be outside very much, so you don't have to worry about warm clothing. I think you should just go with slacks, maybe your new khakis that I packed for you. I think your light blue, long-sleeve oxford shirt with an open collar would be fine. And how about your navy-blue sport coat to top it off? I think that would be nice. Casual but distinguished. What do you think?"

"Very wise, my dear. Very wise. Why is it that you are so smart in so many different ways? And while I think about it, how is it that you packed just the right items for me to wear on this brief trip?"

Connie laughed, her blue eyes twinkling. "Just one of my gifts, I guess."

Following his wife's advice, Jack got himself dressed and ready for his trip to Weaverton.

The trip was a pleasant one. Route 30 was fairly busy, as usual. During the last thirty minutes, the GPS took Jack through some of the beautiful hills and valleys of Pennsylvania, meandering along Route 663. Even the small towns he passed through were a pleasant experience. Of course, Jack was feeling so positive about this whole new adventure; it's unlikely anything would have felt unpleasant to him today.

The staff meeting was scheduled for 10 a.m., and Jack arrived in the church parking lot fifteen minutes before that. There was a man in a bright red shirt and blue jeans sweeping off the front steps leading up to the main entrance of the church building. He looked up and nodded with a pleasant smile.

He was a big man, at least six feet tall, with a shock of blonde hair. Laugh lines at the sides of his eyes seemed to indicate that he was a positive person, easily led to laughter. He walked over to the driver's side of Jack's car and greeted him with a strong handshake as the new pastor climbed out of the car.

"Hi," a booming, friendly voice announced, "I'm Jim Clemmer, the custodian here. We actually met on the day of your trial sermon, but there's no way you would remember that with all the people shaking your hand that day. Welcome to Grace. I look forward to working with you. By the way, I like the way you preach."

Pleasantly surprised and certainly feeling welcome, Pastor Jack extricated his hand from the rather large but warm grip of his new coworker, who was still shaking it, and said, "Well, Jim Clemmer, I feel like I have been properly greeted. Thank you very much. Let me get some things out of the car, and we can go inside."

"Do you need any help?"

"No, but thank you. It's just my Bible, a file folder, and a notepad." Reaching across the driver's seat to grab these items, Jack closed the door and joined the custodian as they took the steps to the entrance.

Jim kindly opened the door, one of four entrances to the church, for his new pastor to enter. Standing just inside the door, the two men surveyed the scene before them. Across the spacious vestibule and fellowship area was a row of doors, each of which led into an office.

Although the signs on the doors informed Pastor Jack of the purpose of each office, Jim explained, "This here office on the right is for our Sunday school superintendent, Nancy Williams. She's been running that for a long time now. Then next to her is the music director's office. I'm sure you've met Sally."

"Yes, Sally Erb," responded Pastor Jack. "We have talked quite a bit already."

"Then to the left," continued Jim without hesitation, "is where Linda Hartman runs the church." He looked at Pastor Jack with a twinkle in his eyes, and out came this boisterous laugh. Everything about this man seemed to be big and joyful. "Just kidding, Pastor."

"Well, you may be right. It's been my experience that the church secretary is absolutely essential to keeping things going in the church. I'm certainly not threatened by that. In fact, if you really want to know, I welcome it."

"Well, good," boomed Jim Clemmer. Continuing his task as a self-appointed tour guide, he went on, "And this is your office. It was just recently redecorated. I hope you like working here."

"I'm sure I will," Jack assured him.

Jim's big voice and laugh must have alerted Linda that they had arrived. The door to her office opened, and she came out to greet the men with a smile on her face and a warm "Hello."

Jack had chatted with Linda for a few minutes during fellowship time on the day of his trial sermon. From the little conversation they had that day, and by telephone since then, he was looking forward to working with her. And he told her so.

Linda was sort of tall, maybe about five-foot-nine, he would guess. She was a little to the right of average weight for her height but certainly not what one would consider fat. She had long, brown hair that reached her shoulders and wore a nice flowery blouse with navy-blue slacks, business casual, he thought they called it. Jack never thought he was good at judging ages, but he would guess Linda was definitely into her fifties.

As the three of them were talking, another person unexpectedly emerged from Linda's office. She looked familiar, yet he didn't know who she was. Then it dawned on him. She looked familiar because she resembled Linda.

Linda explained, "This is my sister Loreen. You will eventually meet all of us. There are five of us sisters. You have yet to meet Lindsay, Lois, and Lilly. I'm the oldest," she explained, "and Loreen is the baby." This brought forth a little groan from Loreen.

"I thought it would be good for us to have our staff meeting downstairs in the meeting room if that's okay with you," Linda continued. "Loreen will fill in for me while I'm out of the office."

Pastor Jack nodded his approval with a smile. She did run things, he thought. That was good within certain parameters.

"Sounds good to me," said Jack.

Just then, the main door opened, and in came two women. Jack

184

recognized them right away. It was his music team: music director Sally Erb and accompanist Anita Garcia. They were a kind of Mutt and Jeff duo, or maybe more like Jack Spratt and his wife. Anita was as thin as a rail with clear, dark mocha skin. Sally was short, wide, and pale. It was hard to imagine two more divergent people in their appearance.

He was thinking, *I could say as they stand side-by-side that they look like the number ten, but that would be unkind.* He smiled to himself. The most important thing is they came in together, worked well together, and seemed to belong together. They were a team. That was so encouraging to Pastor Jack.

As the newly arrived staff members were chatting with one another, the main entrance door opened once again, and the final elements of the crew arrived. Melissa Weiss, the volunteer youth director, and Nancy Williams, the Sunday school superintendent, completed the team. No introductions were needed because he had met these two women on the day of the trial sermon.

Melissa had this engaging smile on her face. She projected a sense of excitement just by being there. Pastor Jack could see why the youth were drawn to her leadership.

Nancy was an older woman, perhaps late fifties or early sixties. She had a round face, plump cheeks, and a countenance that said, "I really like you" and "everything is going to be all right." Jack liked her immediately, as he suspected the children in Sunday school did as well.

As the chit-chat began to ebb, Jack got the attention of the group so they could move on to the actual purpose of the day, taking the first steps to becoming a unified team of leaders. "Thank you all for being here and even on time. I'm impressed. You will find rather quickly that I like to start things on time. I'm not legalistic about it, but I do appreciate promptness. It says you care about others...as I know you do, or you wouldn't be here and involved in Christian ministry. I'm going to turn things over to Linda to tell us where we're meeting."

"Thank you, Pastor. I thought the best place to meet would be in the meeting room on the lower level. I have a coffee pot brewing there. Nancy was kind enough to bring us some of her homemade pastries to enjoy. Thank you, Nancy." The superintendent, smiling ear to ear, held high her bag of treats, followed by a smattering of applause from the group.

"Jim and I set up two of our rectangular folding tables in the room," added Linda. "That way, we can sit around the table for our meeting. I hope that's okay, Pastor."

"Absolutely! Let's get started. Lead the way, Linda." And they were off down the stairs to the basement area.

As they entered the familiar meeting room, memories of the first interview Jack had with the pulpit committee back in July rushed to the front of his mind. He smiled as he thought of the people he had met and the questions they asked. And now, here he was again, less than four months later, not as a prospect but as the new pastor. How quickly that time had passed.

As everyone took the time to get a cup of coffee and a sticky bun before settling down at the table, Pastor Jack was pleasantly surprised to see an electric teapot on the serving table accompanied by a small bowl containing Irish breakfast teabags, his favorite.

"My, my Linda, you are efficient. How did you know I'm a tea drinker and not a coffee drinker? And you even have my favorite kind of tea."

"Oh, I have my ways. It's amazing what you can find out just by asking questions and observing what people do."

"Well, I really appreciate the effort," he said while preparing to pour some hot water into a mug.

Linda interrupted him. "Oh, no, Pastor. This is your mug right here." And she handed him a ceramic mug that was bright blue on the outside and white on the inside. It was inscribed with bold black letters in script reading "For Pastor only!"

"Now I really feel like I've been officially welcomed. Thank you, Linda."

Chapter 27

GETTING TO KNOW YOU

Everything was ready for Pastor Jack's first meeting with his new staff. When everyone had settled around the two long tables, he opened their meeting with prayer. He was seated at what might be called the head of the gathered tables. To his right, along one side, were his secretary, Linda Hartman, and the youth director, Melissa Weiss. Opposite him, at the foot of the tables, was Nancy Williams, the Sunday school superintendent, and to her right, Sally Erb, the music director. Finally, on Pastor Jack's left were accompanist Anita Garcia and the custodian, Jim Clemmer.

As a tool for him to begin to get to know the staff members and to help them learn more about each other, he used what is called "The Quaker Questions." This is a series of three questions that begin with easy-to-share information and lead to more in-depth thoughts from each person.

First, he asked each one of them to briefly describe the house they lived in when they were seven years old. Pastor Jack began the sharing to set the tone for the conversation. After the others all shared their information, he asked them, "How was the house heated that you lived in when you were seven years old?"

When everyone had shared again, he asked the last question, which was designed to help them open up with more personal information about themselves. "What was the 'center of warmth' in that house? Was it a place like the kitchen where you shared all your meals, a time of year like Christmas around the Christmas tree, a person like your grandmother who always had room on her lap for a child looking for a hug? What do you feel was the center of warmth in that home? Tell us about it."

When all the sharing was completed, each staff member was surprised at how much they had learned about each other in such a simple way. Even though they'd known each other for years, this little exercise made them feel even closer than before.

"Okay, let's take a short break," Pastor Jack instructed. "It's eleven o'clock. Let's get back together in fifteen minutes. I want to learn even more about you, where you live, where you're from, your family, and things like that.

"Before you leave today, I want to make an appointment with each one of you to meet individually with me later this week. That's when I want to learn about what you do at Grace Church, what you would like to do, and what you expect of me. Then, during our final time together this morning, I will tell you about myself, what I like to do, how I like to operate, and my hopes and dreams for our ministry together here at Grace."

Around 11:15 a.m., Pastor Jack called the group back together. "I guess I should have begun our meeting with this information. People always want to know what to call me. I really don't care how I'm addressed. Most people, I've discovered, like to call me Pastor Jack. Others could never call me anything but Reverend Whyte. I'm happy to be called simply Jack. At the church in Connecticut, many of the teens and one older woman in her eighties liked to call me 'the Rev.'" That prompted a few laughs around the table.

"I want people to call me whatever is most comfortable for them. I find that's often tied directly to the church culture in which they were raised. So, it's up to you. Okay? Now...tell me more about yourselves. Once again, this is for me to get to know you, but also for all of us to get to know each other better."

The staff members found they were feeling more comfortable sharing about themselves than they normally would. Apparently, the Quaker Questions in the first hour had broken the ice and made it more acceptable for them to talk freely.

To get the ball rolling, Pastor Jack said, "Why don't we just work our way around the table?" Turning to his right, he said, "Linda, would you mind starting the sharing time?"

"Sure, I'd be happy to. Well, I've been a secretary here for eighteen years.

I'm married to Bob for thirty-five years next week. Yay! We made it! We have two children. Bob, Jr. is thirty-two and an IT specialist with SpecTech in Norristown. He has two children. Our daughter, Evelyn, is thirty, and she and Tony have a daughter.

"Since the children have married and moved away, Bob and I are empty-nesters, and we love it! We live conveniently a few blocks up the hill from the church and just off Church Street about two blocks. If you're interested, Pastor, Bob owns his own TV sales and repair shop. If you need help in that area, he's really good at what he does. He'd be happy to see what he could do for you."

"I can vouch for him," added Melissa. "We bought a TiVo system to record programs on our television, and we couldn't figure out how to get it set up. Bob came over and got it going, and it works very well."

"I'm glad to know that. Thank you," acknowledged Jack. "Why don't we continue with you, Melissa? Tell us about yourself."

"Okay. Most people already know about me. I've been volunteering with the youth ministry here for about six years. My husband, Sam, and I have been married for almost seventeen years. We met at Muhlenberg University. Married shortly after graduation. We were lucky enough to both get jobs teaching in Weaverton. I teach math in middle school. Sam teaches Phys. Ed. and coaches the varsity track and cross-country teams."

"I don't think you folks know this yet," added Pastor Jack. "But Connie and I are experimenting with homeschooling this year. I mention that only to say to you, Melissa, I may be calling you to help me understand some of my oldest son's math. He's in eighth grade."

"Certainly; let me know if you need assistance. Sam and I have three boys. Sammy, ten years old, is a jock. Marty is eight and the comedian of the family. Andy is seven and was a complete surprise. We thought we were finished building our family after Marty arrived but, oops, Andy joined us. And we're thrilled with all three of our guys.

"If you think of it, you could send up a prayer for Andy. We've discovered he is dyslexic and really struggles with school. There are some new developments to help with this, but it does bring us quite a few challenges."

"We will definitely be praying for you and Andy," assured Pastor Jack. "Is there anything else you would like to share?"

"I don't think so. Oh, yes, I forgot to mention where we live. We're about three miles southeast of the church on Rock Road, near Heartfield. Also, as Anita and Sally already know, Sam and I love contemporary Christian music. I use it for our worship times in youth group here at Grace. I hope that's not a problem, Pastor."

"That is far from a problem, Melissa. In fact, our family likes it also, as well as the old hymns of the church. In the church we came from in Connecticut, I introduced some contemporary Christian music in the services with my guitar."

"Oh, good. We may have to get you to bring your guitar to some of our youth meetings."

"I'd welcome the opportunity. Okay, let's move to your right. Nancy, how long have you been Sunday school superintendent?"

"It seems like forever, but I love doing it. I'll be celebrating twenty-five years on the job next fall. So, it's just over twenty-four years now. I'm originally from Bethlehem, which is where I met my husband, George, through mutual friends. We moved here because of my husband's work. He was an electrician. As most of you already know—but you don't know, Pastor—George developed cancer and fought it for almost three years. He passed away two years ago." Nancy choked up and fought back the tears. "As you can tell, I'm still not over it."

"That's understandable," counseled Pastor Jack. "It takes a long time to heal from such a loss. How long were you married?"

"Forty-one years, and they were wonderful years. We never had children, but we had each other, and it seemed that was enough for both of us. I think that may be why I've spent so many years working with children at church."

"I would think your ministry met a need the church had as well as one you had. Thanks for all your work for the Lord, Nancy. Now let's hear from

Sally Erb, our illustrious music director. Sally, would you tell us about yourself, please? Did you grow up in this area?"

"No, I was born and raised in Hendersonville, Tennessee."

"Tennessee?" commented Melissa. "Now that's a surprise. I never knew that."

"Yep. I grew up just outside Nashville in a little country home near the Cumberland River. Me and my parents and my little brother, Tim. Well, he's not little anymore."

"That's a long way from Nashville to Weaverton," observed Jim. "How in the world did you find out about our little country church?"

"Well...that's a long story," hesitated Sally. "I don't know if I should get into that right now."

"We have time, don't we Pastor?" encouraged Melissa.

"Sure we do," said Jack. However, sensing a deep-seated concern in Sally, he added, "But if Sally wants to save that information for another time, that would be fine."

"Thank you, Pastor," said Sally very quietly. "It's just that...it's kind of complicated." She was talking to Pastor Jack but looking questioningly to Anita, her partner in ministry, perhaps for some kind of support.

With a knowing look of understanding on her face, Anita smiled and nodded slightly. "I think you should tell them."

"Really?" pleaded Sally.

"I think it would be good for you and for all of us if you explained. We all love you, Sally. You know that."

Pastor Jack interjected warmly, "I don't want you to feel any pressure, Sally. This is up to you."

"I appreciate that. I really do. Ummm...well..."

There was an almost tangible silence for a few moments until Pastor Jack said gently, "Maybe we should go on to something else."

"No," interrupted Sally, with a kind of resolve. "No, I want to tell you how I got here."

"Okay, then. Just take your time."

Chapter 28

SALLY AND ANITA

Sensing so much loving support around the meeting table, Sally began her story. "As I said, I was born and raised in Hendersonville, just outside Nashville. I have always had an interest in music. My mother was a big influence in that regard. It was almost expected that I would have a career in music. And living so close to Belmont University, which has a phenomenal Christian music, worship, and arts curriculum, it was quite natural for me to become a student there. I majored in piano, worship, and music direction." She paused. "This is a long story, but I'll try to make it short."

"You can tell us as much or as little as you like," counseled Pastor Jack.

"Thank you. So...when I was a junior at Belmont, I met this really nice guy named Bruce Erb. He was a transfer student from a school near Philadelphia. Bruce was majoring in the audio-video curriculum. It was called 'worship support ministry.' We hit it off right away. In no time at all, we began dating. By our senior year, we were talking about marriage. My parents really liked Bruce. To make a long story short, we were married three months after graduation.

"Because of Bruce's connections in this area, we both got jobs near Philly. I was a part-time pianist and organist for a small community church near Germantown. Bruce joined a few of his hometown friends who had formed a recording studio for musicians. His technical training at Belmont was a big help for their work.

"Less than two years after we moved to southeast Pennsylvania, Bruce confessed to me that, working in his hometown, he ran across his high school sweetheart. They had broken up four years earlier. That was one reason he left the area and transferred to Belmont. Suffice it to say, he told me he still had strong feelings for this girl and had been seeing her for a few months. Apparently, I was more of a rebound than his true love.

"Very sadly, he decided he no longer wanted to be married to me. After a long time of tears and counsel from friends, Bruce said he was sorry for hurting me, but he wanted a divorce. Fortunately, we had no children to consider." She paused to wipe tears from her eyes. Others in the group were also tearing up.

"Finally, I decided not to fight it, and after a lot of thinking and crying and praying, I agreed to end our marriage. But, being practical during some lucid moments, I realized I would need more than a part-time job. I felt like such a failure, and I didn't want to go back to my hometown. I was afraid people would brand me as the girl who failed at her marriage. And I didn't want to continue where I was. That would be too painful. That's when I heard from some friends of friends who lived near us, about this lovely little church in Weaverton, near where they used to live.

"They heard the church had a small choir and needed a new music director." She looked at Anita, who nodded in encouragement. "So, I applied and got the job. And that's how I got from Tennessee to Weaverton." She paused and smiled. "And I'm so glad I'm here. I'm not crazy about the route I had to travel to get here. But I really feel at home here. Thank you for accepting me."

Melissa responded. "We're also happy you're here and a part of our family. I'm sorry if I caused you any discomfort in asking my question earlier...yet I'm grateful you felt free to share your story with us. I feel even closer to you now than I did before." Nods and comments around the room confirmed Melissa's words.

"Thank you for telling us your story, Sally," Jack said reassuringly. "I know it was difficult. But I believe it was good for the group and I'm convinced some healing for you is going to result from opening up to us about that tough time in your life. Would you mind if I prayed for you about that?"

"Not at all, Pastor. In fact, I would really like that. And while you're praying, let me add one more thing for you to pray about.... I can't believe I'm saying this, but I think it's right. I wasn't always this size physically. From the time Bruce told me about his girlfriend, I found comfort in food. It has been a growing experience," she joked, "but in some ways, not in the right direction." She saw looks of understanding from around the room. "So, while you're praying, Pastor, I could use some divine help in that area as well."

"Absolutely! Let's pray. Our loving heavenly Father, we come to You with praise and thanksgiving for who You are and what You have done to show us Your love and acceptance. We realize that all of us have things that You know about in each of our lives that we have kept to ourselves over the years. We thank You for Sally and her willingness to share a great hurt from her past.

"We have two requests to make of You, Lord. First, we ask You to heal the hurt in Sally's heart and mind. We're not asking You to remove the memory of that hurt. We're asking You to heal the hurt so that, when she remembers, she will see the entire experience, one segment at a time, with new eyes. Help her to see that You were with her during that difficult time and all the times since then and that You love her.

"We also ask that You would work healing in her life in the area of eating. Set her free from any bondage that has developed over the years and any negative eating habits that have developed; set her free from any wrong desires in that area of her life. We thank You in advance for the many loving ways You are already beginning to answer our prayers. In Jesus' name. Amen."

"Thank you, Pastor. I'm sorry I talked so long."

"No apology necessary." At that point, everyone rose from their chairs and, one by one, gave Sally a hug and a word of encouragement.

"Why don't we take a break for a few minutes?" advised Pastor Jack. "We'll get back together soon to finish up our time together."

As the staff returned to their seats around the table, the atmosphere grew more and more personal. Each one found it easier to comment and agree with things someone else said, often identifying with one or more items being shared. A real sense of warmth was enveloping the room.

It was Anita Garcia's turn to share about herself.

"I have been accompanist here for ten years. My husband is Hank. His real name is Henrico, but don't you ever call him that."

"Are you originally from the area?" asked Pastor Jack.

"No, actually, I was born in Cuba."

"Cuba? Now that's information I didn't expect to hear from you."

"Yep, born in Cuba but came to the United States when I was only five years old."

"Now that's a story I would like to hear," prompted Pastor Jack.

"I think we'd all like to know more about that," added Melissa.

"Okay. Well...my family lived in Cuba when Fidel Castro took over that country in a revolution against Batista in 1953. After Castro aligned himself with Russia, things got pretty nasty in the country. Under both Batista and Castro, there were waves of emigration to the United States.

"It was in 1980, under lots of international pressure, that Castro agreed to open the port of Mariel to those who chose to leave Cuba. He resented this pressure and chose to take advantage of this opportunity for his own ends. Of the 125,000 people who emigrated to the United States during the Mariel boatlift, Castro included 16,000 criminals he wanted to get rid of and foist on America. Very sad.

"My parents couldn't afford passage on one of the merchant ships that helped with this project. They hoped to come to America later. Their good friends, the Maldonados, offered to take me with them and care for me until my parents could raise enough money for the trip. It was a radical idea, but my parents agreed because they were concerned for my well-being if I remained in Cuba.

"When we crossed the Florida Straits and landed in Miami, we were warmly welcomed. A local church mission committee worked with immigration to arrange for us to find a home. We stayed in temporary housing just outside Miami until we were moved to Akron, Pennsylvania.

"To make a very long story shorter, over the next two years, it became clear to Mr. and Mrs. Maldonado, through correspondence with my parents, that my folks were not going to be able to come to the United States very soon, if at all. As it turned out, that open window to leave from the port of Mariel closed six months later. So, the Maldonados arranged for me to be adopted. And at age seven, I became Anita Walker. It was both a happy and sad time, but the Walkers raised me as their own."

"So, how did you end up here?" wondered Pastor Jack.

"I went to Millersville College. It's Millersville University now. I majored in piano and organ with the hope of working in a church someday. After graduation, I got a job here. Hank and I met at a Christian retreat for singles. That was nineteen years ago. We dated for two years and are now married for seventeen. And they said it wouldn't last," she teased.

"By the way, Pastor, Hank's father, Roberto Garcia, is pastor of the Heartfield Hispanic Church of God. Hank works with the firm of Sweeten and Fulton as an accountant and loves his work. We have two daughters. Traci is fifteen, and Michelle is thirteen. I love working in my vegetable garden in my spare time. Our lovely home is in the newest development in the area called Pine Mills Estates. The name is actually fancier than the development. And my good neighbor two blocks away is Sally Erb."

"That's an amazing story," noted Pastor Jack. "But I have to ask, what happened to your birth parents?"

"We corresponded regularly with them and tried to talk them into coming here. They said the red tape was too complicated, and they felt they were getting too old to make such a move. Sadly, they died three years ago, much too early in life, within six months of each other. Once my father died, I think my mother just gave up and didn't want to continue on without him. But they're with Jesus now, and I'm sure we'll see each other again in the Lord's timing."

"Thank you so much for sharing your story, Anita. I really need to ask you an important question, but I feel a little awkward asking it. As a dark-skinned Hispanic woman, how do you identify yourself in today's changing culture?"

"Thanks for asking that, Pastor. It used to be fashionable to say I'm black. Then the nomenclature changed so that 'African-American' was the official designation."

"But you're not African. You're Cuban," commented Nancy.

"Well, yes and no. I guess I'm a Cuban American. But the fact is, my ancestors came to Cuba as migrants from Haiti. All black Haitians came from the slave trade that arrived from western Africa. Anyway, today I would be considered a woman of color, I guess. But that's a bit strange too. We're all one color or another. As far as I'm concerned, I'm a lover of Jesus and a child of God. And I'm just an American!

"By the way," Anita continued, "did you know that more than fifty years ago, the US government passed a law that said any Cuban that moved to the United States and lived here for one or more years was considered a resident? No other people have been granted that privilege. I always thought that was cool. Anyway, I don't need any other designation or label. I'm a dark-skinned American who was born in Cuba with Haitian ancestry, and I'm a Christian. That should be enough. I think the Bible only talks about one race, and that's the human race."

"You are absolutely right, Anita," Jack confirmed. "Paul talks about that in Acts 17:26. Thanks again for opening up to us. That was very interesting. Okay.... Jim Clemmer, we have yet to hear from you. Talk to us."

"Well, after those stories from Sally and Anita, my life seems pretty boring. But here goes. I live just a half mile south on Weaverton Road with my lovely wife, Sylvia. We've been married just eight years. I'm a retired Marine. I spent twenty years in the service. But I'm sure you've often heard, 'Once a Marine, always a Marine.'" And his big laugh filled the room.

"Let's see. What else can I tell you? I have a stepdaughter, Brenda. She's from Sylvia's first marriage. Hmmm, what else. Oh yes, I love working with wood. I like to make furniture and such things. In fact, the oak communion table in the front of the sanctuary...I made that shortly after I started working here."

"That's amazing!" said Pastor Jack. "I've admired that more than once. That is a beautiful work of art, Jim."

"Thanks. I get a lot of pleasure out of doing things like that. I think that's enough about me."

"Thanks to all of you for sharing," concluded Pastor Jack. "I really think we're establishing a firm foundation for us to build our future ministry together. That was my plan in scheduling this first meeting. I hope to add to that when I meet with each of you individually later this week.

"Now then, all I have left on my agenda is to share some information about me, my family, and the way I like to conduct ministry. Does anyone have other items to add to that?" With everyone looking from one to the other and no comments being made, Pastor Jack ended the meeting by sharing a bit more about himself.

Chapter 29

INFORMAL ECCLESIOLOGY

It was Pastor Jack's turn to share about himself with his new staff. "I grew up not too far from here in Cedar Street, Pennsylvania. Yes, that's the town's name. Not a street. Very odd. I don't actually know how that happened. My family is staying there with my parents during this moving process. My mother was a teacher for many years. My dad owns Whyte Construction Company. Since retiring, Mom has helped him in the office with finances and scheduling. I'm an only child. My parents tried hard not to spoil me. I'm not sure how successful that worked out." Everyone smiled.

"My wife, Connie, and I have been married almost fifteen years. We met at a Christian summer camp where she was a counselor, and I was the youth leader. We have five children, three girls and two boys. John, Jr. is almost fourteen. We call him Johnny. Sarah is eleven. Megan is nine. Paul is seven, and Suzy is just five years old. You might see a pattern there." This time everyone laughed.

"I enjoy playing the guitar. So, Sally, you will find me doing that occasionally during the service, sometimes as an illustration during my sermon. I've written quite a few songs, so you will find me suggesting from time to time using one of them during worship."

"I look forward to that," said the music director.

"I recently discovered what my style of ministry is. That question was asked by the pulpit committee, and my wife informed them...and me...what it is. It seems that I pray a lot. And when I believe God is telling me what to do as a congregation, I will present it to the church leadership." A chorus of "goods" percolated up from around the table.

"If the leadership approves, we go ahead with it. If they don't approve it, I'll keep praying about it until either they or I change our minds." This brought more smiles to all the faces in the room.

"Although I recognize my position as the final authority on most matters concerning ministry, you will find that I don't take advantage of that position. You'll find me asking for your ideas and your opinions of my ideas. I try to be open to all possibilities, so please don't hold back if you have something to share.

"Also, I like trying temporary experiments from time to time to see how folks react. If I get really positive feedback, I very likely will move the experiment from temporary status to standard practice. A member of the leadership team in the Connecticut church explained my approach this way. He observed that 'we are a pastor-led church, but not a pastor-driven church.' I kind of like that." More smiles from the staff.

"I'm a fairly organized person," continued Pastor Jack. "During my early years in ministry, I used to say that a clear proof that God is real and powerful is the fact that the church was growing and doing well in spite of the fact that I was the pastor. Eventually, I asked God to grow in me the spiritual gift of administration. Over time He answered that prayer. Within twelve months, I had the entire next year's events as well as my preaching and teaching schedule planned and posted on my office walls." This time, Linda's smile was the biggest one.

"Of special interest to Anita, Sally, and Linda, you will find very soon that I will give you a printout of my sermon titles, my Scripture texts for each sermon, and the theme of each message for the next three months. Keep in mind, however, these things are not written in stone. I'm always open to the Lord changing my mind somewhere along the way. As I mentioned to you, Sally, for at least the first two months, I want you to choose the hymns we'll sing. At that point, we'll see if I want to be involved in those choices. I want us to play that one by ear.

"Let me give you my theological reason for this approach. Now we're getting into what theologians call ecclesiology. That's a fancy name for 'the study of the church and how it works.' I'm convinced that the Lord has one plan for each worship experience. I get the seeds for that theme in my prayerful planning of each message. While you, Anita and Sally, are praying as well about the music for these services, I'm convinced the same Spirit that inspired me will be guiding you to the exact music we need to make the entire worship experience a unified and inspiring experience for all.

"I like to use the image of a wind tunnel through which a large fan is moving air from one end to the other. No matter where we enter that long tunnel, if we allow the wind to move us, we'll find ourselves going in the same direction. That's the way it is with the Holy Spirit. If we're open to His influence, we'll find ourselves moving together in a beautiful way without necessarily even consulting with one another. Does that make sense to everyone?" Verbal and nonverbal confirmation from the staff followed his question.

"You will find early on that I get excited when I step into the pulpit to share my message after we sing a hymn or hear a special song by the choir or a soloist that affirms the theme of the morning. It reinforces in my mind and spirit that the Lord is indeed in charge of the service. Are you all with me on this?"

"Yes!"

"Yes!"

"Absolutely!"

"One more thing you need to know about me. I'm a delegator. I used to think I should do everything myself and then just delegate the areas I don't have time to do. You might remember that Moses tried to do it all, according to Exodus 18, and failed miserably. That's how pastors get burned out. The Lord made it clear to me that is *not* the biblical approach to ministry."

Opening his Bible, Pastor Jack continued. "In Ephesians 4:11 and 12, we read that God 'gave some as apostles, and some as prophets, and some as evangelists, and some as pastors and teachers, for the equipping of the saints for the work of service, to the building up of the body of Christ.' That tells me that the work of the church is to be primarily done by what Paul sometimes calls the saints. And the saints are not just a few special people called pastors.

"Since I'm a pastor and teacher, according to this passage, my primary calling is to help all of us discover what gifts God has given each of us as part of the body of Christ. Further, my job is to train people, equip them if you will, to use their own gifts, your own gifts, to do the work of the church. In this way, the body of Christ will be built up, edified, and become vibrant. Is everyone with me on this?" Everyone nodded again.

"Let me point out," he continued, "that you are already doing your jobs as saints of the church. Sally, with your music. Anita, with your performing talent. Linda, with your administrative skills. Jim, with your woodworking and good work ethic. Nancy, with your love of children. And Melissa, with your dedication to the church teens. The seeds of our shared ministry are already being planted with the work you are all doing right now.

"So let me explain. Proper delegation is this. I delegate all that I can, allowing each church member to use the gifts he or she has discovered and has learned to use. My job is to help people find their spiritual gifts and equip or train them. And I'm called to do those things that can't be delegated. When this approach is used, I find the church to be an enthusiastic body of believers who are excited about the way God is using each one in our ministry together. The old adage that 20 percent of the people do 80 percent of the work in the church should not be our church model. Are we still on the same page here?"

"That makes all the sense in the world," responded Linda.

"Sounds good to me," added Melissa.

All showed signs of enthusiasm at Pastor Jack's approach to ministry as he laid it out before them. "A major goal will be for us to help people find and use their gifts from God here at Grace Church. Okay, then, that should be enough from me for now, unless someone has a question or comment."

"I do have one question," said Linda. "How do you make all this happen with our regular church members?"

"Excellent question, Linda. We do it gradually and systematically. It will begin with all of us praying about it, asking for divine guidance. It will continue with me planting seeds in my preaching. The Lord has already given me direction for the first series of sermons He wants me to preach. It's going to be basic stuff, sort of like Vince Lombardi, coach of the Green Bay Packers.

One year he began his first summer training session by standing in front of his players with a football in his hand. And he said, 'Men, this is a football.' That's pretty basic.

"The series the Lord has prompted me to preach will include a number of messages on each of these themes. First, who is God? Second, who are you? And third, who are we as a church? I hope we can build on this foundation, perhaps ever so slowly, the kind of church God wants us to be. Is that helpful, Linda?"

"Completely!"

"Are there any other questions or comments...? Hearing none, let's wrap up this meeting. If you would each take time to corner me before you leave, I want to make an appointment with each one of you to meet with me later this week. If you can't squeeze that in this week, we'll aim for next week. Thanks again for your work and for being here today. I look forward to our time of ministry together."

As the individuals formed a line with calendars or cell phones in hand, Pastor Jack singled out Jim Clemmer. "Jim, would you mind being the last one in line? I wanted to ask you for a favor."

"Fine with me," Jim said and happily headed for the sticky buns one more time.

After the last person had gone, Jack approached Jim, who was licking the last bit of sticky bun goo off his fingers. "Jim, I know you just had a sticky bun, but I was wondering if we could have lunch together."

"Sure, there's always room for more."

"Would you have some time now to show me around town, point out areas of interest, places to eat, where to shop, and things like that?"

"If you're buying lunch, I have plenty of time," Jim joked.

"Okay, then, let's do it." They both waved to Linda and her sister Loreen as they headed out for an excursion around Weaverton and lunch together.

Chapter 30

DISCOVERING WEAVERTON

The little town was too small to have suburbs. When you left the borders of Weaverton, you were immediately in the country. Grace Church and its parsonage were located near that borderline, five or six city blocks downhill from the southeast edge of town. With farms surrounding the church property and spreading out beyond the cemetery, this was definitely country. That meant that when Pastor Jack and Jim Clemmer left the church building to make a tour of Weaverton, they headed up the hill on Church Street toward town.

"This is Church Street," explained Jim from the passenger seat of Pastor Jack's car. Actually, the car was not Pastor Jack's. He was driving his father's Honda Accord, leaving the family van for Connie and the children to use at PopPop's if they chose to take a trip somewhere while he was away.

"Church Street," continued Jim, "is the eastern boundary of the town. Its name comes from the fact that there are three churches on the street. We're at the southern end. Up the street is the Weaverton Mennonite Church. It's just three blocks ahead of us on the left. Did you know that Weaverton was settled by the Mennonites back in the 1700s?"

"Yes. I think Lucy Geisinger mentioned that to us."

"Yep, there's about five different Mennonite churches in and around Weaverton. Then at the northern end of Church Street is the Brethren in Christ Church. One thing we have plenty of in our area is churches. Now, at the stop sign up ahead, you'll want to turn left onto East Broad Street. That will take us into what you could call downtown Weaverton. You said you wanted to get lunch, and that will take us to some good places to eat."

"Oh, good. I'm really hungry."

"Well, let's go around the traffic circle here to the right. Why don't you pull into that big parking lot, and I'll point out some things to you."

"Aha, train tracks. Do you still have train traffic in Weaverton?" asked Jack.

"Passenger service stopped a long time ago. There are occasional freight trains that come through during the night. What we still have here, though, is a good place to eat. It's called The Station Restaurant. Some of our folks bought the old railroad station building, gutted it, and turned it into a good little place to eat. They specialize in soups, salads, and sandwiches for lunch. They're only open from 10 a.m. to 2 p.m., and it's best to make reservations. This large parking lot is the site of the Olde Weaverton Inn. It was conveniently located next to the railroad station."

"Boy, that was really convenient."

"Yes. And it was a going business for a long time. Henry and Daniel Weaver settled the town in the late 1700s, and one of the first buildings they erected was the Weaverton Inn. It was owned and operated by their descendants for many years. People came from all over to stay at the inn and enjoy their fine dining. But after many years, the structure itself was becoming unsafe, and it was too expensive to repair.

"Meanwhile, new, modern motels were opening up just north and east of here along the highway, and that was drawing a lot of business away from the old inn. The final blow came about twenty years ago when a fire started in the middle of the night from a gas leak in the basement. Fortunately, no one was injured, but the entire building was destroyed. After some negotiations, the family sold the property to the town of Weaverton. The town council decided not to erect another building on the site. Instead, they cleared the area and paved this lot to provide much-needed parking for downtown shoppers and workers."

"It sounds like you have some good community leaders in Weaverton."

"Yes, they're mostly good planners," agreed Jim. "They've been working hard to revitalize the town." Then changing the subject, he pointed across

North Main Street and said, "That three-story building over there is the local drug store, Long's Pharmacy. A number of businesses rent space from Mr. Long on the second and third floors for their offices. To the left on the southwest quadrant of the circle is our local bank. The vice president is a member of Grace. Back here, to our left, is a craft shop. It was another old building with a store that went bankrupt. A group of investors bought them out and turned it into a craft store and workshop on the first floor with apartments on the second and third floors."

"Downtown seems to be pretty much alive and not falling apart like many small towns," observed Pastor Jack.

"Absolutely. We have a large percentage of residents who realize the importance of buying locally. So...if you're still hungry..."

"By now, I'm starving," joked Pastor Jack.

"Okay, let's turn right and head up North Main Street."

After lunch, the two men continued their tour of Weaverton with Jim as an excellent tour guide. Jack congratulated himself on his decision to ask Jim to help him become familiar with these new surroundings.

As they got back in the car, Jim pointed out another place to eat. Just a little further down the block on the opposite side of the street was a neon sign flashing the name "Frank's Place."

"If you just want to hang out with some of the local citizens, you can't do better than Frank's Place. Frank is a really funny guy and runs a nice establishment. You can only get lunch there. The menu is very limited but also very good, especially their homemade soups."

Continuing his travelogue, Jim pointed out, "Down here on the right again is the dentist we go to. Dr. Dieterly has been the dentist in our town since the day the Liberty Bell got cracked. Or at least it seems that way. He left us for a few years to be a missionary in Haiti before returning to Weaverton to settle down and continue his practice here. We like him because he's very gentle and clearly knows what he's doing. And a plus for you is that he's very good with children."

In another part of downtown, Jim pointed out a small, local grocery store and a sports equipment shop. The town hall and police station were in a building together only a few blocks from the highway that provided the town's northern boundary. On the other side of the highway was a mall with a large grocery store, a pharmacy, and a pizza shop. And something else that immediately caught Jack's attention was a Christian bookstore. On the western edge of town was a park that included a beautiful pool with facilities for showering and changing.

After more maneuvering around Weaverton, Jim mentioned, "The closest hospital we have is about five miles northeast of here. It's called Lakeview Memorial Hospital, and it's quite good. If you're interested and have the time, I'd be happy to show you how to get there."

"That would be very helpful, Jim."

When the tour was over, the men returned to the church building. Pastor Jack checked in with Linda one more time.

"I'll be heading back to my parents' home now. But I'll be back tomorrow to make a tour of the parsonage. The whole family will be with me. We'll probably look like an army of ants swarming over the property. The children are really excited about choosing bedrooms and such things. Is there anything else we need to talk about before I go?"

"No, Pastor. I think we're good here. Oh, did you get a key to the parsonage?"

"Yes, I have that on my key ring."

"I also have the garage door opener for you to attach to your sun visor. Do you want to take that with you as well?"

"Good idea. Yes, I'll take that. Anything else?"

"No, I think that should do it. I look forward to seeing you sometime tomorrow morning."

Chapter 31

Parsonage Exploration Day

"Revelation Song" by Philips, Craig, and Dean was pouring out of the six speakers on the family van CD player. It was one of those songs that were favorites of the entire family, but none of the children heard it. Given the high decibel level of their excited chit-chat in the rear seats, they were totally oblivious to the beautiful strains of the worship song.

Jack and Connie were aware of the almost tangible excitement pervading the van. They looked at one another with knowing smiles. They would be arriving at the church parsonage in less than ten minutes, and during the almost two-hour journey that morning, the children had asked their parents a total of three actual questions about their new home. The rest of the time was spent imagining, maneuvering, planning, and laughing on their own.

As they pulled into the church parking lot, Pastor Jack stopped and texted Linda that they had arrived and were about to start their exploration. He would talk to her later in the morning.

Jack thought it would be fun to enter the house through the underground garage. He was hoping it was not loaded down with storage items for the church and would be open to them. He drove across the parking lot and entered the parsonage driveway. Moving slowly down the gradual incline, he reached up to the sun visor and pushed the button on the automatic door opener Linda had given him the day before.

All of a sudden, a quiet anticipation replaced the chattering of the previous two hours. All eyes were focused out through the windshield. The only sounds were the quiet running of the van's engine and the rumbling of the garage door as it slowly moved up and disappeared into the ceiling of the garage. Totally clean and open to their access, Jack noticed that there was actually room for two cars, one behind the other. *That will be helpful*, he thought, *but then again, it would probably require some tricky schedule planning.*

Jack broke the silence. "Okay, gang, we're here." A raucous cheer went up from the other six members of the family. The clicking of seat belts being unfastened all at one time was followed by the noise of the sliding side van door opening. Out scurried five children who ran through the door into the basement of their new home. Their parents followed closely behind.

The first room they entered had a concrete floor. Along the right wall stood a washer and dryer.

"Hey, look," cheered Connie, "we have a laundry!"

Above these appliances were two small windows, about twelve by twenty-four inches, and near the ceiling. If one were to climb up onto the dryer and look out those windows, there would be a clear view through the recently washed glass to the backyard of the parsonage and beyond that to the pond and the few white Charolais cattle they had seen during their first visit. Along the far basement wall in front of them were cabinets and shelves for storage. There was a door in the wall to the left leading into the other section of the basement.

Dad encouraged them with a nod of his head, and the children opened the door, flicked on the light switch, and came into what looked like it could be a family room. Paul, the family geek, immediately noticed outlets on one wall and attachments for a large-screen television. He pointed this out to the family, and everyone began to chatter about how nice this room was...an unexpected surprise for the children. When Jack and Connie had previously toured the parsonage, of course, they had already seen this large room.

The floor was covered with a dark blue wall-to-wall carpet. *Very nice*, thought Connie, *as long as they had no water drainage problems*. More cabinets and shelves for storage were situated along the wall to the right. Conversation revolved around what furniture they had and what they might need to purchase to furnish this room. Connie's gift for interior decorating was already moving into second gear. It would reach full speed once they ascended the stairs to the first floor.

The stairway next to the door was in the center of the basement. Ascending the stairs and opening the door to the first floor, they were faced with three doors in front of them. The door to the left opened into a small room.

"This will be my study," noted Jack. "If you walk through it, you'll come to a door leading to the outside and to the church building itself."

They closed this door and moved to the center. The middle door opened to reveal a powder room.

Opening the door on the right, Connie explained, "This is where we'll have most of our homeschooling activities. The desks PopPop made for you will fit in here nicely and leave room for the other equipment we already bought. It will be so convenient to have that powder room next door and Daddy's office across the hall for those times when he'll be helping with school. I think this setup is just perfect for us. And for those times when any of you want some quiet time to study, we have the living room available."

The children thought this all made sense. They appreciated the advance thinking their mother had done. Quite frankly, though, they were more interested in heading upstairs to see the selection of bedrooms.

Connie led the way once again to the right. There was a rather large living room with a huge bay window along the left wall that looked out onto the covered porch and the front lawn. The front door was near the corner to the left of the bay window.

Moving again to the right, Connie led the family into a dining room and then around the corner to the open kitchen with nice appliances and lots of counter space. The open plan of the first floor was in the shape of a circle that wrapped around the central stairway.

"I don't suppose anyone wants to check out the second floor, do they?" asked Jack.

With that, there was a mad scramble for the stairs leading to the second floor and bedrooms to be discovered. Jack and Connie just smiled and gave them a few minutes to explore the second floor on their own. Because there were only four bedrooms for five children, it had already been agreed that Sarah and Megan would share a room again. It was actually their idea. They had become even closer than before, very likely because of their adventures in the Connecticut treehouse during the closing weeks of summer.

Arriving at the top of the stairs, Jack called for the children to join him in the central hallway. "What do you think, gang? Have you come to some sort of agreement about who gets what rooms?"

"Megan and me..." began Sarah.

"You mean 'Megan and I,' don't you?" prompted their teacher-mom.

"Yeah, sorry. Megan and I would like the large room to the left. It has enough space for our two beds and our dressers."

"That sounds reasonable," noted Connie, giving a slight smile to her husband. They had had the same thought.

Johnny said, "I would like the bedroom over here, next to the girls," he indicated the room situated above his father's study and next to the large bathroom." He wisely added, "The biggest adjustment is going to be how the five of us are going to manage with only one bathroom. It's big, but not that big."

"Yes," added Connie. "We've been thinking about that. I guess we're going to have to create some kind of a schedule."

"Why do they have only one bathroom when they have so many bedrooms?" wondered Sarah.

"Yeah, that seems a little weird," added Megan.

"We have to remember," answered Connie, "when this house was built a very long time ago, people didn't take showers and wash their hair every day the way most people do today."

"Really?" asked Johnny.

"Absolutely," said Jack. "My dad told me that, when he was just a young boy, he spent a week's vacation with his aunt and uncle and their four children on a farm in the country. He was a bit surprised when Saturday night came, and all the children took turns taking a bath in the same huge washtub filled almost to the brim with hot soapy water."

"Come on, Daddy, you're kidding us," exclaimed Sarah.

"No, PopPop swears it's true. And you'll never guess where they set up this bathtub. It was in the kitchen!"

"How did they do that?" Sarah wanted to know. "They could never fit all the kids in one tub."

"You're absolutely right," continued Jack. "They just figured out who was the cleanest one. He got in the tub first. Then they took turns until the dirtiest child took a bath last."

"That's disgusting," commented Paul.

"To us, that's disgusting. To them, so many years ago, it was normal. At least they had running water in the house and didn't have to go outside to an outhouse. That's what my great-grandparents had to do," added Jack. "And the outhouse was across the street from their home. But at least it was a two-seater." He smiled.

"Now you *are* kidding," said Johnny.

"Nope. Absolutely true. And they used an old Sears catalog for toilet paper."

"What's a Sears catalog?" asked Suzy.

"Before there was the internet," explained Connie to her youngest, "you could order things by mail from a big book...but not email."

"That's kind of odd," Suzy replied.

"What's really odd," contemplated Johnny, "is having a two-seater. Who would you want to sit with while in an outhouse?"

"Good question," agreed Jack. "Good question. And I must admit I have no idea what the answer to that question might be."

Connie interrupted, "As intriguing as this conversation might be, we still have room assignments to consider. We still have two bedrooms along the left wall of the hallway leading back to the master bedroom and two children without bedrooms. Who is going where?"

Paul spoke up. "Suzy wants to be next to you and Daddy, so I'll be in the first room, and she'll take the second one."

"I'm impressed, gang. You worked this out very well."

There were proud smiles on the children's faces. "Well, you didn't hear all the negotiations," commented Johnny, "but in the end, it all worked out."

215

The second-floor tour ended with a look at the master bedroom with its en suite bathroom.

"If necessary, from time to time," suggested Connie, "we may have to share our bathroom when things get a bit crowded or even work something out with the powder room downstairs."

"But none of you are allowed to use my shaving equipment in the master bath," teased Jack.

With some good-natured laughing, he led the family to the door just outside the master suite and up the stairs to the attic. It was pretty much just empty space. Although in the far-right corner of the first room, next to a closet door, was an ancient hand-cranked record player. It had a large trumpet for amplification. *It looks just like the logo on the RCA Record label*, thought Jack. *I wonder if it still works.* While the other family members explored the second attic room, Jack wandered over to this antique. *Why look here, five 78 RPM records. I have got to try this out.*

He lifted the cabinet lid and placed an old, heavy 78 RPM record on the turntable. The label said "Chopin's Polonaise" by Jose Iturbe. Jack cranked the extended handle on the right side of the cabinet, and the round platform began to turn rapidly. He placed the old record on the turning table, lifted the arm inside the cabinet, and touched the sound needle to the record. Immediately, the scratchy strains of the classical piano composition filled the room. Hearing the surprising sounds, the rest of the family came running back to see what was going on.

"What's that?" asked Paul, pointing to the source of the music.

"It's an old, old, old record player."

"What's a record player?' asked Suzy.

"It's how people used to listen to music many years ago...before CDs, and iPods, and cassette tapes, and 8-tracks, and 45s, and LPs and HiFi players."

"Huh?" was all Suzy could manage to say.

"And look, Connie, there are a few old 78s here. One of them is the Glenn Miller orchestra playing 'Moonlight Serenade.' Would you like to dance?"

"Not now, dear," she replied.

Even though there was a lot of coaxing from all five children, Connie refused to dance and laughed good-naturedly. "Maybe another time," she said with a smile on her slightly blushing face. "I think right now we should get back on track with our agenda for the day."

Accepting the fact that Connie was not, at least presently, going to be persuaded to dance with him in the attic, Jack switched gears. "You know, these ceilings are high enough. In the future, if we need it, the church might agree to do some renovating up here to create another bedroom. Of course, we would have to extend the HVAC system to this floor, and that could be expensive."

"We'll have to cross that bridge if we actually come to it," said Connie. At that point, Jack decided it was time to go next door to talk to his secretary while the rest of the family moved from bedroom to bedroom, talking about what furniture could go where.

"Hi, Linda."

"Hello, Pastor. How has the tour been going?"

"It's been great. The children were most interested in who would sleep where. They've been talking amongst themselves for a few weeks about the possibilities. When they actually could see the size and location of each bedroom, it went rather smoothly. How are things going here? Are we all set for Sunday?"

"Yes, we're having a little Thank You Luncheon for our interim, Pastor Stevenson, on his last Sunday with us. Molly Young and her team are working on that. What I will need from you, Pastor, is the bulletin info for the following Sunday."

"I actually have that for you on my iPad. I also have my preaching schedule, Scripture texts, and themes for the next three months. I have it all here in my briefcase. I'll email it to you while I'm here so you can make sure it comes through all right. If you could make a copy then for Sally, Anita, me, and yourself, I would appreciate it. Just put my copy on my desk."

"I can see that I'll have to make some adjustments to work with such an organized pastor," joked Linda. "But I think I can manage. It's going to be a refreshing change if you don't mind my saying so."

"No, I'm happy you're open to working with me on this. In time, I'm hoping we can have the entire church calendar for the year set up with activities, dates, responsible leaders, and anything else that will help things run smoothly."

"Oh, boy," said Linda. "This is going to be fun."

Pastor Jack had to laugh at her response. "Is there anything else today that I need to know about?"

"No, I think we're ready. I printed out the schedule for your interviews with the staff that you set up yesterday. It's on your desk with any mail that came in that you might want to look at. I'm sure you remember that your first appointment will be with Sally Erb tomorrow at 11 a.m."

"Thanks for doing that, Linda, and for putting it on my desk so I have it to refer to during the week. But I also have the schedule on my cell phone, so I'll remember when to come in during the rest of this week. I guess I'll see you tomorrow before I meet with Sally. I'll keep my office door open until I can get Jim to put a window in there."

"Right. I'll be here."

"Now, I'm going to see what I've missed over at the parsonage. I'm sure they've made a few plans I need to know about. Then, I'm going to show them around Weaverton, thanks to the tour Jim gave me yesterday. See you tomorrow. Feel free to call me about anything."

"I will. Enjoy the rest of your day. And have a safe return trip to your parents."

On their way back to Nana and PopPop's house, the van that was very noisy with exuberant children's chatter on the way to the church that morning was very quiet. As they were approaching Cedar Street, Jack's cell phone rang. He handed it to Connie, who answered the call.

With a concerned expression on her face, Connie nodded her head slowly and said, "I guess there's nothing else we can do. We look forward to seeing you then."

"What was that about?" asked her husband.

"It looks like we're not going to move into the parsonage on Friday. That was the furniture movers. It turns out they had the furniture from two different families in their moving van. They ran into some trouble unloading the first family's stuff, and it took a lot longer than they expected. That plus the fact that the weekend is almost upon us. They wanted us to know they won't be arriving with our furniture until Monday morning."

"Whoa! At least we have a place to stay for a few more days. I'm sure my folks won't mind. Now that I think about it, I'm so happy I told the church leadership to have the interim pastor preach one last time this first Sunday in November. I thought the reason was that I expected to be exhausted from all the moving, unpacking boxes, and arranging furniture on Friday and Saturday. It turns out the reason is that it looks like we're still going to be staying at my parent's home over the weekend. Once again, I'm sure the Lord knew this was going to happen and protected us from what could have been an uncomfortable situation."

"We can talk to your parents about this when we get there," added Connie, eyes brightening. "Do you know what would be nice? How about we take advantage of these extra couple of days and worship with your parents at their church in Cedar Street?"

"Good idea," said Jack. "They talk very highly of the church and their pastors. We're almost at their place now. Let's see what they think about that idea."

Chapter 32

WEAVERTON, HERE WE COME!

Monday, the new moving day, had arrived. Nana made sure she was up early to prepare a hearty breakfast for the family. She knew it was going to be a busy day, maybe even a very tiring day for everyone, and she wanted to make sure they started off with a good, nutritious meal.

The atmosphere in the big, grey van was very upbeat as they drove back to Weaverton. There wasn't a sense of being frantic and overly excited, but everyone was looking forward to how events would unfold throughout the day. Conversations were pretty much evenly divided. Sometimes it was Jack and Connie chatting in the front seat while the children talked at high speed in the rear of the van. Sometimes one of the children would ask one of them a question, and all ears were tuned to the answer. Other times it was just very quiet while busy minds imagined how the whole moving-in process would unfold.

Perhaps the biggest concern was where to park the moving van for the unloading process. Parking in front of the house on such a narrow two-lane street and so close to where Weaver Road formed a "T" with Church Street would probably create a traffic hazard and very likely be dangerous.

On the other hand, parking on the edge of the church parking lot near the walkway was a long trek, especially considering how many items had to be unloaded. In the end, however, that seemed to be the only sensible thing to do.

The truck driver had texted Connie the night before with their estimated time of arrival. Traffic cooperated with the Whyte family, and they arrived at the parsonage about a half-hour before the moving van. Jack parked the family van in the church lot, out of the way. Connie had time to station the children at key places and gave each one instructions to help the movers take everything into the house.

Five-year-old Suzy was the greeter at the end of the walkway and the official opener of the door to the back screened-in porch. Eight feet further on, seven-year-old Paul would hold the door open for each person passing into the dining room/kitchen area of the house. Both of these children were instructed to close the door after each load was carried through to avoid inviting interested insects into their new abode. If Paul saw the word "kitchen" or "dining room" on a carton, he would indicate where the men should go. Or he would point ahead to his sister, who was waiting for them.

Eleven-year-old Sarah was stationed at the foot of the stairs leading up to the second floor. She would check the label on the carton or the tag attached to the piece of furniture and point the way straight ahead to the living room, around the corner to the left and the homeschool room and Daddy's study, or indicate the path up the stairs to the second floor.

Nine-year-old Megan would be waiting to direct the men into the homeschool room or her daddy's study. If Sarah sent the movers up the stairs, thirteen-year-old Johnny was there to lead them to the proper bedroom. Jack and Connie would roam from room to room and floor to floor throughout the process, sometimes having been beckoned by one of the children to give specific instructions concerning the intended locations for each item.

When the lumbering moving van worked its way slowly across the parking lot, Jack caught their attention. He went to the driver's side and indicated to the men the only safe place to unload. Since the moving van had a side door, it worked out well to pull the truck parallel to the backyard and extend a ramp out that side door to the walkway leading up to the screened-in porch where Suzy would be waiting with her usual big smile.

Jack told them the process they had set up to make it as easy as possible for them to do their work. If an item was labeled family room, it should be taken down the sloping driveway and placed in the open garage. All other items were to be carried up the walkway, where the children would give them directions to the proper location for each item.

Everyone had fun with their sentry posts throughout the house. But they were certainly not like the Queen's Guard in London with their high bearskin hats, stoic expressions, and precision movements, or, more precisely, no movements at all. In between loads from the moving van, there was plenty of running around the house and chatting about the items already unloaded.

The movers were very pleasant and appreciative of the system that had been set up to make things easier for them. When they knew it was going to be some time before the next item would be brought in because of the need to move things around in the truck, the men would let the children know they had a few minutes for a break. That gave them the chance to get a quick snack or run down to check out the pond or the cattle in the neighboring field.

When the movers took their morning break, each child went scurrying to their designated bedroom to unpack what items were already there. The entire moving process was a wonder to behold. With each family member doing his or her part, everything, as far as they knew at the moment, ended up in the right location.

When it appeared to Jack that the truck was almost empty, he used his cell phone to order everyone's favorite sandwiches, chips, and sodas from Jersey Mike's. Connie was signing the final paperwork when Jack hopped into the family van and headed off to pick up his order for an early supper. Meanwhile, the children enjoyed unpacking cartons in their bedrooms and placing their treasures where they thought they should be.

Jack returned with his bag of goodies, and the wonderful aroma of Philly cheesesteaks spread throughout the house. All of a sudden, everyone discovered they were hungry.

"Come and get it!" shouted Jack. The rumbling of six pairs of shoes on the hardwood floors could be heard as everyone followed their noses into the dining room. As they sat around the table, they discovered they were not only hungry; they were a bit tired as well. It was good to relax for a moment.

When they were pretty much into the meal, Jack said, "What about taking a tour of the church building after supper? Anyone interested?"

The cheers indicated they were. Connie showed them the big trash bag where refuse should be tossed. When all was cleaned up, the family followed Jack out the door located in his study, down the two steps to the concrete walkway that curved its way across the gently sloping lawn and into the backdoor of the office wing of the church building.

Just inside the door and to the right was the church secretary's office. Tapping on the door frame, Pastor Jack invited Linda to meet the entire Whyte family.

"Kids, this is Mrs. Hartman, my official secretary. Linda," indicating each child in order by tapping each one on the head or the shoulder, "this is Johnny, who is thirteen."

"Almost fourteen," the boy interjected with a smile.

"Sarah, here, is eleven. Megan is nine. Paul is seven. And Suzy is five."

"Five-and-a-half," she added.

"And you already know Connie, but we won't tell you how old she is." Everyone chuckled.

"The children haven't seen the inside of the church building yet," continued Pastor Jack, "so I thought it would be good to give them a tour while we take a break from moving in."

"That sounds like an excellent idea," confirmed Linda. "I can travel along with you in case you have any questions about any of the facilities."

"That would be very helpful," answered Pastor Jack.

"I'll just put a note on the door, turn on the church answering machine, and we'll be ready to go."

While she took time to take care of those details, the children wandered around the lobby, checking things out, up and down, and all around. Sarah and Megan commented to their mother how nice Mrs. Hartman seemed to be.

Linda began the tour by leading them across the lobby and down the eight hardwood-capped steps to a door on the right that led into the sanctuary. *Ooohs* and *aaahs* were heard all around as five pairs of young, amazed eyes took in the beauty of the worship center for the first time.

The next stop was back up those eight wide, wooden stairs and down the hallway to the left that led to a large fellowship hall with a nicely-appointed church kitchen. A set of stairs took them down to the Sunday school classrooms. Linda, who apparently had a good memory, indicated to each child the room his or her Sunday school class would meet. Each child was impressed with how bright and colorful each room was. She ended the tour with the warm and richly-appointed meeting room.

"This is where your mother and I had our first meeting with the committee that talked to us about the possibility of coming here to Grace Church," explained Jack.

After a few brief questions, the group went back upstairs, where they thanked Linda for the tour, and Jack led them into his office for a peek at where he would be doing a lot of his work, particularly pastoral counseling. As they looked around, he excused himself to check in with Linda about any messages or information she needed to give him before they went back to the parsonage to do more arranging of furniture, clothing, and countless other items.

Empty cartons and packing paper were still strewn everywhere. It was Connie's intention to see that all the empty boxes would be broken down and all the trash placed in garbage bags and put next to the dumpster in the church parking lot. This was to be done before bedtime.

Not one person, adult or child, complained about going to bed that night. In no time, as excited as they were, all were asleep in a matter of minutes. The last question on their minds was, *I wonder what life is going to be like in our new home.*

Chapter 33

BEGINNING THE NEW NORMAL

Everyone seemed to have had a good night's sleep. This made Connie happy. As good as the experience of moving in had been, she knew they had to get the children back on a schedule for homeschooling. Any more organized unpacking would have to take place late in the afternoon and early evening.

Connie had set the alarm to get up early. She wanted to get things organized for studies, and Jack wanted to get some of the basic ingredients for breakfast and lunch in an early run to the market.

Connie decided the best thing to do was to continue with the daily schedule that worked so well in Connecticut. From 8 to 8:30 a.m. was time for devotions and getting dressed. At 8:30 a.m., they would gather around the dining room table for breakfast, leaving time for clean-up. Classes ran from 9 a.m. to around 2 or 3 p.m., with a break for lunch. This didn't always mean time in class at home. Sometimes there was a field trip and often a time for a walk and some healthy exercise at the beautiful city park in Weaverton.

This was Connie's plan for this second day in the parsonage, even though she knew it would not be an ordinary day. They would begin with class time around the dining room table and in various locations in the living room. Jack's parents would be arriving mid-morning with the desks Tom had made for the children. After they moved them into the official homeschool classroom, they would get reorganized there after lunch.

Jack's schedule called for him to be at the church office by 9 a.m. to get things on track for this new ministry. Connie would call him when his parents arrived, and he would come home to help unload the new desks. The plan was to have the whole family give Nana and PopPop a tour of the parsonage.

Jack would follow that up with a tour of the church facilities while the children went back to their schoolwork. When lunch was ready, whatever they happened to be able to prepare with their limited supplies would be shared in the dining room. That was the plan, but no one really knew how the morning would go. It was clear, however, that Jack had to spend some time in his church office.

Shortly after 10 a.m., Tom and Janet arrived in their pick-up truck. PopPop had unloaded all of his construction equipment to make room for five desks for the children. In the passenger seat in the double cab, Nana had very carefully placed a couple of surprises for the family. That included her special homemade macaroni and cheese with breadcrumbs on top, which was the cheesiest anyone had ever tasted. The children loved it even more than the Kraft mac and cheese some of them could make on their own with a little help from their mother.

Janet also brought a few cans of Campbell's cream of tomato soup. She had concluded a long time ago that it was difficult to improve on such a classic. Nana's surprises ended with a one-pot meal for their dinner.

"Janet," protested Connie, "this is just too much."

"Well, I knew you wouldn't have time to prepare much on your first day in your new home, so I decided to relieve you of that responsibility."

"I do appreciate it, but I feel bad that you went to so much trouble."

"No trouble at all," Janet responded. "Actually, PopPop made the Hookie Special for your evening meal and enough for you all to have it warmed up tomorrow for lunch."

"What's Hookie Special?" wondered Paul.

"When I was a younger man," explained PopPop, "I was a volunteer fireman."

"Really?" exclaimed Paul.

"Yes. I was a member of the Cedar Street Hook and Ladder Company. Everyone called it "the Hookies." We had a fancy kitchen for special meals in the firehouse, and many years ago, Bert Smith, we called him Smitty, came up with this great recipe. He called it Hookie Special. It's made of browned smoked sausage, diced and cooked potatoes, and kidney beans in a delicious thick sauce."

Noting the strange look on Paul's face, PopPop added, "It may sound like a strange combination, but when you smell it, you'll want to dive in right away. It's one of the few meals I like to cook for Nana and me."

"I have to agree with PopPop," added Connie. "You're going to love it. I promise."

"We can heat up the mac and cheese for lunch," Nana suggested. "How about setting the oven at a nice low temperature, and we can heat it slowly while we take care of other business? And that includes bringing in your desks."

Connie called Jack at the office to let him know it was desk-moving time. Then she and Janet took care of things in the kitchen while PopPop and the children ran out to the pick-up truck. At this point, everything that Connie had hoped would happen during the morning came off without a hitch.

After tours of the parsonage and the church building and a delicious lunch courtesy of Nana, Tom and Janet headed back home to Cedar Street. The children went back to their new classroom, and Jack returned to his office.

———————•———————

Pastor Jack wanted to get started with what he called a "schedule frame" for the next three months. This was a large calendar attached to his office wall. In this frame, he could plug in events noting who was responsible for each one. He would also list the title, text, and theme for each Sunday service and sermon.

He was determined not to shake things up, especially during the first months of his pastorate at Grace. He wanted to get as much information as possible from Linda concerning what was done in the past and what the congregation would expect, particularly in the near future, with Thanksgiving and Christmas approaching. No other season shouted "tradition" like the Christmas season, and he wanted to be sensitive to that.

On the other hand, something that his music director, Sally Erb, told him during their private meeting together had piqued his interest. It turns out that she was involved in the drama department while a student at Belmont University. In fact, she had been involved in drama while a high school student as well. Sally's path ran parallel to Pastor Jack's. Adding even more interest to this area of ministry, according to Sally, her conversations with Melissa indicated some interest among the church youth in drama as well.

When Pastor Jack mentioned that he had written a short one-act play about Christmas while at the Connecticut church, Sally began to imagine this would be an excellent program for the family service held each Christmas Eve at 6 p.m. That service always included hymns and Scripture and a reminder of the true meaning of Christmas. As Pastor Jack described the play he wrote, Sally recognized this drama would do exactly the same thing but in a different format.

She and Pastor Jack realized it was a change without much change. Yes, Christmas was approaching rapidly, but Sally was willing to put the extra time into producing this play. She felt, with Pastor Jack's help, this could be successfully done. Her eyes lit up as she considered the idea.

Pastor Jack later explained this possibility to Linda. "I really like that idea," she said. "My suggestion would be that Sally should do all the announcing about this play. If it comes from her, there's little chance that anyone will balk at something new. The family service is always a little different each year, so this won't sound any alarms for our most tradition-minded members, especially if it comes from Sally."

"What an excellent idea. I'll contact Sally again later today, and we can talk about the best way to move forward with this program. Yay!" Pastor Jack was getting excited. He knew this would be good for the church because it would show them that they were capable of some things they didn't know they could do and that they had gifts and abilities God gave them that could be used in many new ways.

As he thought about it, Pastor Jack realized this would fit in perfectly with the three-part sermon series he was beginning this coming Sunday. In November, the theme would be "God Is…" and would set forth the basics about the nature, character, and ways of God.

In December, the focus would be "You Are..." and would explain what it means to be a child of God and how He loves and blesses us and wants to use us for His purposes and by His power. This would fit in perfectly with the Advent season with its focus on the birth of Jesus, who invites us to be children of God.

January would find the congregation hearing messages based on the theme "We Are...." In this series, Pastor Jack would talk about what it means to be a church with only one body but many members and only one head, Jesus Christ. Referring to the list of sermons he had given to Linda, he said, "Look at this. It all fits together. This was God's idea all along. I was hoping I was in tune with His plan for us, and now I'm convinced I was right. This feels so good, Linda. *So* good."

She just laughed and clapped her hands. Working with this new pastor was going to be a lot of fun. She was sure of that.

Chapter 34

SOME FIRST THINGS

It was the first full day of school in Pennsylvania for the Whyte family in their new classroom with their new desks. A big question was whether or not the children could do their schoolwork in such close proximity without distracting or disturbing each other.

In Connecticut, they were scattered around the dining room table and some upholstered furniture in the living room. Now they were all in one room. It was a good-sized room, but they were all together. As the day progressed, small adjustments were made. For example, on one occasion, Johnny moved out to the living room to finish a project he was working on that needed a bit more concentration. The good thing was that many of their subjects were video classes on the computer. With the use of earbuds, the possibility of distractions was very limited.

Jack did what he could to help things run smoothly for their homeschool. He also wanted to make sure everything went well on what he considered to be his first full day in the church office. He had texted Linda to let her know he would be there at 10 a.m. after he helped Connie get the school day off the ground as efficiently as possible.

Making his way through his home study to the back entrance of the church building, picking up his Bible and church calendar on the way, Pastor Jack was right on time at ten o'clock. He did not like to be late.

He began with a brief session with Linda in her office. He wanted to check on any messages she had for him, any phone calls he would have to make, and any thoughts she had about items he should check out. He then filled her in on his usual routine.

"My Sabbath is normally on Tuesdays. That's my day of rest from my work. I obviously can't take Sunday off. Saturday is too busy leading up to Sunday,

233

as well as an optimum time for a few family activities. And Monday is usually packed with things I have to follow up on because of events or conversations on Sunday.

"Actually, for years, it wasn't my practice to take a day off at all," continued Pastor Jack. "I figured I was too busy for that. I would say that I took a few hours off here and a few hours there. Till the week had run its course, I had probably taken about twenty-four hours off. But the elders of the church in Connecticut didn't accept that practice. They said if we were going to take the Bible seriously, and I do, I had to take a full twenty-four-hour day of rest when I did not work at my job. In fact, they required it of me. So...I experimented and found that Tuesday works best for me. That means I'll be in the office on Monday but not on Tuesday. I'll ask you please not to call me or schedule anything for me then."

"How do you handle emergencies that happen on Tuesday?" Linda wanted to know.

"Good question. I'm not legalistic about my day of rest. If it's a true emergency, you need to let me know, and I'll follow through. Now, I'd like to sit down with you for a chat about specific church members. Who is sick at home or in the hospital? Who needs to have me talk to them by phone or in person because of something they're dealing with right now? Who do you want to warn me about? Is that acceptable?"

"Absolutely," responded Linda. "Do you want to have that sit-down right now?"

"There's no time like the present. Let's do it."

Except for a few interruptions from phone calls, all went well. A few minutes before noon, Pastor Jack headed home. He checked in with Connie and the children, tucked the store list into his shirt pocket, and headed out for his store run of the day. Jack enjoyed these trips to the store. He often encountered interesting people or those who needed a word of hope or encouragement.

Jack returned with eight bags of groceries and two small plastic bags of supplies from the drugstore. While he and Connie unloaded the items, Jack reported on his trip.

"You're not going to believe what I discovered in downtown Weaverton today. I'm surprised Jim Clemmer didn't tell me about this."

"What did you discover?" Connie asked.

"I went into Long's Pharmacy on Broad Street. Would you believe they have an old-fashioned soda fountain in the left rear corner of the store?"

"Really?"

"Yes, really. It's a pretty smart thing to have when you think about it. How many times have we gone to pick up a prescription and had to wait twenty or thirty minutes with nothing to do? Well, at Long's Pharmacy and Soda Fountain, that's actually on the marquee. You can sit down on one of the bar stools and have a soda or a cup of coffee or tea. And they have cupcakes, muffins, donuts, cheese, and peanut butter crackers. They even have shoofly pie."

"You really checked this out, didn't you?"

"I did! I was flabbergasted. It's like a horseshoe-shaped counter that seats about ten people. Against the back wall, in front of a counter-to-ceiling ten-foot wide mirror, is an old-fashioned soda dispenser. I can see me stopping in there on a regular basis to meet the people in town, make friends, and learn the latest about what's going on in Weaverton."

"Good idea, honey. Good idea. Now, how about lunch? Did you make some good buys at the grocery store?"

"Yes. As you suggested, I picked up some items to help the children make their own sandwiches for lunch with tomato soup. We can save the leftover Hookie Special for dinner. The kids really liked my dad's special one-pot meal."

"Good. Would you mind calling them to the table? I'll put things out and let each person make their own."

Conversation around the table focused on how class time had unfolded that morning. With some good ideas shared by all and some simple adjustments to be made, everyone seemed happy about the new set-up for school.

———————————

Later that week, it was Connie's suggestion that they should all make another visit to the education wing of the church building to familiarize the children with their new classrooms. She had Suzy particularly in mind when she suggested this. Fortunately, everyone thought it was a good idea. It was Friday afternoon when they got around to it after class time was over at 2 p.m.

Jack was visiting a church member at Lakeview Memorial Hospital. Thanks to Jim Clemmer, he knew how to get there. This was when Connie and the children took a second tour of the church classrooms. Much to their surprise, and by the wonderful grace of God, the teacher Suzy would have for her Sunday school class was getting the room ready for Sunday morning.

When they entered the kindergarten classroom, there sitting cross-legged on the floor was a pretty, gray-haired lady with copious curls piled on top of her head. She wasn't that old. Just very gray. She had the sweetest smile anyone could imagine. With a sparkle in her eyes, she looked up at Connie and the children and welcomed them into the room. Being on Suzy's level made it a very non-threatening encounter for the five-year-old.

While Suzy held Connie's hand, the lady looked lovingly into Suzy's eyes and said, "Hi, I'm Savannah Partridge, your Sunday school teacher. You can call me Miss Savannah. What's your name?"

Suzy seemed enthralled by what appeared to her to be some sort of exotic creature.

"My name is Suzy. We just moved here."

"Well, welcome. I hope I can see you again, maybe this Sunday."

Suzy Whyte just nodded her head in silence.

"Hi, I'm Connie Whyte, Suzy's mother. We just moved into the parsonage on Monday, and this will be our first Sunday in church. I'm so glad you happened to be here when we were taking this little tour."

"Since I don't believe in coincidences, I'm sure the Lord had something to do with it," smiled Miss Savannah Partridge.

"I'm sure you're right," agreed Connie.

Meanwhile, the other four children stood side-by-side behind their mother and sister, seemingly mesmerized by this woman sitting on the floor in front of them.

Paul broke the spell. "Do you suppose she lives in a pear tree?" he whispered, followed by stifled giggles from his siblings as they quickly eased out of the room in search of their own classrooms.

"Thank you for being here," said Connie. "Suzy has been hesitant about starting in a new class. Your being here has been very helpful. I'm sure she's thinking her full name is Suzannah, and that is so much like Savannah. And yes, we will both see you on Sunday morning." Then to Suzy, "Do you want to say goodbye to Miss Savannah?"

"Goodbye, Miss Savannah," said Suzy very quietly.

"Goodbye, Suzy. I look forward to seeing you on Sunday."

Still holding her mother's hand, Suzy walked out of the classroom while looking back over her shoulder at this mystical person she had just met. Starting a new class might not be so bad after all.

———————•———————

The first Sunday as the pastoral family of Grace Church was a busy one. All the children were up and ready early with no coaxing from their parents. No one complained about dressing properly for Sunday school and morning worship. The breakfast Connie prepared was consumed with vigor. After last-minute checks of attire, and only one button on Paul's shirt needing adjustment, the family headed out through Jack's study door and into the church building.

They were warmly greeted by church members they met along the way. Thanks to the two tours the children had made of the education section of the building, they all knew where to go when they descended the steps to the lower level. They were welcomed in the hallway by greeters who asked their names, gave them nametags, and had them sign in. They were informed that the younger children would remain in their classrooms after Sunday school was over and only come back upstairs when one of their parents came to get them.

Connie was pleasantly surprised when Suzy released her hand and trotted down the hall and into her classroom to greet Miss Savannah. Paul went into the primary class for grades one through three. Megan headed over to the class for grades four and five. Sarah and Johnny were together in the middle school class. Each child felt fairly comfortable in this new setting.

There was a lecture class for adults in the meeting room taught by attorney Scott Porter. Other adults went to the Fellowship Hall, where they enjoyed conversations, coffee, tea, and donuts. Pastor Jack and Connie had the opportunity to meet some more members of Grace there, some for the first time and many for the second time.

In the sanctuary, before the worship service began, there was a time for announcements about things coming up in the life of the church. Sally, the music director, took this opportunity to announce that this year's family service on Christmas Eve was going to take the form of a special Christmas play. They would need an older couple to play the role of grandparents and another couple to be the parents of four children, all getting their home ready for the celebration of Christmas. The play was called *Our Family Tradition*.

There would be music, Scripture, and an explanation of the Christmas story by the actors in the play. Any interested members were instructed to see Sally or Anita after the service or call the church office this week. There was what seemed to be some positive hubbub in the congregation following the sharing of this announcement. *A good sign*, thought Linda and Sally.

This first service that Jack led as senior pastor of the congregation went surprisingly well. The music was anointed and inspiring. The special music presented by the choir under Sally and Anita's leadership was outstanding. Just before the sermon, the first of a three-part series on who God is, the congregation sang the old standard hymn "Holy, Holy, Holy, Lord God Almighty."

It was the perfect introduction to this first basic message prepared for the flock of believers now under Pastor Jack's care. As he preached, his constant unspoken prayer was that those worshiping that day would come to understand how great God is and how much He loved every one of them. The comments Pastor Jack heard following the service seemed to indicate that for most of the people, his prayer had indeed been answered.

Chapter 35

FRANK'S PLACE

It was on Wednesday that Pastor Jack spent more than an hour starting to go over the names of members of the congregation. He used the church's pictorial directory and prayed over each family as he looked at their photos. He had not yet met most of them, so for those he did not yet know, he prayed a general prayer for good health and a hunger to know the Lord.

For those he had met, like Officer Harold Bender, Sally, the Hartmans, the Garcias, the Geisingers, the Highlands, and quite a few more, he was able to pray a more specific prayer for God to be working in their lives. This took him through the first third of the congregation. He would continue this practice every week of his pastorate at Grace Church.

Today, the plan was to meet more of the church members personally. When he had talked to Linda about the people he should focus his attention on, she noted the seven shut-ins of the church. At his request, Linda called and made appointments throughout the day with each of them, people who, for various reasons, were not able to come to church to worship. In addition, Pastor Jack made a follow-up visit to the hospital to see the member he had prayed with last week.

For lunch, he decided to stop in at Frank's Place. It wasn't that he couldn't have had lunch at home, but he wanted to work on getting to know as many people in the area as possible. Also, he thought it was good for the people of the community to meet the new pastor in town. When he entered Frank's Place, he was not expecting what he found.

To the right of the door, as he entered, he saw two horseshoe-shaped counters side-by-side. Behind the counters along the wall to the right were a grill, a coffeemaker, and a milkshake mixer. Over the grill was a stainless-steel vent to remove aromas and odors from the food prep area. To the left of the grill was a glass-enclosed and brightly lit refrigerated case with meats and cheeses and various ingredients for making sandwiches. And to the left of that glass case was an assortment of bread and rolls. To the right of the grill were two large urns, each having a label attached to the front describing the homemade soup contained in each one.

A big man, at least six-foot-two tall, was working over the grill with his back to the entrance. Hearing someone enter, he turned around and, with a warm smile and a big voice, said, "Welcome to Frank's Place. In case you wanna know, I'm Frank." And then he laughed heartily. "Find yourself a seat. The first counter is for normal people. The second one is for characters and crackpots." His smile turned up slightly on the right with a glint in his eyes as he watched to see where this new customer would choose to sit.

"I think I probably belong at the second counter," said Pastor Jack with a grin.

Frank's hearty laugh filled the room. "I'll be with you shortly," he announced. "There's a menu in front of you. Specials for the day are up there," he noted, pointing to a blackboard to his left above the glass-enclosed sandwich ingredients. He was not a handsome man, but certainly not unpleasant looking either.

Jack studied the man and the menu. Frank had a thatch of hair around the sides and back of his head with a few wisps on top. His eyebrows were thick and bushy. He wore a full-length white apron, already dirty from wiping his hands there during food preparations so far. The long apron did not hide the fact that the man had no waist. He appeared to be someone who liked people. That would go a long way toward bringing in customers and, hopefully, with good food, bring them back.

Frank was the only one waiting on customers. He checked with each one to find out what they wanted. He would then prepare what they ordered along that long wall behind the counter.

Frank approached Jack. "So, are you new in town or just passing through?"

"I'm new in town. I'm the new pastor at Grace Church."

"Well, welcome to Weaverton, Reverend. I hope you like it here. It's a great place to live, not perfect, but really good. Hey, folks," he announced to the patrons, "it's the new reverend in town." There were a number of greetings from both counters. "So, what can I get you for lunch?"

"I see you have homemade vegetable soup and also potato soup. I think I'd like a bowl of the vegetable one. Is there beef in that soup?"

"Beef in my vegetable soup?" asked Frank incredulously. "I don't put beef in my beef stew; why would I put it in my vegetable soup?" And his laugh once again filled the restaurant, joined by the guffaws of a smattering of "characters and crackpots" around the counter.

"Just joking, Reverend. No, today it's just vegetable soup. On other days it's vegetable beef soup. Do you still want a bowl?"

"Absolutely," said Jack.

"Coming right up. Did you want crackers with that?"

"Yeah, as long as I don't have to pay extra," he said with a smile.

Frank laughed again. "I think I'm going to like you, Reverend," he said.

"I hope so," said Jack, "because I already like you."

"Good. That's good," said Frank to himself as he approached the urn containing vegetable soup.

When he finished and paid for his lunch, Jack said goodbye to Frank and thanked him for the meal.

"You come back again, Reverend. We'll save a seat for you at the second counter. I think that's right where you fit."

Jack just laughed as he left the restaurant amidst applause and laughter from the customers at the second counter.

"Well, that was fun," he said to himself as he headed for his car and his other shut-in appointments for the day.

It was almost 5 p.m. when Pastor Jack returned to the church office. Linda was just getting ready to leave.

"How did your visits go?" she asked.

"They went pretty well. Thank God for GPS. Do you have any messages for me?"

"I put them on your desk. I'll see you tomorrow?"

"Absolutely. I look forward to it. Enjoy the rest of your day, Linda."

As Linda left through the main entrance of the church and locked the door behind her, Pastor Jack checked the messages on his desk. Then he left through the side door and followed the walkway to the parsonage.

He met Connie as he walked through his study, and she was leaving the homeschool room. Almost in unison, they asked each other, "How did your day go?"

Connie answered first. "We're really moving along nicely with school right now. I'm feeling really good about it. And I'm learning a lot myself. It's mostly reviewing things I learned before, but some of it, especially in history, I'm learning for the first time. Johnny was studying Gettysburg, and the details they get into are fascinating. There's a book called *Killer Angels* about Gettysburg that I'd like to get. Terrible title but apparently a wonderful book."

"I think I heard about that. It's part of a trilogy, I think. You know, I can get that for you as an eBook if you want me to."

"Let me think about that. It just might be a good book to add to Johnny's reading list. Anyway, I think everyone is making progress. We'll know how much progress they're really making when they get some testing done. That won't be for a while unless we have them go to public or Christian school next year. If we do that, there will be some testing before they start new classes in the fall. What did you do today? I know you were going to be visiting some shut-ins. How did that go?"

"Really well. But before I get into that, where are the kids?"

"They're all downstairs enjoying their new family room. Do you remember we talked about the need to get some additional furniture for down there?"

"Sure. Have you thought about what we need?"

"I have, and I think the most efficient and least expensive thing to do is to buy some big beanbag chairs."

"I love that idea," said Jack. "When you say 'big,' do you mean big enough for the father of the family? If they want to fight me for them, I think I'd win. I'm a lot bigger than any one of them."

"But what if they gang up on you?"

"Oooh, scary thought. Joking aside, I think beanbag chairs are an excellent idea. We'll have to ask around about where to get them in the area. Not to change the subject but aren't we getting close to supper time? I only had a bowl of soup for lunch, and I'm getting hungry."

"Yes, it's in the oven and on the stove. We're having meatloaf, mashed potatoes and gravy, and green beans with almonds."

"Mmmm. One of my favorites. Why don't I tell you about my lunch and a couple of my visits after supper? I think the children will get a kick out of one of my adventures for the day while we're eating."

"Okay, let's do that. Why don't you go have fun with the children while I finish up food prep? I'll call down to you when it's time to eat."

Chapter 36

SARAH'S MISSION

As they sat down to eat, Connie commented, "I heard a lot of giggling and howling from the basement. What was going on down there?"

"Oh, just a little bit of wrestling here and there," answered Jack. "I was testing out your theory about the beanbag chairs. I think you're right. One-on-one, I'm still a winner. When they gang up on me, though, I'm in big trouble, especially as big as Johnny is getting."

There were a lot more giggles around the table.

"Okay, everybody. Let's thank God for this meal and for the wonderful lady who prepared it for us. Let's pray."

With that, all hands reached out to the person next to them, all heads were bowed, and Jack led them in a prayer of thanks.

After the children shared about their day, Jack said, "I met some new people today from the church, and I think you'll enjoy hearing about one of my visits in particular." So, between bites and while the family continued their meal, Jack briefly recounted his encounter with one particular shut-in.

"I stopped in to see three ladies in the church. Apparently, everyone simply calls them 'the sisters.' They live together in a two-story red brick house on Leroy Lane, just about two miles south of here. Connie, you would love this house. I'll take you along on a visit sometime. As I said, it's red brick with classic white shutters and dark green trim above each window, the kind of accents you don't see in new homes. They have a covered front porch with white-tooled balustrades. And there's a hanging wooden swing at one end of the porch."

"Oh, just like the one I'd like to have on our front porch."

"Exactly. These three sisters are Ellen, Emma, and Abby Schultz. Ellen and Emma are the two older sisters and are both widows. Their husbands died some years ago, and they never got remarried. Abby, the youngest sister, has never been married. But she is the most interesting one. She's the only shut-in, meaning she can't get out of her home very often. Ellen and Emma are in church every Sunday, but Abby never attends.

"Ellen said to me shortly after my arrival that the main reason I was visiting them was probably because of their younger sister. They excused themselves to let me have a private talk with Abby. She's a little thing. Grey hair tied up in a knot on the top of her head, wearing a long, figured dress in rather dark colors. She had very little color in her face and didn't smile much. I felt sorry for her from the very beginning. She just sat there rocking slowly in her high-backed rocking chair the whole time."

"She sounds sort of sad," said Sarah.

"You're absolutely right," said Jack. "Very sad. I made the mistake of asking her how she was doing."

"Why was that a mistake?" asked Paul with a mouthful of mashed potatoes. "That seems like a nice thing to do."

"Ordinarily, it would be a nice thing to do. When I asked her how she was doing, she began a twelve-minute description of all the problems she had, whether real or imagined. From now on, when I visit her, I'm going to talk about how beautiful the day is, how nice her home is, and things like that. I need to get her to think about more positive things. It was the apostle Paul who wrote to the Philippians that they should spend time thinking about what is good and true and pure. He said if you do that, you will know the kind of peace God wants for you."

"That sounds like a good plan," encouraged Connie.

"Now, here is some interesting information at least one of you will find fascinating. Before Ellen and Emma left the room, I asked if they would mind telling me how old they were. Ellen is seventy-two, Emma is seventy, and Abby will be sixty-seven on her next birthday, which is coming up in just a few weeks, December third."

"Hey, that's my birthday!" shouted Sarah. "I'll be twelve. Boy, that means she's fifty-five years older than me."

"You're right," said Jack. "That's a lot of years. I told her I would visit her again on her birthday. I want to make it a positive experience for her."

"Can I go along with you, Daddy?" pleaded Sarah. "I could make a birthday card and give it to her on her birthday."

"Of course, if you want to. I'm sure she would like that."

"Yay! I'm going to make a house call with Daddy. This is going to be fun."

"Just don't ask her how she's doing," prompted her big brother Johnny.

"I won't. I'll only talk to her about good stuff."

"In the meantime," suggested Connie, "if her name comes to mind, it would be good to pray for Abby Schultz."

"Can we pray for her now," asked Sarah.

"Absolutely," answered Connie. "Do you want to pray?"

"Sure." Everyone put down their eating utensils and grabbed hands as Sarah began. "Dear God, we're really happy we're here in our new home, and we're sorry Miss Schultz is not so happy in hers. Make what hurts her feel better and help her to feel so much better that she can get out of her house and come to church. Thank You. Amen."

"Thank you, Sarah. That was a fine prayer," said her mother.

"Now, before we ask Mommy if she has any dessert for us, I want to remind you of one of the rules in the Whyte house. If you learn about a member of the congregation," said their father, "it is not for you to tell anyone else about him or her. It is for you to be able to pray for them. Got it?"

"Got it," resounded around the table.

"Okay, Mommy. How about dessert?" Jack was still hungry.

"Well, there's only dessert if you're interested in chocolate brownies."

More cheers went up all around the dining room.

"Whose turn is it to clear the table?" asked Connie.

"That would be me," confessed Paul.

"Let's get it done, then. The sooner the table is cleared and the dishwasher loaded, the sooner we eat brownies. Oh, and did I mention we have ice cream to serve with the brownies?"

More cheers went up, and Johnny even offered to help his brother clear the table so they could have dessert that much sooner.

Season IV

The Holidays

Chapter 37

A Corporate Inferiority Complex

The day for the Christmas play auditions had arrived. Pastor Jack and Sally were both excited about the possibilities. Linda had made multiple copies of the play for distribution to those who would arrive for the audition. She also made a small sign to be taped to the main entrance that said "Auditions in the Sanctuary." Although there would be a lot of music for this play, specifically Christmas carols, they wouldn't be getting into that yet, since this was only an audition. Nevertheless, accompanist Anita Garcia was there to observe.

Pastor Jack, Anita, and Sally had prayed together for the right people to show up for the auditions. They believed God would work all that out.

The first people to arrive were the Williamsons, Aaron and Evelyn. They were what anyone would call a sweet couple, probably in their early seventies. They both had white hair. Evelyn's was a beautiful color without adding any chemicals to the mix. Aaron's was wavy but also thinning quite a bit. They both exuded warmth and confidence. You could tell they were obviously still in love.

The Williamsons admitted they had never done anything like this in their many years together as husband and wife. "We just thought it would be fun to try something new," explained Aaron.

Next to arrive was the Hartley family. Alex and Kate were the parents of Steve, who was sixteen, Jessica, "call me Jessie," who was fourteen, and Nate, who was twelve. As Pastor Jack got to know them briefly, he learned that they all had a real interest in drama.

Alex was a big man, just over six feet tall, with a brilliant smile and a pervading attitude of good humor. He owned and operated Hartley Reno and Repair. He was the "go-to guy" for the local high school when they produced their class plays. Alex would help them by constructing the flats and other necessary props for their sets.

His interest in drama was clearly reinforced and even fueled by his marriage to Kate, who'd been a drama major in college. In fact, they met when he was helping to create the set for a college production of Shakespeare's *As You Like It*, and Kate was one of the actors. Kate, with dark hair and matching dark eyes, was diminutive alongside her big husband. It seemed their interest in drama spilled over into their children. When Steve, Jessie, and Nate were in elementary school, they started to put on little dramas they created in the family's large basement, inviting friends to be their tiny audience.

These seven people were the only ones who contacted Sally after her announcement about the production. When no one else came forward, she made a follow-up announcement that any interested members should just show up on Saturday at 10 a.m. even if they hadn't contacted her.

Therefore, Pastor Jack, Sally, and Anita chose to wait a few more minutes for any stragglers to arrive. While the Williamsons and the Hartleys chatted away, the three leaders stepped aside to have a little conversation themselves.

"Let me tell you a little something about Grace Church, Pastor," Sally said. "I'm sure you'll discover this very soon anyway. This congregation is full of good and, in many cases, talented people. But they don't think they're good enough to do things like act in a play. You will often hear someone say, 'We're just a little country church.'"

"Then how did you manage to get such a fine choir out of this group? You have fifteen talented singers there."

"Thank you. Yes, they do a good job, but it took a few years to, little by little, add to their number and their confidence."

"Sally, you've brought to mind something Pete and Lucy told me early on in our relationship with Grace," added Pastor Jack. "They said the pulpit committee had been told they would probably never get a good pastor for this church because it was so small. Apparently, that negative opinion of themselves has spread throughout the congregation."

"Yes," Sally agreed. "That idea just reinforced the poor attitude these people have about themselves and what they might be able to accomplish."

"I'm hoping my first series of sermons may help with that. The Lord has made it clear that every message for my first three months here must emphasize the irrefutable fact that God loves these people individually and as a group of believers. I'm getting the sense that the whole congregation unknowingly has a kind of inferiority complex, the idea that they can never do anything significant. I wonder if it was part of God's plan that we use this play to help them see that they can do something special and worthwhile."

It was Anita's additional insight that broke through any negative thoughts in Pastor Jack's mind. "You know," she said, "we prayed that God would send the right people for this audition. So, these must be the right people. We have the Williamsons for the grandparents and the Hartleys for the family. An additional benefit is that we've avoided any feelings of competition among our members. No one will feel hurt because they didn't get chosen. Everyone who showed up will get a part in the play. I would say we're in good shape here, Pastor. We just need another actor for the role of the youngest child."

"I like your attitude, Anita," said Pastor Jack. "And I think I might have the solution to where to find a fourth child. We produced this play last Christmas in Connecticut, and my son Paul, who was six at the time, played that part. He really enjoyed it. I think he might consider doing it again if I ask him."

"This is getting exciting. Can you ask him right now?" encouraged Anita.

"Sure. I'll just call Connie's cell phone and talk to him. The family is having a painting party in one of the bedrooms at the moment. Why don't you two chat with our actors while I take care of this? Encourage them to skim over the script."

Everyone in the Whyte family liked their rooms. Johnny really liked his location. It was a corner room with two windows, one on the east wall looking out over the backyard and the pond, the other looking out toward the church. The only problem he had was the color of the walls. It was what he called "little girl pink." Not a good color for an almost fourteen-year-old boy. The family had a painting party to take care of that glaring problem just days after they moved in.

Today, they were having a second painting party for Sarah and Megan's room. The wall color there wasn't bad. It's just that the girls wanted a color that fits their personalities. They decided that color was "springtime lilac."

Custodian Jim Clemmer had come in early to apply that special tape painters use to make sure you had good, clean edges. Then he and Johnny moved all the furniture to the center of the room and covered everything with sheets of plastic that were already splattered with dozens of colors from previous painting projects.

Connie and the children were in the midst of attacking and transforming their assigned portion of the walls when Connie's cell phone rang. Wiping her hands, she answered it.

"Hello, Jack."

"Hi, honey. How's the painting going?"

"We're having lots of fun. There's paint everywhere, most of it on the walls," she laughed. "How are things going with your auditions?"

"Well, at first, I was disappointed with the number of people who showed up. But now I'm convinced God has His hand on this whole thing. I'll tell you more after lunch. It's actually quite amazing. What I need right now is to talk to Paul."

"Okay, I'll get him for you."

"Hi, Daddy," said his son.

"Hi, Paul. You know we're having the first read-through of the Christmas play we did last year."

"Right."

"We have all the people we need, with the exception of the youngest child of the family, the part you played last year."

"Yessss?"

"Do you think you could bring yourself to do that part again this Christmas Eve? You did a great job last year, and I know you enjoyed it. What do you think?"

Silence. Then, "Yeah, I guess I could do that. It was fun, and I won't have any trouble memorizing the lines again. There weren't that many, to begin with. Sure, I'll do it."

"Great. Now, do you think you could drag yourself away from the painting party to do a read-through of the play right now? We're in the sanctuary."

"I think they'll be fine here without me." He suddenly sounded very grown-up. "I'll be right over." With that, he turned the phone over to his mother and announced, "I'm going to be in the Christmas play!"

"Oh, okay then. I think we can get this done without you. I must say, your father is full of surprises. You might want to wash up a little before you head over there."

"Okay. Bye." And with that, her actor son was gone.

"Good news," said Pastor Jack to Sally and Anita. "Paul is on his way over. Let's get this show on the road."

When they were all together in the sanctuary, Pastor Jack addressed the group. "Sorry for the delay, and thank you all for being here. I will admit to you I was hoping for a whole bunch of people to show up for this audition. But then Anita reminded me that we specifically prayed for God to bring to the audition the people He wanted to have in this play. Obviously, you are those people. So, look around you. This is the official cast of *Our Family Tradition*. Congratulations!"

Sally asked if anyone had a chance to look over the script. "I have," said Kate, "and from what I've seen in a cursory look, I really like it. It even has a touch of mystery concerning what the youngest child has hidden behind his back the whole time."

"There are some good laugh lines in there as well," added Alex. "This is going to be fun."

"Good. And our eighth cast member has just arrived. He is a veteran actor, my son Paul. He played the role of the youngest child last year at the church in Connecticut. He's been called out of retirement to reprise his award-winning performance," joked Pastor Jack.

"Thanks a lot, Daddy." To the other actors, he said, "It's a fun play. I think you'll all have a good time with it."

"Okay, let's read through the script. Sally and I will be doing the directing. We may make some comments about how things should happen onstage and other kinds of logistics while you're reading, but primarily, we just want to hear you read your parts. And Anita, if you have any questions or suggestions, feel free to add them as well."

———————————

After the read-through, when the others had left for home, Sally, Paul, and Pastor Jack remained, chatting just outside the sanctuary. When Jack saw how late it was getting to be, he turned to Paul and said, "Okay, son, let's head home and see if the painting is finished."

Chapter 38

TIME FLIES FOR BUSY PEOPLE

It's true that the busier you are, the faster time seems to fly by. The Whyte family was very busy with homeschooling, painting, organizing rooms, and family plans for Thanksgiving dinner, all while continuing to unpack. Would that never end?

Paul was feeling sort of left out, so he decided he wanted his room painted blue as well. But he wanted one dark blue wall and three light blue walls. Was there an artist hiding somewhere in there behind all that geeky tech stuff he loved so much? Maybe. As for Suzy, she was just content to have the bedroom next to her parents, whatever the color.

The Christmas season would soon be upon them. There were family plans and individual dreams to deal with as November whisked by and December beckoned them forward. Of course, church activities always ramped up quite a bit during the Christmas season each year. In addition to the usual activities, there were special events and services.

Actually, for Pastor Jack, Christmas and Easter were his easiest times of the year, or at least they had been. After being at the Connecticut church for a number of years, he had learned well how to delegate and to whom to delegate. That meant that most of the extra responsibilities, and some of the usual tasks as well, were given to various members of the church who had the gifts to take them on.

He would not be able to do that at Grace this year. He didn't know the people well enough to know who had the gifts and abilities to share in the joys of ministry, particularly at this special season of the year. But that would come in due time. One of the most fulfilling areas of pastoral ministry for Jack was helping people discover the gifts God had given them and helping them learn how to use those gifts.

He loved watching lights of recognition go on in their eyes when Christians learned about their unique gifts from God. Even better was seeing their sense of joyful satisfaction when they actually ministered to someone and gained new confidence as a disciple of Jesus. That was one of the things that made his ministry so rich and fulfilling.

Yes, it would be like starting over again, just like he did in Connecticut, but it was so worth the effort. In the meantime, the Christmas season this year was going to be very busy for Pastor Jack.

The Christmas play was moving along nicely. Rehearsals and blocking and directorial comments from Pastor Jack and Sally all worked together to produce wonderful signs of progress. They were sure all the actors would be ready for the one-time performance at the 6 p.m. Christmas Eve Family Celebration.

Creating a stage for the performance was the tricky part. Fortunately, they had two very creative and gifted men in Alex Hartley and Jim Clemmer. The difficult part was having a stage that allowed free movement for the play itself yet was removable for conducting worship services in between rehearsals.

They decided to conduct early rehearsals in the Fellowship Hall. Closer to performance time, a cleverly-created portable yet sturdy stage was set up in the chancel of the sanctuary for the actors to get accustomed to proper blocking. Alex arranged to borrow a few flats from the high school drama department for this purpose.

Sally and Anita were working diligently on Christmas music. The choir was practicing Christmas carols to be used as part of the Christmas Eve play. One of the songs, "Away in a Manger," would be sung by a special children's choir. Sally and Anita put out a call for children to learn this one song for the play. Rehearsals were to begin soon, and most of the Whyte family children were more than likely going to be a part of the production. Johnny wasn't sure he qualified for "children's choir" anymore.

One interesting development slowly unfolded when members of the church discovered the play was written by their new pastor. Talk about this fact began to generate more and more interest in attending the play. In addition, many members began to tell non-members about this gifted new pastor at Grace Church. He was not only a nice guy and an excellent preacher, but he was a writer as well.

"You oughta come and see the play!" they encouraged their friends. It looked like some of the collective sense of inferiority that "we're just a little country church" was beginning to crumble a tiny bit.

Another gradual development was causing significant conversations among the Grace Church members. Each week, it became apparent that a few more people began attending Sunday services, some members and some from the community. Slowly, the word was beginning to spread about this new pastor at Grace, and people wanted to check him out.

Obviously, this gradual increase in attendance did not go unnoticed by Pastor Jack. He was sure the series of sermons God had directed him to preach had something to do with this development.

The clear direction he received from the Lord was that these first messages were to be informative, inspirational, and encouraging. They were not to be challenging. These people were not yet ready for a challenge. They had to know more about themselves, their God, and the Spirit-inspired Bible before they were ready to be challenged. Not only that, Pastor Jack had to build up a kind of trust account with them.

The members had to know he loved and cared for them before he was able to challenge them to grow and perhaps even change some of their ways of living. Pastor Jack knew that was an important part of his ministry and his calling from God. He was going to continue to trust the Lord to let him know when to turn that important corner on their journey together. Meanwhile, his messages seemed to be drawing new people to Grace Church. That was very encouraging.

For Connie, her major area of responsibility continued to be homeschooling. From her perspective, that was going very well. The children were learning and growing. She was learning as well. The areas where Jack took responsibility were very helpful in relieving some of the pressure. They had become an even stronger team than before as they shared this responsibility and respected the available time and knowledge each one brought to the project.

On the horizon was Thanksgiving dinner. Connie was famous for her savory roast turkey that was filled to overflowing with her special bread stuffing. Each week, Connie would save a few slices of whatever kind of bread they were eating that week, including the crusts that nobody wanted. She placed them in a large freezer bag to keep until Thanksgiving. All the different varieties of bread mixed together made for a great stuffing.

Jack, who had learned to bake from his mother, loved to create one or two of their favorite pies, pumpkin certainly being one of them. His flaky pie crust recipe was so well-known that several women's groups in Connecticut had actually invited him to teach them how to make it.

So much was going on in the Whyte house that important events could sneak up on them. It was the week after Thanksgiving, when the family was having even more leftover turkey for dinner, that Jack said, "I have an important question to ask. Does anyone know what tomorrow is?"

"Yes, I do," said Sarah with a big smile. "It's my birthday!"

"Do you remember who else has a birthday?" asked Jack.

"Yes, that lady who lives with her two sisters," acknowledged Sarah.

"That's right. Ellen, Emma, and Abby Schultz. You might also remember that I promised you we would visit Abby on your shared birthday. Do you still want to come along?"

"Yes, I do. And I want to make a birthday card for her. Can I use some of the art supplies we have in our classroom to do that, Mommy?"

"Of course you can," answered Connie. "We can count that as part of your art class."

"Oh boy. This is going to be fun!"

The next morning couldn't arrive soon enough for Sarah. Immediately after breakfast and devotions, she began creating Abby's birthday card. She used lots of bright colors, creating a scene of flowers with a bright yellow sun shining down on them. On the inside of the folded card, she printed, "Happy Birthday, Abby Schultz. From your new friend, Sarah Whyte."

When she was finished, Sarah rushed into her father's study to show him the results of her efforts. "Do you think she'll like it?" she asked.

"I have no doubt about that. She's going to love it, Sarah. I made an appointment with the sisters to visit them today at two o'clock. We'll leave about ten minutes before that."

"Oh wow, this is going to be great. Thanks, Daddy." With that, she rushed off to tell her mother the time of her important appointment.

"That's wonderful," her mother encouraged. "Now you'll have time to work on your history reading before you and Daddy leave if you can manage to settle down."

"Yeah, I can do that," Sarah smiled.

When they arrived at the Schultz home, they were greeted at the door by Ellen, the oldest sister, and invited to come in. They were pleased to see Sarah with Pastor Jack. He introduced his daughter to the sisters one at a time.

When Sarah met Abby, the sisters were very surprised to see her walk quickly over to the rocking chair and give Abby a big hug. To say Abby was surprised would be an understatement, but the look on her face was priceless when Sarah gave her the handmade birthday card and said, "Happy Birthday. I made this for you. My birthday is today too."

Ellen and Emma stood back and watched with their mouths open as an intrigued Abby began a quiet but animated conversation with Sarah, asking her how old she was, what grade she was in, what she liked to do, and more.

Pastor Jack just smiled proudly as he saw Abby literally blossoming under the unselfish efforts of his now twelve-year-old daughter.

The visit ended with a prayer from Pastor Jack. With a final hug and a promise from Sarah that she would write to Abby, the visitors left the three sisters amazed and strangely refreshed. This simple visit was one they would never forget. It planted seeds of change in Abby they could have only hoped for.

Chapter 39

MERRY CHRISTMAS EVE!

Christmas began with the production of *Our Family Tradition* at the 6 p.m. Family Christmas Celebration. Immediately following the previous Sunday morning service, the construction team led by Alex and Jim had brought the various parts that would become the stage into the sanctuary from the Fellowship Hall.

They permanently erected the flats that had been created to look like the Wellington family living room. They set a partially-decorated Christmas tree about six feet tall in its proper place. After the set was ready, the actors, singers, and directors had plenty of time for final rehearsals.

Christmas Eve had finally arrived. People were excited and surprised as ushers handed them programs upon entering the transformed sanctuary. If they decided to come back for the 11 p.m. candlelight service, they would be surprised again by how the sanctuary was brought back to its traditional Christmas beauty.

More and more people entered the little country church on the corner of Church Street and Weaver Road as the time for the early evening service approached. By 6 p.m., the sanctuary was full, including quite a few people from the community who were not members of Grace Church.

Pastor Jack enthusiastically welcomed the crowd, the biggest he had ever seen in this sanctuary. "We are happy to see so many people celebrating the birth of Jesus this evening. That will be our focus in both of our services today...the birth of Jesus. I want you all to realize that the presentation of this play is more than a drama. The play is the sermon for this worship service. You will find that to be true as the play unfolds."

He then opened their time together with a prayer, asking for God's blessing on the event. He asked especially for confidence for the actors on stage. The congregation was invited to stand and sing together the first Christmas carol of the evening, "Joy to the World."

After the carol, Pastor Jack continued, "Now, let me invite you to enjoy our message for this Family Christmas Celebration as our actors and singers present *Our Family Tradition*. By the way, you will hear a number of Christmas carols during the presentation. I encourage you to sing along. Also, I believe the sanctuary is a great place to express how happy we are to be God's children. So, when someone onstage says something funny, you have my permission to laugh."

As hoped, that remark relaxed everyone who was not already comfortable and caused laughter to spread throughout the sanctuary. Just what Jack wanted. With that, the actors entered the sanctuary from the front right door, chatting as they walked, some carrying cartons containing Christmas tree ornaments. They were welcomed with applause from the audience.

To begin the play, Jim Wellington, the play's father, welcomed everyone into their living room and introduced each family member to the audience, beginning with his in-laws, Chester and Verna Gruver. The first laughs of the play occurred when this Grandma and Grandpa teased each other. Then Jim asked his wife, Allison, and oldest child Sherry to explain the Wellington family Christmas tradition.

Stepping forward, Allison said, "Thank you for joining us. We love Christmas so much because it reminds us of God's never-ending love for all people."

"Yes," added Sherry. "Whenever I see a painting of Mary and Joseph, looking with such complete love at their newborn child, Jesus, I think about how much love God has for us that He would send us His only begotten Son at Christmas."

"As a family," added the play's mother, "we remember each year what Christmas means while we decorate the tree. Each person takes a turn hanging an ornament on the tree. As the ornament is placed there, that person tells the family what that symbol tells us about Christmas."

"It's really fun," concluded Sherry. "You'll love it! Each of us has been looking in the cartons for the symbol we want to talk about this year."

One intriguing character in the drama was the youngest family member, Jeffrey. This was the role being played by Paul Whyte. He just sat on a bar stool the whole time with his hands behind his back and a cat-that-ate-the-canary grin on his face.

As each family member revealed the ornament they chose to put on the tree and what it meant to them regarding the true meaning of Christmas, and as each carol was sung by the senior choir and the newly-formed children's choir, young Jeffrey sat quietly, waiting for his turn. All he would say was that he was holding on to Christmas behind his back.

Finally, the reveal took place, and the young boy proudly showed them he was holding the figure of baby Jesus in the manger. When Grandpa asked him why he chose that ornament, Jeffrey said, "Because you can't have Christmas without Jesus, Grandpa." And everyone applauded.

As Jeffrey hung his ornament on the Christmas tree with confidence, his actor father invited everyone to hear the historical account of the birth of Jesus recorded in Luke 2:1–7. Then Jim asked the audience to open their hymnals and stand to sing "Silent Night" together with the actor family on stage.

At the conclusion of that favorite Christmas carol, Pastor Jack pointed to the stage actors and choir members and said, "I think these people did a fabulous job. What do you think?" The sanctuary erupted with enthusiastic applause. "And let's not forget Alex Hartley and Jim Clemmer and their crew who created the set and have set it up and taken it down many times in these last few weeks." The applause continued. "And, of course, our music director, Sally Erb, and our wonderful keyboard artist, Anita Garcia." More applause.

"Before you leave," Pastor Jack continued, "I want to remind you of our candlelight service this evening at eleven o'clock. You are all welcome. Come back and bring a friend or two. Our actors and singers will be upfront now as you leave. Feel free to talk to them and let them know what a great job they did. And don't forget that, on Sunday, we have Sunday school at 9:30 a.m. and morning worship at 10:45 a.m. That will be your last opportunity this year to worship the Lord."

Then raising both hands high and toward the congregation, he said, "May the peace of the Christ child dwell in your hearts and bring many blessings to you and your families. Go in peace."

While Anita played more joyful Christmas music, the crowd dispersed, many of them congratulating the actors who had come down from the stage and were standing in front of the sanctuary. All of the Whytes huddled around Paul and told him how great he had been.

"Once again, Paul," said Johnny, "you were the star of the show." This caused Paul to grin from ear to ear.

Things had pretty much quieted down as Jim and Alex quickly worked with their crew to take down the set and get things ready for the 11 p.m. candlelight service. The ushers had kindly remained and were in the process of collecting programs that had been left in the pews, some having fallen onto the floor. When the sanctuary looked presentable again, lights were turned out, doors were locked, and the building was left to itself until it would be invaded again in less than four hours for the next service.

Jack and his family retired to the parsonage. Relaxing in the living room, he announced with a big smile, "You will never guess who was in church tonight."

"Tell us," said Connie.

"The sisters, all three of them, Ellen, Emma, and Abby. This is the first time in years that Abby has come to church with them." He looked meaningfully at Sarah. She just grinned from ear to ear.

"Isn't it amazing what a little love and attention can accomplish? Thank You, Jesus. And thank you, Sarah. You have done something very important," her father told her.

Once again, Sarah just smiled. She couldn't be happier. This was her best Christmas gift ever.

Dinner on Christmas Eve had become a tradition. It was always beef stew simmered for hours since early in the day. After dinner, many presents were placed under the Christmas tree in front of the bay window in the living room. The parents had secretly stashed away other presents that would be placed around the tree after the children were all in bed for the night.

In Connecticut, they had a fireplace in their living room. Christmas stockings were always hung from the mantel, waiting to be filled with little surprises. Since there was no fireplace in the parsonage, it was decided to fasten the stockings to the stair railing leading up to the second floor. The stockings fit there perfectly and looked rather nice. It was quite decorative.

After the children were all in bed, and Jack had his usual kiss, hug, and blessing with each one, he and Connie relaxed before placing all the extra gifts and goodies that had to be taken care of. Jack returned to the church around 10 p.m. to help get things ready for the candlelight service.

A candlelight service was not a tradition Jack had practiced before, but he liked the idea. The only problem for him was that he was a more alert worshiper in the morning than he was in the evening. He was generally a morning person. He just had to fight through that mental block and take charge. With the Lord's help, he knew he could do it.

Pastor Jack was encouraged. Once again, the sanctuary was filled with worshipers. Each person received a candle with a wax catcher attached. The format of the service was simple. They followed a traditional order that had been creatively put together by previous pastors.

Beginning in the Old Testament with the prophecy of the Messiah to come and proceeding through biblical passages that unfolded the story of salvation and pointed to the birth of Jesus and then to His second coming, everyone was able to hear a beautiful summary of the good news told in Scripture. Each Bible passage was teamed with a musical number, either a Christmas carol, a hymn, or a special presentation by the choir or a soloist. Pastor Jack added his personal touch to the service with brief comments he would make about the passages before and after reading them to the congregation.

The service concluded with the passing of the light from a large candle on the communion table to the candles of each individual in attendance. This was done while they sang "Silent Night." To make it easier to hold on to a burning candle while singing a hymn, the lyrics of "Silent Night" were printed in the church bulletin. The sanctuary lights were dimmed, and the lighted candles were held high while singing the final verse. After Pastor Jack gave the blessing, he asked everyone to leave quietly and enjoy the celebration of the birth of Jesus.

When he arrived home, everyone was asleep. It would take him a little time to wind down from his busy evening of activities and responsibilities. After a pleasant cup of decaffeinated tea with two chocolate chip cookies he found in the cookie jar, Jack was ready for bed. Tomorrow would be another busy day, especially for Connie.

Chapter 40

MANY NEW BEGINNINGS

It was the beginning of a new year, one that was pregnant with all kinds of possibilities for God to work in the lives of His people. Starting on the first Sunday in January, Pastor Jack began his third four-part sermon series.

The title of his first series in November had been "God Is..." in which he did his best to reveal the nature, character, and ways of God in all His splendor. Embedded in each message was the underlying theme of "God loves you." Pastor Jack had no doubt God told him to include that basic truth as a key part of each message.

During the December Advent season, the second four-part series was titled "You Are...." In this series, Pastor Jack emphasized how people are fearfully and wonderfully made by God and what it means to be a child of God. The wonder of the birth of Jesus, who came to bring the gracious and free gift of salvation, fit in perfectly with the celebration of Christmas.

Once again, in this second series, he emphasized, "God doesn't love you because of who you are or what you've done. He loves you because of who He is." A key verse for this series was 1 John 4:9: "By this the love of God was manifested in us, that God has sent His only begotten Son into the world so that we might live through Him."

The new year was beginning with the third and final four-part series. The theme of this one was "We Are..." and focused on what the church is and what it means to be part of the church.

By this time, worshipers at Grace Church, both members and visitors alike, had been hearing the underlying positive message that God loved them. By January, many of these people had actually begun to believe this truth for the first time. It was finally sinking in.

Pastor Jack began his first message in the new series by defining what the church is. "I am willing to bet that all of you have made the same mistake that I make over and over again. We say we're going to church or 'I'll see you at church' as though the church were only a building or location of some kind. What does the Bible say the church is? The church is not a building. It is the people of God. In a sense, you can't really go to church. If you've asked Jesus to forgive you for your sins and to be the Lord of your life, you're a child of God and a part of the church. We don't go to church. We go to the building where the church is gathering. Look around you and see the church.

"We also need to realize that just because we're in the church building, that does not mean we are automatically part of the body of Christ. Someone wisely said, 'Spending time in a church building does not make you a Christian any more than spending time in a garage makes you a car.'" Gentle explosions of laughter bubbled up around the sanctuary and quietly dissipated.

Pastor Jack continued, "Another wise man said, 'God has no grandchildren.' What did he mean by that? He was trying to say, 'I am not a Christian and a part of the church just because my parents were. I need to become a child of God myself in order to become a part of the church of Jesus Christ.' It's an individual choice, a personal decision that each one of us has to make at some point in our lives.

"For many of you gathered here on this first Sunday of the new year, this may be that day of decision. Do you believe Jesus is who He said He is? Do you believe He did the things the Bible tells us He did? Do you believe He died on the cross and was raised on the third day to pay the debt for your sins?

"If you've been with us more than one Sunday these last two months, you've heard me say every week that God loves you. I only told you that because God made it clear to me that I was responsible for letting you know that truth. And I know that some of you are toying with the idea in your mind that you want to make sure you are a child of God and, therefore, part of the church, but some of you are also thinking that you're not worthy of God's love and acceptance.

"Well, you are absolutely right. You're not worthy of God's love. None of us is worthy of God's love. Let me repeat what I said in my sermon the Sunday before Christmas. God doesn't love you because of who you are or what you have or have not done. He loves you because of who He is. I usually say God loves me in spite of what I've done.

"Let me wrap up this message by telling you a story. But first, I want to tell you about a miraculous coincidence that shows us how God works. Just before I began this message, we all sang the beautiful hymn 'Amazing Grace.' Sally didn't know I was going to tell you the story of John Newton as part of my message today when she chose that hymn. But we both pray every week about our part in the service. Sally picks the music. I decide what to preach. And here we both ended up at the same place. That is evidence of God moving in our midst. He is good.

"I want to introduce you to John Newton, the man who wrote 'Amazing Grace.' He was from England. He made his living as the captain of a ship deeply involved in transporting people from Africa to be sold as slaves. Apparently, God was chasing after him for a very long time before he finally gave up.

"Captain Newton couldn't take the spiritual and mental pressure anymore. Finally, he confessed to God the terrible life he was living and asked for God's forgiveness. And then he surrendered his life to God. His experience is the root of the words he wrote in this hymn. 'Amazing grace! How sweet the sound that saved a wretch like me! I once was lost, but now am found; was blind, but now I see.' That was John Newton's own life story. He finally realized the wretch that he was and accepted the fact that God loved him anyway.

"Are you worthy of God's love? No. Does He love you anyway? Yes. So, I want to pray with you right now. I'm not going to ask you to raise your hand or stand up or come forward. That's just not my style. But if you are ready to say, 'I've made that choice. I want this new year to mark the beginning of my new life as a Christian,' I want you to tell me today or later, if you're making that decision today, that you're praying with me right now. By the way, some of you are saying, 'I think I already made that commitment, but I'm not sure.' Then let's make sure today. Let's pray.

"Our loving heavenly Father, I come before You seeking Your grace and forgiveness and acceptance. I believe Jesus is Your Son and that He died so I might be forgiven for my sins. I want to be a part of Your family. Accept me as Your child. Assure me of Your gift of salvation and the certain hope of eternal life with You in Your heavenly realm. I pray in Jesus' name. Amen.

"Before we sing our closing hymn, I want to make this announcement. Three weeks from tomorrow, on Monday evening at 7 p.m., I'll be starting a new Bible study group. We will go through the letter of James verse by verse. If you're interested, come ready to learn. Don't worry if you think you don't know enough about the Bible to attend. I'll be doing most of the talking.

"This study will tie in with the next series of sermons I'll be preaching starting in February, also based on the letter of James. It's a great study, especially for people who have just committed their lives to the Lord. It's very practical and answers the question, 'How do I live now that I've given my life to Jesus?'"

Turning to his right, Pastor Jack said, "Sally and Anita, is it possible that we could change our closing hymn and sing 'Amazing Grace' one more time?" Immediately Anita began playing the introductory notes of that wonderful hymn.

Following the hymn and before sharing the benediction, Pastor Jack reminded any who had made a personal commitment to Jesus to let him know today or sometime this week. They would talk about how to grow as a disciple of Jesus.

Pastor Jack and Connie stood at the church door together, as was their usual practice, to shake hands with worshipers as they left the sanctuary. A half dozen or so indicated they had made a new commitment to the Lord and would be attending the new Bible study. A few said they thought they had made a commitment in the past but wanted to make sure of it today.

Connie noticed a young lady waiting at a distance for everyone else to leave. She was about five-foot-five and probably in her early twenties. It looked like her shoulder-length dark red hair was in need of unsnarling and washing. She wore no makeup, and her drab, pale green figured dress was rather wrinkled. Her winter coat didn't appear warm enough for the day's temperature. She seemed so forlorn, yet she had a definite grin on her face that made her eyes light up just a bit. They were almost green in color.

The young lady finally made her way across to Pastor Jack and Connie and introduced herself. "Hi, my name is Laurinda, Laurinda Francis. Yeah, I know; I'm one of those people with two first names."

"It's good to have you here," Connie began, feeling a kind of affinity with Laurinda Francis.

"I just wanted to tell you I'm convinced God led me here to your service today," explained Laurinda. "I felt God was telling me to come here to find out about Jesus. I've been homeless for a few months now, and I'm trying to find my way back. And Pastor, I think your message was the first step for me to do just that. I'm happy to say I prayed that closing prayer with you, and although I have a smile on my face right now, I can assure you I did not have one at the beginning of the service."

"Well, Laurinda, we're really happy about your new beginning. Welcome to the family of God," assured Pastor Jack. "We certainly want to know you better, and if there's any way we can help you with your situation right now, we'd be more than happy to try."

Connie reached out a hand to Laurinda and, with a warm smile, said, "I'm going to guess you don't have any plans for lunch. Am I right?"

"Right," nodded Laurinda shyly.

Then with one eye on her husband for his approval and getting a nod, Connie said, "Why don't you join our family for lunch? That way, we can get to know you better and we'll see where things go from there."

"Oh, I don't want to impose," responded Laurinda.

"No imposition," added Pastor Jack. "It's good for God's family to break bread together."

"Just follow me," Connie assured her. "We just live next door. But prepare yourself to deal with five noisy children when you come through our door. I promise you; it won't be quiet."

Chapter 41

About Laurinda

It was time to do something to help Laurinda with her living situation. As Jack and Connie walked with her through Jack's study and into the living room, all they could hear was squealing from the three girls as Paul chased them around the living room, trying to tag one of them. Johnny was just lounging on one of the stuffed chairs laughing hysterically.

"Whoa, whoa, whoa, what's going on here?" Jack's voice boomed into the fracas. "What is going on?"

Johnny, allowing a few words to sneak out between gales of laughter, said, "I think we're learning how fast Paul is and if the girls are faster."

"Yeah," agreed the girls.

"Well, you may not have noticed it in the midst of your experiment, but we have a guest for lunch. Her name is Laurinda Francis, and I would appreciate it if you wouldn't scare her away."

"Why don't you guys go down to the family room while Daddy, Laurinda, and I get lunch ready?" their mother suggested. "When things are ready, we'll call you."

While the children disappeared, Connie invited Laurinda to join her in the kitchen to help get lunch ready. "I hope you like ham and split pea soup, Laurinda. I made it with some of the leftover ham we had from Christmas dinner. We can also put out the makings for sandwiches and let each one make their own."

"That sounds good to me. I haven't had a home-cooked anything for a long time."

"While my husband is in the study unwinding from this morning's activities, why don't you tell me about yourself?"

"I actually come from a fairly well-to-do family, growing up on the mainline near Philadelphia. I was never very popular in high school, but by the time I was a senior, I had started going to parties a lot. I did a lot of drinking. I often came home drunk. I was somehow protected from taking drugs or smoking. Maybe that was God. I don't know. Somehow those things really disgusted me. But the booze was another thing.

"My parents warned me, but I didn't listen. At the end of my senior year in high school, they finally said they'd had enough of my attitude. They said I was an embarrassment to them and that if I didn't want to change and follow their rules, I should just leave. So, I got out. Looking back on it now, almost four years later, I know I was really dumb, but I wasn't thinking very clearly at the time. I was being stubborn. I guess I got that from my dad."

"Where did you go? Where did you live?" wondered Connie.

"I started hanging out with some of my friends, especially some of the older kids I used to party with. That worked for a while, but they were pushing the idea of getting me to try drugs. That really scared me, so I took off on my own. When I was telling my story one night at a bar, two girls there said they were looking for someone to share the cost of their apartment. If I got a job and helped with the rent, they said I could stay with them. So, I started slinging burgers at McDonald's and was able to move in with them for quite a while."

"How long did that last?" asked Connie while heating up the ham and split pea soup in a pot on the stove.

"I continued to work at McDonald's for a long time until one of my customers wanted to know if I wanted a better job. She said she needed a live-in companion who would keep the house clean and help prepare meals and so on. I would have room and board and money to spend. I was happy to try something new. So, I quit the burger business and moved in with this lady. She was really nice. Actually, she was an artist, and as far as I could tell, a really good one."

"So, you were happy there," commented Connie.

"I was for a while."

"What went wrong?"

"After a few months, she said I could make even more money if I would pose for her as a model. I was flattered in the beginning. But when she asked me to pose in the nude, I figured this was going in a direction I didn't like at all. I liked the money, but I didn't like it that much. I thought if I agreed to pose like that, the next step might be one I did not want to consider."

"What did you do?"

"I left. That evening while she was sleeping, I packed up my things and left."

"Where did you go? Where did you live?"

"I had made enough money over time to be able to afford a little used Honda Civic. And that became my home for the next few weeks. Then, Sunday morning, I was driving down Church Street when I came to Grace Church. First of all, I liked the name of the church. I was convinced God was telling me, 'Go into this church. Someone will tell you about Jesus.' So, I did."

"All I can say is 'Wow.' That sure sounds like the God I know," commented Connie.

"I don't think anyone could have kept me from entering Grace Church at that moment. And sure enough, your husband told me about Jesus. It was wonderful. It was like a hole in my heart was immediately filled, and I felt good about myself for the first time in years."

"I'm so happy for you, Laurinda. Look, let's get Jack and the kids in here for lunch. Afterward, we can talk some more about your future."

"Sounds good to me."

While they all sat around the dining room table, enjoying the delicious homemade soup and sandwiches, Laurinda was thinking, *I haven't felt like I was part of a family like this for years. This is good. It's like these people accept me as one of their own. God is so good.*

After lunch and after dishes and food items were all put away, Jack suggested the children head to the family room again. He wanted to talk to Laurinda some more. But before doing so, he asked Connie if they could have a brief chat in his study.

"I've been doing some thinking and praying about Laurinda, and one thought keeps recurring in my mind. Connie, what do you think about asking Nancy Williams, our Sunday school superintendent, to take Laurinda in for a while? It's an idea that I just can't seem to let go of."

"I would agree that Nancy has a lot of love to share," Connie responded. "She's been banging around that big old house for two years now since her husband died. I think she might be ready for a new adventure."

"And who better to disciple Laurinda than Nancy? I think she would be perfect for this."

"I think you're right, Jack. It sounds like God. Why don't you call her and see if she agrees? I'll spend a little more time with our guest."

When Jack came out of the study, he had a big smile on his face. "Laurinda, I have an idea for you to consider. One of our members, who is in her sixties, has been living alone for two years now since her husband died. When she heard we had a new friend who could use a place to stay, she quickly agreed. If you're interested, she would love to have you stay with her. You would be good for each other. She has a nice guest room and would also like to help you grow as a new Christian. What do you think? Are you interested? She lives just a few blocks from here."

"Whoa, this is moving pretty fast. Let me think about it for a few minutes."

"Sure, go ahead. Take your time. Keep in mind, if it doesn't work out for you, you don't have to stay with her. But we think you'll really like her."

After some serious thinking, Laurinda looked up again and said, "Okay, I think I'd like to give it a try. What do I have to do?"

Connie said, "I'll take you there. Just follow me in your car."

When they arrived, Nancy welcomed Laurinda with a warm smile and open arms. Connie stayed long enough to be sure Laurinda was feeling comfortable. "If you have any questions for me, Nancy has our number. Feel free to call me any time. And Nancy, you might want to make a trip to the Rummage Sale room at church to fill out Laurinda's wardrobe."

"What a great idea," she said. "We can do that tomorrow. Oh, this is going to be fun. I'm so glad you're here, Laurinda. This old house has been empty for too long. Now tell me. Are you interested in a cup of tea or coffee? How about some homemade cookies?"

As Connie quietly made her exit, she was thinking, *God, You are so good. You had this all worked out, didn't You? Thank You so much.*

Season V

Spring

Chapter 42

SEASONAL CHANGES

Seasons in southeast Pennsylvania seem to change more than four times a year. The transition from winter to spring is a classic example. There is often a great deal of snow in February and March, but maybe not. One never knows.

Once temperatures begin to rise, hinting at the arrival of spring, a few days of warmer weather might be interrupted by cold or even freezing temperatures. Blooms would start to burst forth on flowering trees, only to be shocked by freezing temperatures or even snow just a few days later. Then when everyone is convinced that spring has officially arrived, here comes a blast of hot air in the upper eighties for a day or two before sliding back into proper spring weather.

A contributing factor in the Weaverton area was its location just east of the Appalachian Mountains. Whatever weather was occurring west of that range might never make it into their valley. Sometimes it seemed like a weather system would sneak south past the Appalachians to the Mason-Dixon line and then shock Weaverton with a snowy impact or sweltering heat moving up from the southwest.

The seasons were obviously changing if one could only figure out which season it really was. Just because the calendar said it was spring often meant nothing at all. But it certainly made life interesting.

By the start of spring, Pastor Jack was already well into his series of sermons based on the letter of James. He was coordinating those messages with the new Monday evening Bible study.

The plan was simple. He would preach on a passage from James' epistle on Sunday morning. The next evening from 7 to 8 p.m., he would lead a study of that same passage and the surrounding paragraphs. This way, the Bible study participants would already have some basic information before going into their study time.

The Monday night study was open to anyone who wanted to attend and learn more about the Bible. It was particularly important for those who had made a recent commitment of their lives to the Lord and became part of the family of God. Jack knew that many pastors and church leaders would recommend that "baby" Christians begin their new life by reading the Gospel of John. He disagreed with that.

Jack didn't think new Christians wanted to study theology and the life of Jesus. Uppermost in their minds, in his opinion, were the basic questions: What do I do now? How am I supposed to live now that I'm a Christian? Even though the great Protestant Reformer Martin Luther had called this letter of James an "epistle of straw," Jack believed it was one of the most practical books in the Bible for living a new life as a child of God.

The Bible study room was set up with three rectangular tables in a horseshoe configuration, with chairs already placed only along the outside edges. At the open end of the horseshoe, Pastor Jack had a small adjustable music stand to hold his Bible and his teaching notes. There was a padded stool for him to sit on in front of the class, with a whiteboard placed right behind the stool. Jack liked to use the whiteboard to jot down important points and illustrations that might help explain what he was teaching.

Signs were placed at strategic points in the building to direct participants to the downstairs meeting room. Jack had initially been hoping for maybe a dozen people to dwindle into the first night's study, but twenty-one students had crowded into that first meeting room. Pastor Jack laughed and told them, "I think we'll have to choose a larger room next week." Everyone agreed, but they were willing to crowd in together for that first evening. It made them all feel like they were a part of something important. By now, weeks later, even more eager learners were gathering around a larger horseshoe of tables that had been moved into the Fellowship Hall.

After opening in prayer each week, Pastor Jack explained in simple terms and conversational English his understanding of James' letter. He had initially told the class that scholars believe this letter was written shortly after

Jesus' death and resurrection by His own younger brother to churches that were increasingly scattered abroad during the first century. Now Jack was expounding on each verse in turn as he moved through the five chapters of this book.

Pastor Jack encouraged people to ask questions or make comments. During the first few sessions, nobody did that, but they all seemed very much interested in what their pastor told them. Some even took notes. Gradually, after more than a month, a few questions began to pop up.

Starting and ending promptly was very important to Jack, so he always concluded his teaching precisely at 8 p.m. He figured if attendees were sure when the session would end, they could schedule other activities afterward with confidence they could keep any such appointments. But he also invited those with personal questions to come and chat with him afterward. A handful of people had started to do just that.

One of these was a man with a most pleasant smile on his face. Jack estimated he was in his later sixties. He was short, only about five-foot-one, and balding with a halo of gray hair, sort of like a sixteenth-century monk. Fat cheeks and twinkling eyes caused Jack to think about one of those little statues you see on lawns here and there, a kind of green gnome, except he wasn't green. He had a very warm voice, a wonderful New England accent, and a love for chatting.

"I've been in the area only a few weeks now," he said, "and I've been looking for a good church where the pastor preaches the Word of God. You do that. And you do it well."

"Thank you."

"I wanted to check out this Bible study as well to see how you handle yourself. I'm impressed. You have a gift. You make the Bible come alive. You make it understandable, and I appreciate that. If you don't mind, I'll be back again next Sunday for worship and Monday for Bible study."

"We would love to have you join us. What's your name?"

"Oh, my goodness, I guess I forgot to tell you. It's Scott. Scott Langhorne.

And I'm really happy I found this church. I've been sampling lots of churches these last few weeks, and I think God has finally brought me home. Thank you, Pastor Jack. I'll see you next week."

"Well, thank you, Scott. I look forward to seeing you again. God bless you."

Jack closed things up after everyone left and headed home with a smile still on his face and a prayer on his lips. "Thank You, Lord, for a great study session. I wasn't just pleased with the numbers but with the attitude of the people. There was a positive atmosphere and an openness to learn more from the Bible. Thank You."

When Jack arrived home, just a short walk to the side door of the parsonage, things were surprisingly quiet. Everyone was in the family room enjoying a *VeggieTales* CD on the television. Monday night was a free night in the Whyte house with nothing specifically scheduled. That's why Jack felt free to schedule his Bible study for Monday evenings.

Now Tuesday night was another matter altogether. He would never schedule a church meeting on Tuesdays. It was sacred territory for the family. Tuesday night was family game night with popcorn and something juicy to drink. The family loved the fun of games like Farkle or Yahtzee or The Game of Life with its noisy little spinner. On a crazy night, they would play Twister and end up tangled on the floor in fits of laughter. It was fun living in the Whyte house.

As soon as Jack took off his coat and headed into the family room, the quiet atmosphere was interrupted by the jarring sound of Connie's cell phone. She was hesitant to answer it. She just had a bad feeling about it. But answer it she did.

Chapter 43

An Unpleasant Interruption

"Hi, Mom," Connie hesitantly began the telephone conversation. "What's going on?"

"It's your father, Connie. He's in the hospital, but don't worry. He's fine."

"How can he be fine if he's in the hospital?"

"Well, it's a good visit to the hospital. We have answers to those questions that have gone unanswered for many months."

"You're talking about him passing out, aren't you? Like he did last summer at the beach?"

"Yes," replied Marilyn. "You remember, I'm sure, that we were waiting for him to get one of those event monitors."

"The one that he was supposed to carry around with him and place on his chest if he knows he's going to pass out?" asked Connie.

"Yes, exactly. Well, he's been carrying that thing around with him for more than four months, and nothing happened. Well, at least until today. He was home for lunch and felt one of his spells coming on. He told me, and I watched him lay down on the sofa, open his shirt, and place the cell phone-sized monitor on his chest. When he passed out, I made sure the monitor stayed on his chest. A few minutes later, when he came around, he told me he was feeling fine, just a little tired as usual. We had to call the number on the monitor and send in the test result."

"How do you do that?" wondered Connie.

"It's really quite simple. It's a matter of pushing one button."

"Then what happened?"

"In a few minutes, they called us and said we should take him to the hospital for further observation. And that's where we are now."

"How is Daddy feeling now? Is he okay?"

"Oh, yes, he's fine. He had an EKG, and they hooked him up to a temporary pacemaker. He'll get a permanent one tomorrow morning."

"So, it's definitely his heart, then."

"Absolutely. In fact, an unusual thing occurred while we were here. We'd been in his room for about two hours when he felt another spell coming on. That doesn't happen often, but it was great that it happened while he was in the hospital and hooked up to their telemetry. God is so good. They were able to see his heart activity throughout the entire episode. That's when they told us the amazing truth. His heart stops for fifteen seconds at a time before it kicks in again. That's what makes him pass out.

"And by the way," Marilyn continued, "they gave us a printout of his heart rhythm during that last spell. It shows he flatlined for fifteen seconds, and then his heart started again. We'll show it to you when we can get down there again. The reason they put him on a temporary pacemaker right away is that they didn't want to assume that the next time his heart stops, it will start again. Anyway, it's ticking away quite nicely at the moment. Now we're tired but elated at the same time. We finally got the answers we've been seeking for so long."

"But why is this all happening, Mom? And why is it happening now?"

"The doctors don't really know for sure. They think it may just be a congenital thing that didn't manifest itself until now. God apparently gave us three electrical impulses to keep the heart pacing. If the first one fails, a secondary cell will click in. In your father's case, it seems like that doesn't happen until maybe the third backup gets things started again. I'm not sure about all that medically, but that seems to be what's happening."

"I don't know what to say. I'm upset that Daddy's in the hospital, but I'm glad there's finally something they can do for him. Getting a pacemaker, then, will take care of his passing out?"

"Yes, dear, that will keep his heart working through what would have been an episode. The pacemaker he gets will, in the beginning, not actually pace his heart. It will just act as a permanent monitor. Then, whenever the implanted pacemaker senses that his heart is going to stop, and maybe that secondary electric cell won't do the job, the device will kick in and take over until his heart's own built-in pacemaker gets going again. Again, I'm not totally sure about all the science, but that's generally what will happen."

"And he gets this pacemaker tomorrow?"

"Yes. It's smaller than those old cigarette lighters and thinner. It's implanted under some of the chest muscles. He'll be home tomorrow afternoon after a brief session to program the device."

"Does he have to do some kind of physical therapy or anything like that?"

"No, not at all. In fact, the only restrictions are that he can't run and jump around for a couple of weeks. When they implant the pacemaker tomorrow, they'll insert two wires into his heart. The ends of those wires, after a few days, are held in place because the heart tissue grows around them and holds them there. It never ceases to amaze me how God's creation and modern medical science work so well together. The thing is, if Daddy is jumping up and down and jogging during these first few weeks, it will be difficult for that binding in the heart to take place."

"This is all so hard to believe. At least I'm glad he has such a loving nurse to take care of him," said Connie.

Laughing, Marilyn said, "I do my best. But I think he pays more attention to the nurses in the hospital than he does to the one he married. Anyway, we have a follow-up appointment with his new cardiologist in a few weeks just to see how things are progressing and to remove the staples from the surgery. We're very pleased with this new development, Connie. We hope you can relax about it now. Everything's under control."

"Thanks, Mom. We'll keep both of you in our prayers. Please keep us informed."

"We will, honey, we will. Bye now."

After reporting on that conversation to Jack and the children and calming down any fears that were trying to creep in, they had an impromptu family prayer session for both Grandma and Granddad. Soon it was bedtime when Jack had more individual prayers with his children and later with his wife.

Chapter 44

PLANNING FOR SPRING PLANTING

Spring has sprung.

The grass is riz.

I wonder where the flowers is.

Connie had a big smile on her face. She remembered that cute little rhyme about the season change. She planned to answer that question about the flowers and hopefully grow some vegetables as well. She was looking forward to the first appearance of bright red climbing roses on the trellis at the side of the house near the willow tree. She could just imagine cozying up to one of the blossoms and taking in the wonderful aroma. Not all roses smell. But these did.

The big plan was to establish a vegetable garden at the lower end of the backyard close to the pond. The ground leveled off in that location and got a lot of good sun as well. She had mentioned to Lucy Geisinger, now her good friend, that she was hoping to get started soon on a vegetable garden. Lucy offered to contact Kenneth Sloane to see if he could be of any help.

Kenneth, a member of Grace Church, owned and operated a landscaping business. It was Lucy's thought that he might be willing to save Connie a lot of time and effort by using his rototiller to initially break ground for the garden. Sure enough, when contacted, Kenneth was very happy to offer his help. Once again, Connie was so pleased with the friendly nature of the members of their new church. She thanked God one more time for making it all possible for them to be at Grace.

Connie's plan was to make this gardening project not only a family affair but a homeschool project as well. She would work with Suzy and Paul, her youngest two, on a game of identifying the vegetables and the plants they come from. That would include a trip to the Weaverton public library to find some picture books, taking advantage of the library cards each member of the family had recently acquired.

The older children would learn about Gregor Mendel, a ground-breaking biologist from the 1800s, and his amazing discovery of genetics while experimenting with hybrid pea plants. Connie would focus on the specific principles of dominant and recessive genes passed on from parents to children. Johnny and Sarah, the middle-schoolers, would also watch a homeschool video on genetics and write a report on what they learned.

She hoped to take them all on a field trip to the local grocery store to focus on what vegetables and fruits were there and for the older children to learn how to read labels. This would then prompt a later discussion for the middle-schoolers about commerce and economics. The younger ones would be included in discussions about how products are processed and moved by various means of transportation from one country to another and from one state to another. Then they would learn at their various grade levels about how this would affect the price of the produce.

———————•———————

Tuesday was Jack's day off, and the entire family was going to load up the van after breakfast and devotions and head to Home Depot. On this field trip, the goal was to choose starter plants for the garden as well as lettuce and radish seeds. Connie's plan was to start small this year and hopefully expand a little each year.

This first year she hoped to plant tomatoes, peppers, parsley, lettuce, and radishes, all wonderful ingredients for fresh salads. With Kenneth Sloane's help and Jack's digging efforts, she wanted to start an asparagus bed as well. In her reading, she discovered it's a good idea to plant strawberry plants next to the asparagus. They apparently kept bugs and pests off one another.

She would plant a row of asparagus, a row of strawberries, and a walking row and then repeat that pattern one more time. Hopefully, in a year or two, they will have some of these fresh ingredients for their meals.

An excited and chattering Whyte family piled into their van and headed off on the short excursion to Home Depot. With simple instructions for staying together and not wandering off, they left the parked van and entered the huge store. It was almost overwhelming to see all the possibilities for purchase at the garden center.

Fortunately, there were lots of signs and even a few workers to direct the Whyte family through aisle after aisle of green and glorious plants. Johnny was assigned the task of operating the flatbed cart that was big enough to hold the plants, plant food, and potting soil they would be buying.

It became a family decision-making project as they chose which plants to purchase. There were so many to choose from. Little debates arose as to which plant was the nicest of all they had displayed before them.

Finally, they ended up with two beefsteak tomato plants, one plum tomato plant, two green, two red, and two yellow pepper plants, a small flat of strawberry plants, and twelve asparagus roots. They also got seeds for Black Seeded Simpson Lettuce and both red and white radishes. Since childhood, Connie had loved sandwiches made with sliced and salted white radishes and lots of butter.

In the herb department, Connie limited her purchases to parsley as well as apple mint for iced tea. Since the apple mint grew like weeds, two small plants would provide an endless supply for them, but it had to be hemmed in, or it would take over everything.

"Do we have all the gardening tools we need?" wondered Jack.

"No," answered Connie. "First of all, we need to pick up a good shovel so you can dig those deep rows for the asparagus."

"Oh, I'm sorry I asked," joked her husband.

"Yes, dear." Connie made a cute face at him. "And we could use a couple of spades, a three-pronged cultivator, a rake, and a hoe. Oh, and we're going to need a long hose that reaches from the outside faucet at the rear of the parsonage all the way down to the new garden. While we're at it, we should probably get one of those things that let you coil up the hose neatly at the side of the house."

"I saw some tools over at the edge of the garden center," informed Megan, pointing to the right.

"Why don't you ladies stay here with the cart," suggested Connie. "The boys will go with me to pick out the tools we need. I think the three of us can carry them all. Well, maybe Sarah should come with us to help." Off they went, leaving Dad and the other girls behind.

After everything was assembled and they checked out at the register, Jack winced as he saw how much this project cost. Noticing his expression, Connie reminded him how much they would save in food costs later when the harvest came in. "And the tools are a one-time purchase. We'll have them for years to come."

"Yes, I know," he said, "but it still smarts at the moment."

Johnny carefully guided the flatbed cart to the rear of the family van. Everyone helped to load their purchases in the back. Five family members climbed into the van and waited while Johnny and Paul made sure the cart was returned safely to its proper location.

On the way home, Connie explained, "Mr. Sloane will be at our house this afternoon around one o'clock with his rototiller to get the ground ready for our planting project. That's going to be fun to watch. When he's done, we're going to smooth out the ground and prepare the area for the planting. It's going to be a lot of work but a lot of fun as well. If we don't get it all done today, we can finish the project tomorrow."

"How big an area is he going to plow?" asked Jack.

"He said he'd determine that when he sees how many plants we've selected."

"Sounds good to me," replied Jack as he drove the family home.

The Whytes were just finishing lunch when they heard a knock at the backdoor. Looking out the window, they saw Kenneth Sloane waving to them from outside the screened-in porch. They welcomed him in, and Jack introduced the family members to him.

"So, are you all ready for a big project?" he asked them.

"Yeah," was the unanimous response.

"Okay. I already unloaded my rototiller. My understanding is you want to plant your garden toward the lower end of the yard. I think that's a good location. Let's go out there. Tell me what you're going to plant, and we'll decide how big to make this plot."

The family left the house, and like a group of wanderers behind a pied piper, they made their way to the end of the backyard in the wake of Kenneth Sloane.

"We really appreciate this, Mr. Sloane," remarked Pastor Jack on the way.

"Please call me Ken," he responded.

"Okay, Ken. If you don't mind, though, our children will call you Mr. Sloane."

"I understand. That's fine with me. So, tell me what you're going to plant." Connie explained what they had purchased that morning and that they were making it a homeschool project.

Ken surveyed the area and said, "Well, I won't say you have a big project, but it's certainly at least a medium-sized project. My suggestion, just because it takes up so much room during the preparation process, is that you plant the asparagus first. In fact, if you don't mind, since I'm here, I'd like to help you dig those asparagus trenches, Pastor. After that, you can put in your strawberry plants. Then, my suggestion is that you wait until tomorrow to put in the rest of your plants and seeds. Taking care of these first two plantings will take most of the afternoon. Does that make sense?"

"Well, you're the expert," said Pastor Jack. "But, yes, it does make sense to me."

"Yes," agreed Connie, "I can see where we'd be trampling on some of our other plants if we waited to plant the asparagus until later. This is so kind of you, Ken. We really appreciate your help."

"Well, I'm doing something I love to do, so I'm happy to help with your garden. And since you said you've made this a homeschool project, I'd be happy to answer any questions your children might have about plants and God's wonderful way of making things grow."

"I just might take you up on that. Thank you. So, while you're doing your thing, we'll get out of your way. Meanwhile, the children and I will unload the plants and the tools we bought today. We'll put them on the screen porch for now, except for the shovel and rake you'll need, Jack. And Jack, maybe you and Johnny can bring those bags of potting soil and plant food here to the edge of the garden when Ken is finished running his rototiller."

"Sounds like a plan," agreed Jack. Within minutes, the new garden began to take shape.

Chapter 45

CATCHING UP

The children were all in bed. It had been another busy day at home for Connie and at church for Jack. They were relaxing on the sofa in the living room. They rarely utilized this space in the house. Now it was good to just sit and unwind.

They were close enough to hear the children if they were needed for anything, being just at the foot of the stairs. In this relaxed state of mind, with Connie drinking her cup of black decaf coffee and Jack sipping his Irish breakfast tea and munching on some chewy, fresh-baked cookies, they were sharing the events of the day and their recent blessings from the Lord.

"How has the Monday evening Bible study been going?" Connie asked.

"As far as numbers go, we now hover around thirty people each week. Laurinda is there every time. And did you know Ron Young has also been attending regularly?"

"No, I didn't. But that's good to know. If anyone should be learning more about the Bible, it would be the president of the church council."

"There's something else you don't know about Ron."

"What's that?"

"The reason he's attending Monday evenings is that he's a part of that group in January that committed their lives to the Lord for the first time. I challenged them to come to Bible study and learn how to grow as new Christians, and Ron accepted the challenge."

"Wow. Who would have thought that the president of a church council had never committed his life to the Lord?"

"Oh, I'm sure that's the case in a lot of churches."

"You're probably right."

"By the way, have you met Scott Langhorne?" Jack asked. "He's new in the area and has been a regular at Bible study. I like him a lot."

"I don't think I've met him yet. What does he look like?"

"Well...I've never said this out loud before. He's only about five-foot-one with a balding head, and he reminds me of one of those yard gnomes. Please don't tell anyone I said that," laughed Jack.

"Oh, yes. I know who you're talking about. I've seen him on Sunday mornings. A very pleasant man, isn't he?"

"Absolutely. And one of the more interesting developments with Scott is that he's become friends with Patty Clemmons. They sit next to each other at every Bible study and are always chatting."

"Patty Clemmons? Isn't she almost six feet tall?" smiled Connie, imagining the two of them standing side-by-side.

"Well, she's not quite as tall as me, so I would guess about five-foot-ten. They make a very unusual couple."

"Do you see a relationship in their future?"

"I wouldn't doubt it. They're both eligible. She's a widow, and his wife died more than ten years ago. They seem to have a lot in common. And they both love the Lord."

"Wow, a Bible study romance. What more could you want?" joked Connie.

Jack just laughed. Then he said, "I met someone else you don't know."

"That's not hard to imagine," said Connie, "unless they walk through this house."

"I finally met our other neighbor across the street, Emory Townson. He and his wife, Gladys, live in that big, beautiful stone house. It sets back on the rise above the meadow and is surrounded by some beautiful pine trees. You might remember he's CEO of Philly Cheese Soft Pretzels."

"Those pretzels are sooooo good. I love them with that mustard dip they have. Where did you manage to meet him?"

"I met Em. That's what he told me to call him...."

"Oh my," interrupted Connie with wide eyes.

"Well, it is," laughed Jack.

"Did you tell him to call you the most holy Reverend John Whyte?" suggested Connie in between fits of laughter.

"As I was saying," Jack spoke slowly, trying to continue with a grin on his face, "I met Em at the soda fountain at Long's Pharmacy. I had stopped in for my usual cup of tea and a piece of shoofly pie, and he came in to pick up a prescription. He was waiting for it to be ready and having a cup of coffee at the counter. I just introduced myself and mentioned that we were neighbors and things just opened up from there. I like him."

"You like everyone, Jack."

"That's not completely true, but I did find him to be a really friendly person."

"I assume you invited him to church."

"Of course, but they already attend the Lutheran church in town. He said they might stop by one Sunday or so just to be neighborly. He also mentioned that they have a shallow pond near their house that often freezes enough in the winter to allow for safe ice skating.

"They even installed permanent lighting around the pond so they can have evening ice skating parties with a campfire and all the trappings. He invites his church youth group to take advantage of their set-up each year and suggested we might want to put ice skating on their pond on our youth calendar for next winter."

"What a great idea. That's one thing I missed this past winter that we often enjoyed in Connecticut. I'm sure our youth director would like to follow up on that. That reminds me, I thought Melissa was going to invite you to lead singing sometime at a youth meeting with your guitar. Did she decide against that?"

"Actually, we talked this past week at the staff meeting precisely about that. I'm going to lead worship at the youth meeting next week."

"That's good. The teens in Connecticut always liked when you did that."

"Speaking of music, there's a new development in our music ministry that I think you'll be interested in."

"Please, tell me more."

"We had a really good staff meeting this week. Well, they're always good. I really like working with these people, Connie."

"You've got a great team, Jack."

"I do. I really do. Thank You, Lord. Anyway, when Sally gave her report on happenings in the music ministry, she told me about something special she has in mind."

"And that is?" prompted Connie.

"Can you believe she wants to do an Easter cantata this year?"

"That sounds like a great idea, Jack, but what made her think of that?"

"Apparently, she's been wanting to do a cantata for a long time. In fact, it's one of the reasons she's been growing and training the choir over the past few years. Sally now believes she's come to the point where she has the right people and the right number of people. It seems like the real turning point for her was the success of the Christmas play we did. She was encouraged by the response of the church members and the support of the community. Laurinda has also turned out to be a fantastic soprano solo voice. By the way, Laurinda now has a job at the grocery store, and she's doing really well."

"That's so great. Has Sally talked to the choir members about the cantata idea yet?"

"Yes, and they had the same thoughts Sally had. Doing that Christmas play has shown them our little congregation can do quality productions to be proud of. When she asked for my blessing on the project, I gave her the go-ahead to make it happen."

"When do you think you'll present this cantata? Have you decided on that?"

"Sure. We figured that Thursday, Friday, and Sunday of Holy Week are already tied up with other activities for most churches at Easter. If we want community people to come and see our production, we'll have to avoid those days. But we're going to be positive and schedule two performances on Wednesday night and Saturday afternoon of Holy Week."

"You *are* thinking big, aren't you?"

"Absolutely. Sally and I think that, with the right advertisements over the next few weeks, we can fill the sanctuary twice. At least, we hope we can. With the right preparation, the support of the congregation, and the blessing of the Lord, this is going to happen. Sally and Anita have been looking for just the right music for this first production, and they've decided on a cantata called "No Greater Love" by John W. Peterson. I've listened to the CD. It's beautiful music and very inspirational. I think it will be a highlight of our Easter celebration. What do you think?"

"I think it sounds wonderful. I can't wait to see it all fall into place."

At that point, Jack smiled contentedly and finished his last cookie. They put their cups and saucers in the dishwasher and quietly headed to bed with smiles on their faces and musical images in their heads.

Chapter 46

PAUL GETS A RASH

The backyard garden was growing very nicely. The children had decided that Johnny and Paul should take on the responsibility of watering the garden because of running the hose all the way from the house to the lower end of the yard and rolling it back up again on the hose storage unit at the side of the house. This required some muscle.

The boys were happy to take on this responsibility two or three times a week, depending on how often God watered the garden for them with the spring rains. There was almost a celebration among the children when Paul reported the first sighting of rows of green sprouts where they had planted lettuce and radish seeds. Squealing sisters joined the boys as they inspected these first sightings.

Ken Sloane, who had helped them get the garden started with rototilling and planting the asparagus, stopped by occasionally to see how their garden was growing. At one point, he reminded Connie of the need to support the tomatoes by using carefully placed tomato cages around each plant. He also stopped by one morning when Johnny and Paul were watering the garden. He showed them how to make sure they watered around the base of the pepper and tomato plants more than just showering them with a power spray.

The boys thought it was more fun to shoot water from the pistol grip hose over the entire garden, but now they understood that might cause some of the plants to become diseased. Mr. Sloane also very generously offered to help them add mulch to the garden to keep the weeds down and help retain water in the soil.

It was only a few weeks before tiny peppers and tomatoes began to appear on the plants. This caused another rush of excitement among the children, not to mention their parents. Paul took on the role of tour guide to pull aside parts of the plants to show the rest of the family where the tiny tomatoes and peppers had appeared. He noticed that his hands and forearms itched a bit afterward but thought nothing more about it. Connie made sure he washed his hands when they all returned to the house to finish their school day.

That evening, Paul found himself scratching his itching arms and hands. It was not long before Connie noticed a rash developing in those itching areas and even on his cheeks. He must have casually touched his face sometime before washing his hands. Everything seemed to point to a reaction to something in the garden, most likely the tomato plants. After a few hours, the developing pink rash became very noticeable, and they decided to call the doctor.

They had already developed a relationship with Dr. Steve Blanchard, who had opened a practice in downtown Weaverton eight years ago, was well-respected by the community, and came highly recommended. Connie called the doctor's office the next morning. The receptionist said Dr. Blanchard would be able to see Paul that afternoon. Jack arranged to be at home with the other children while Connie took Paul for his appointment. It was Jack's scheduled day to supervise science, so everything worked out well.

By the time they got to Dr. Blanchard's office, the rash was even worse. And the itching was, in the words of young Paul, "driving me crazy!" Dr. Blanchard was great with Paul, and they all agreed that what they were dealing with was caused by an allergic reaction to the tomato plants. He assured them it was a common malady and could be dealt with quite easily and effectively.

He prescribed an antihistamine to deal with the boy's reaction to the allergen and a 2.5 percent hydrocortisone cream to apply directly to the rash and cut down on the itching. He cautioned them that it would be a number of days of discomfort before the rash and the itching went away, but it would, indeed, be gone even though Paul might doubt it from time to time. He also told Paul to avoid touching the area around his eyes and to avoid touching tomato plants in the future.

When they returned to the front office, the receptionist informed Connie that she had called in the prescriptions to Long's Pharmacy, and they would probably be ready in about an hour. Since the office already had their insurance information, Connie and Paul headed home. She would ask Jack to pick up the prescriptions. This would give him an excuse to visit his friends at the soda fountain in the rear of the store.

"Well, Paul," said Connie, "it looks like your days as a tomato gardener are coming to an end."

"Can I at least do the watering? Johnny and I have fun doing that."

"I suppose so, as long as you don't come in contact with any tomato plants."

"No problem."

"But let's hold off on even the watering until we get this rash under control. I don't want you doing anything to irritate it. Okay?"

"Okay. I can't wait to get rid of this."

When they got back to the parsonage, everyone was on alert as they heard the garage door open and then close. They all wanted to know what the doctor said. Paul gave a full report and notified Johnny he would be watering the garden by himself for the next week or so.

"No problem," said Johnny. "I can handle it." Sarah kindly offered to help as well.

"What's the treatment going to be?" asked Jack.

"He has to take an antihistamine pill and also put lotion on the rash itself to reduce itching," answered Connie. "If you could go to Long's to get those prescriptions, that would be great."

"Sure. I'll go right away. Meanwhile, Johnny, Sarah, and Megan, you can follow up on that video we watched by completing the assignment in your workbooks. While they're doing that, Paul can take his mind off his itching by watching that same video. And Connie, if you will, maybe you could have Suzy work on an art project as a follow-up to the video."

"Sounds like a plan. We'll all be finished, I'm sure, by the time you get back from Long's. The sooner we start the treatment, the sooner Paul will feel better."

"I'm on my way," said Jack as he headed down the steps to the garage.

———————•———————

Jack came in the backdoor of the pharmacy and saw two people waiting in line to pick up prescriptions at the pharmacy counter. As he passed the soda fountain, he told Millie behind the counter that he would be back for some tea in just a minute. When it was his turn to ask for his two prescriptions, the clerk welcomed him. "It's good to see you, Pastor. I saw we had two orders for a Paul Whyte. I assumed that was one of your children."

"Yes, my seven-year-old, well, almost eight now. He got a rash from working in the garden. Lots of itching."

"Well, your order will be ready in ten or fifteen minutes. We'll let you know. Having some tea in the meantime?"

"Absolutely! Millie's already working on it."

Millie had his tea ready for him when he sat down on the cushioned bar stool. "So, how are things going at your church, Pastor?" she asked.

"Rather well, it seems. We're busy. By the way, here's something you might be interested in. We're presenting an Easter musical program called 'No Greater Love.' We're doing it twice in hopes that people from the community will come as well as our members."

"When's it going to be?"

"The first performance will be Wednesday evening of Holy Week at 7 p.m. We'll do it again on Saturday afternoon, the day before Easter, at 4 p.m. The music is beautiful. We've never done anything like this before, and we're hoping to get a good turnout."

"Well, I must say, I truly enjoyed that Christmas program you put on with that delightful play about decorating the family Christmas tree."

"Glad you liked it, Millie."

"You wrote that, didn't you?"

"Yes, and the actors and singers did a great job with it."

"Well, if this one is as good as that, I'm sure you'll have a lot of people come to see it."

"I'm pretty sure it will be just as good, if not better. Anyway, spread the word. When we get the publicity material, I'll see that the store gets one or two posters."

"Bring a few extra," she suggested. "I can put one up at our church and maybe some other places as well."

Just then, the call came from the pharmacy. "Pastor, your prescriptions are ready."

"Thanks for the tea, Millie. I've got to be going."

Jack picked up his prescriptions, thanked the workers for their efficiency, went out the backdoor to the parking lot, and headed home. He wanted to get these medications to Paul as soon as possible.

The children were all finished with their schoolwork by the time he returned. Paul was trying not to scratch his rash. Connie had found on the internet that putting warm compresses on a rash can sometimes help. She was doing just that in the kitchen when Jack came up the stairs from the garage. Immediately, Connie got a glass of water and gave Paul his first antihistamine for children.

"Do you want to put this cream on yourself, or do you want me to do it?" she asked her son.

"You do it, please."

When she finished the application, Paul said, "It still itches."

"I'm sure it does," his mother said. "It doesn't take effect immediately, but pretty soon, you should feel the difference." And he did. But he was very sad that his gardening was severely restricted for the rest of the season. He really enjoyed it.

Chapter 47

EASTER APPROACHES

The greeting was as loud and boisterous as usual, sort of like Norm being welcomed into Cheers on that old TV show. "Come on in, Reverend. Grab a seat with the rest of the crackpots over here," called Frank from behind the counter. As Jack approached the second U-shaped counter in Frank's Place, all the men welcomed him in various ways, everyone calling him Reverend, just like Frank did.

"Why do you guys always call me Reverend?" Jack asked.

"'Cause that's who you are," laughed Frank. "It says so in your church bulletin. I was there one Sunday, if you remember, and there it was in plain print, 'Rev. John P. Whyte.' So, you're a reverend. We call doctors 'Doctor' and reverends 'Reverend.' You got any other questions?" The other guys laughed with Frank.

Realizing any further conversation on that subject would be a waste of time, Pastor Jack, laughing with them, said, "Yeah, one more question. What's the special for the day?"

"A club sandwich on toast, your choice of bread, and a tossed salad with your choice of dressing," informed Frank.

Deciding to do a little ribbing of his own, Jack asked, "So what makes the special so special, Frank?"

"It's special 'cause I made it, that's what. Now, you gonna eat lunch or just ask more questions?"

"I think I'll have the special on white toast," ordered Jack.

"Good, now we're getting somewhere."

All the still chuckling "crackpots" broke into applause, two of them patting Pastor Jack on his back as he sat down.

As Frank began preparing the club sandwich, over his shoulder, he asked, "So how are things going down there at Grace Church, Reverend? You doin' any good?"

"I think so."

"You got lots of things planned for Easter?"

"Yes, we're presenting our first Easter cantata. We're doing it twice, hoping that lots of people from the community might come and enjoy a night or an afternoon of music at Grace."

"You got special seating for crackpots?" asked Frank.

"All our seats are special, Frank. I hope you all come. It'll be the Wednesday and Saturday before Easter." Then turning to the patrons at the other counter, Pastor Jack said, "You're all welcome too. We'd love to see you at one of the performances."

Placing his sandwich on the counter, Frank asked, "What kind of dressing do you want for your salad?"

"Ranch," answered Jack.

"You gonna put up any posters to advertise this musical thing?" asked Frank while placing a salad and a container of ranch dressing on the counter.

"Sure am. I have some in the car."

"Well, bring a handful in here," said Frank. "We'll all take a couple and put them up here and there."

"Thanks," said Pastor Jack. "I'd really appreciate that. Now let's see how special this sandwich really is."

Frank said, "I know you're gonna love it." And he was right.

The rehearsals for the cantata were moving along well. Sally and Anita worked so well together. A few of the harmonies and some of the syncopations were a little tricky at parts but committed effort over and over again produced the results they wanted.

310

One of the surprises that added to the excitement of the cantata came from an unusual source. An older member of the church, Martha Ritter, approached Pastor Jack with a special suggestion.

"My Henry," she said, referring to her deceased husband, "left me a nice inheritance, and I would like to use some of it to bless people. I was thinking, would you be interested in having the ladies in the choir wear special, sparkly tops for the cantata? I've checked it out on the computer, and there are some really nice selections to choose from. I've been thinking that every lady has a black skirt. All they would need is one of those beautiful tops to add a special sense of celebration to the cantata. And I want to use some of the inheritance my Henry left me to pay for this."

Pastor Jack was a bit surprised at this offer but not at a loss for words. "That's very generous of you, Martha. Thank you. I want to talk to Sally and Anita about it, but if they agree, I'm sure we'll take you up on your offer."

"That's wonderful," replied Martha. "But I'm not quite finished. I would like to pay for the rental of tuxedos for the men in the choir too. It would add so much to the performance to see each man in a tuxedo. My Henry always looked so handsome in a tuxedo."

"That sounds amazing, Martha, and very generous. I'll run it by Sally and Anita. If they give the go-ahead, we'll gladly accept your offer."

To no one's surprise, when Sally and Anita heard about Martha's generous offer, they were ecstatic. When this plan was presented to the choir members, they were stunned but happily so. Up to this point, they were just going to wear black slacks or skirts and white shirts or blouses. This changed everything. It looked like the Easter cantata would be a treat for the eyes as well as the ears.

Palm Sunday, one week before Easter, the children of the church walked down the aisle waving palm branches at the beginning of the service. They led the way for the arrival of the choir, singing "Hosanna, Loud Hosanna" along with the congregation. This alone lifted everyone's spirits and prepared them to worship God. As usual, ever since Christmas, Abby Schultz was sitting in the congregation with her sisters.

At the end of the service, Pastor Jack reminded everyone to continue publicizing the cantata coming up in just three days. "Come on Wednesday night or Saturday afternoon," he told them once more, "and be sure to bring a few friends and neighbors. I've heard the rehearsals, and you are really going to be blessed. The music is inspirational. And there will be some surprises as well."

To say the cantata was a huge success would not be an exaggeration. When the choir entered the sanctuary to take their place up front, an audible gasp rippled throughout the congregation as they saw for the first time how elegantly the choir members were attired. Then with the first strains of the vocals, accompanied by Anita, who brought such amazing sounds out of the synthesizer, one could almost say the audience was mesmerized.

It was good they had scheduled two performances. Otherwise, there would not have been enough room for everyone who wanted to enjoy the inspirational music. With such encouragement for the very gifted people of Grace Church, Pastor Jack could see God chipping away at the corporate inferiority complex he had noticed upon his arrival as their new pastor.

Pastor Jack dismissed the congregation with his usual Aaronic blessing, loosely taken from Numbers 6:24–26,

> *The Lord bless you and keep you. The Lord make His face to*
> *shine upon you and be gracious unto you. The Lord lift the*
> *light of His countenance upon you and give you His peace, this*
> *day and forevermore. Amen.*

Pastor Jack meant that blessing with all his heart. He had come to really love these people in such a short time. He was convinced these were more than just words from the Bible. When he voiced these beautiful words, he was sure that God was releasing an actual blessing into the lives of each person who was open to receiving it.

Chapter 48

REMEMBRANCES AND POSSIBILITIES

It was one of those rainy, dreary "I don't feel like doing anything" days. The Whytes had enjoyed a tasty breakfast of blueberry pancakes with melted butter and maple syrup, crispy bacon from a local butcher, and fresh-squeezed orange juice. With tummies full and completely contented spirits, the entire family was scattered on beanbag chairs and the sectional sofa in the basement family room, just goofing off. It was an unusual gathering. The television was silent, and so were all the family members.

A passage in chapter 6 of the Gospel of John came to Jack's mind as he observed the scene before him. Jesus had just miraculously fed 5,000 men and their families with five loaves and two fish. After everyone had eaten, the apostle John writes, they all reclined on the grass. He used a word that normally describes contented cows lying down and chewing their cud. The apostle notes that "they were filled." Jack thought that was a good way to describe the atmosphere in the family room.

It was Connie who broke the peaceful silence. "I was just thinking. It's been almost a year since we first met Pete and Lucy Geisinger at the Overland church. They were strangers then, but now they've grown into really good friends."

"Do you mean the day Daddy preached at that really big church, and we had strawberry shortcake afterward?" asked Paul.

"Yes," laughed Connie. "That's the day."

"We've certainly made a lot of new friends during these last twelve months, that's for sure," added Jack.

Connie asked the children, "Are you happy with the number of new friends you've made this last year? Since we're homeschooling, it's been pretty much limited to your contacts at church."

The younger children, Paul and Suzy, seemed quite satisfied. It was the older children, Johnny, Sarah, and Megan, who said they would have liked more possibilities for social events, especially sports for Johnny. But no one seemed to regret trying the homeschool approach to education.

"Your father and I have done a bit of research into some alternatives to homeschooling," Connie informed the children. "I'm sure you remember that when we started homeschooling, we weren't sure if it was just short-term or something we would continue to do. It depended on our experience with it and also on what education possibilities would be available here."

"Yes," agreed Jack. "We've been looking into the public school system and also a fine Christian school. Sometime in the next few weeks, we're going to take a tour of both possibilities so you can all get a feel for what the schools here are like."

"The public schools are highly regarded," continued Connie, "but as with most public schools, your father and I would have to be vigilant about what's included and excluded from the curriculum they use."

"That wouldn't be a problem with the Christian school," added Jack. "The only negative about that school is the cost of tuition. Although they do have an excellent family plan that makes it possible for larger families like ours to afford to have our children attend. And, Johnny, like the public school, they have an excellent sports program."

"So, when do we have to make this decision?" wondered Johnny.

"Sometime in the next month," answered his father. "And it will be a family decision. Everyone's opinion counts, the options being homeschool, public school, or Christian school.

"I have an idea," Connie proposed. "Why don't we think back over this last year? Let's talk about our best memories and the biggest blessings from God. I'm sure there are at least one or two or three things that stand out for each of us."

"Good idea, Mommy," said Jack. "Who wants to go first?"

Immediately, Megan blurted out, "I liked the really big elephant we saw at the shore. That was fun."

"Ah, yes, the elephant birthday party," recalled Connie. "That was fun."

"Yeah," giggled Suzy, "that was really fun. And I like homeschooling, too."

"I thought you might mention that," Connie said.

"And I like my Sunday school class too," Suzy added with a smile.

With a huge grin, Paul said, "My favorite memory is still the day you and Daddy almost got arrested looking in the church windows." All seven Whytes broke into laughter.

"Besides that strange moment, Paul, is there any other blessing that was important to you?"

"Well, two things, really. One was being in the Christmas play again. That was a lot of fun. The biggest blessing, though, was getting rid of that itchy rash. I was glad when that was over."

"That reminds me of another blessing for me," said Connie. "I'm thrilled that we have such a beautiful and productive garden. And thanks to everyone for pitching in. It's really growing well. So, who's next?"

"If we're going by age, that would be me," said Sarah. "I like the new desks PopPop made for us with our names on them. Not many people have something like that."

"Very true," commented her father. "Very true."

"I also like my new room and my roommate, Megan," she added, eliciting a big smile from her younger sister. "And I'm happy to have made a new friend with one of the three sisters. Visiting Miss Schultz and now getting to talk to her in church every Sunday is a real blessing for me."

"Anything else?" asked Connie. "Johnny?"

"I'm really enjoying homeschooling, although I do miss the sports programs I'm used to."

"What about you, Mommy," asked Jack. "Any more blessings to add?"

"Well, I'm thrilled with our new home and what we're making of it. And I'm enjoying the church and all the friends we've made and the opportunities God gives us to bless others. But my greatest blessing these last twelve months was when the doctors finally found out why Granddad was passing out. Since he got his pacemaker, everything has been going along nicely. Grandma and I are certainly a lot more relaxed too. How about you, hubby? We saved the oldest and best for last."

"Well, at least the oldest. Yes, I have lots of things to be thankful for this last year. I'm grateful God made it so clear that we were to come here to Grace Church. I have no doubt this is where God wants us to be. And then for all the people who've become Christians since our arrival, and the joy of watching them come alive and grow in their faith. That has been so encouraging.

"I'm also thankful that you guys made the transition from Connecticut to Pennsylvania so easy," Jack continued. "And as usual, it's been fun to watch all of you children grow and mature. I get excited about what God has already done in your lives and what He'll do to bless you as you grow."

"I think this sharing has been a lot of fun," commented Connie while all the heads nodded in agreement.

"Yes, an excellent idea, wifey. This has turned a very dreary morning into a good day to praise the Lord. Wow, what a year we've had. I'm even more excited about the next year God has planned for us."

"Did you have something particular in mind?" Johnny asked his father.

"Well, what would you think about a seven-day free vacation in Fort Lauderdale, Florida?"

"Really?" Now the children were all paying attention.

"Yes. You remember Fred, my best friend from seminary. He learned about a businessman in Florida, an accountant who was so blessed by a pastor many years ago that he wanted to bless other pastors and their families. So, he bought two houses in Fort Lauderdale and filled them with furniture and supplies, even including daily newspaper delivery and a TV guide. He also tacked notes on all the walls to let his guests know what's there and how it works. Best of all. It's all free. The families just have to promise to stay there in the house every night.

"Apparently," Jack continued, "he has everything computerized to handle requests from pastors who want to take advantage of his generosity. I've already put our name in, and now we just wait to see if and when one of these houses will be available to us. Here's an idea. Let's make 'wait and see and expect good things' our family motto for the next twelve months. I'm looking forward to the blessings God has in mind for all of us over this next year in the Whyte house."

Everyone agreed that their father had an excellent idea. They couldn't wait to see what was going to happen next year.

This is the script of the play that was presented

on Christmas Eve at Grace Church.

———————•———————

Permission to copy this script is granted to

the person or group that purchased this book

Our Family Tradition

(or "How We Hold on to Christmas")

A One-Act Play for Church Groups

by

Armand L. Weller

The Set

There is a two-level stage, if possible. The play takes place on the upper level. Those groups that sing at various times during the play will be on the lower level, where they can be seen by the audience but will not block their view of the actors.

If a two-level stage is not practical, it would be good for those who come to sing to be at the side of the stage area rather than on it or directly in front of it.

It is possible to imagine the singing groups to be Christmas carolers. If that is done, a picture window stage right or stage left would be the location through which the family would watch the groups sing their songs.

The Opening Scene

The family enters casually onto the stage that is a living room, ready for a family gathering. The three older children are carrying old cardboard cartons that they set on the floor beside the tree, which is stage right along the side wall of the living room. The family is getting ready for their traditional tree-decorating celebration.

Potential decorations have been stored in cardboard boxes since last Christmas. This is the source from which all family members have already gotten or will get their tree ornament for this year's celebration.

Grandma sits in a rocking chair stage left. Grandpa is standing just to the right of her. There is a fireplace center stage.

Mother (Allison) stands down center stage with her husband (Jim) while the three older children (Sherry, Tom, and Shane—*younger teens or older elementary children*) are searching through the cardboard boxes containing the decorations. They begin to chat quietly about how beautiful all of this is, etc.

Jeffrey, the youngest child (*young elementary*), enters last and stands next to the tree, holding something secretly behind his back. His "cat-that-swallowed-the-canary" facial expression makes it obvious that he is hiding something. Jeffrey climbs onto a bar stool to the left of the tree, where he can see all and be seen by all.

Allison holds on to Jim's arm as he begins to speak to the congregation.

Jim: Hello, everyone. And welcome to our home. My name is Jim Wellington. And this is my wife, Allison. We'd like to invite you to join us in our living room as we get together for our traditional Family Christmas Tree-Decorating Party.

All: (*ad lib*) "Welcome," "Glad you could join us," "Hi, good to see you."

Jim: As you can see, we love to do things together as a family (*all look to the audience, nod, and smile*). And we love to share with others, too. (*Children return to rustling through the cartons.*) Come on in and meet the family. (*Allison goes down left next to Grandma, to the left of the rocking chair.*)

Jim: First of all...(*firmly*) Hey! Take it easy over there, kids! We aren't quite ready to decorate the tree. Remember, we always do this together. Why not be quiet for a few moments...like Jeffrey. (*Jeffrey smiles broadly.*)

Jim: Now, first of all (*he walks up center*), let me introduce you to the best in-laws a man could ever have...my wife's parents, Chester and Verna Gruver. We call them Grandma and Grandpa. You can, too, if you like.

(*Grandma and Grandpa smile lovingly and nod.*)

Grandpa: Ya sure can...any old time. In fact, I remember the time I was first called Grandpa. Why, it was only...

Grandma: (*interrupting*) Not now, Chester. Maybe later.

Grandpa: (*to Grandma*) Oh...okay. (*to the audience*) But don't let me forget to tell you about it. Why, it was the...(*Grandma reaches up and gently places her hand on Grandpa's mouth to remind him to stop.*) (*then to Grandma*) 'Scuse me, dear. Go ahead, Jim.

Jim: (*smiling*) Thanks, Grandpa. (*to the audience*) See, I told you they are neat people. You'll love them. (*pointing to Allison*) And this is my wife, Allison. I love her for many reasons, but most of all, because she makes me believe I'm head of the family.

Allison: But you *are*, Jim.

Jim: See what I mean? (*moves up right between Jeffrey and the older children*) And these lovely creatures are the Wellington children.

(Jeffrey is smiling sweetly, surprise behind his back. Sherry, Tom, and Shane each turn from their cartons of Christmas goodies to smile and wave—but only when their name is called by their father. Then each returns immediately to the boxes.)

Jim: This is our oldest, Sherry. *(Sherry turns and waves and returns to the boxes.)* And next is Tom. *(Tom turns, waves, and returns.)* Then there is Shane. *(no response.)* Shane. *(no response—Jim gets louder)* Shane! *(Tom turns Shane's head and waves his arm for him)* That's our Shane. And this is our youngest, Jeffrey. *(Jeffrey continues to smile)* *(to Jeffrey)* Why aren't you helping to get things ready for Christmas, Jeffrey?

Jeffrey: I *am* ready.

Allison: You're ready so soon?

Jeffrey: I've been ready for a long time. Come on, let's get this show on the road.

Jim: That's a good idea, son. *(to the audience)* I've asked Allison and Sherry to tell you what we're going to do today. Ladies...
(Allison and Sherry walk down center and talk to the audience.)

Allison: Thank you for joining us. We love Christmas so much because it reminds us of God's never-ending love for all people.

Sherry: Yes, whenever I see a painting of Mary and Joseph, looking with such complete love at their newborn child, Jesus, I think about how much love God has for us that He would send us His only begotten Son at Christmas.

Allison: As a family, we remember each year what Christmas means while we decorate the tree.

Sherry: Each person takes a turn hanging an ornament on the tree.

Allison: As the ornament is placed there, that person tells the family what that symbol tells us about Christmas.

Sherry: It's really fun. You'll love it! Each of us has been looking in the cartons for the symbol we want to talk about this year.

Allison: And this year is extra-special for us. Some of the people from church are going to help us sing about the meaning of Christmas while we decorate our tree.

Jim: I think that explains it, ladies. Why don't we get started? (*to the audience*) We always start with the oldest person placing the first symbol on the Christmas tree. We're happy to say Grandpa goes first again this year. (*to Grandpa*) Okay, Grandpa, it's your turn.

Grandpa: My turn? Okay, well, you see, the first time anyone called me Grandpa, I was so surprised. I thought it couldn't be. I was too young to be a grandfather. But, sure enough, when my daughter gave birth to Sherry, didn't they start calling me Grandpa right away. And then...

Grandma: (*gently interrupting*) Chester, they don't want to hear about your stories right now. They want to hear about the birth of Jesus.

Grandpa: Oh, good. Well, why didn't you say so? I like to talk about that even more.

Grandma: Did you pick your symbol for the Christmas tree?

Grandpa: Sure did. Right over here on the mantel. (*He crosses to the fireplace.*)

Grandma: Well, hang it on the tree, Chester. And don't talk too long this year. (*Grandpa crosses to the tree with a star in his hand while Grandma talks to the audience.*) One year he talked so long little Jeffrey fell asleep. And I wasn't far from it myself. (*The family laughs quietly.*)

Grandpa: (*All family members look up to this man, whom they obviously love, as they listen to his words.*) This year I'm placing a star on the tree...right at the top. That's where the star belongs. Way up there where all can see it. The symbol of the star reminds us of the beautiful star in the sky that stopped over Bethlehem, where Jesus was born. The wise men in the East saw the star and followed it as God led them to Mary and Joseph...and their firstborn son, Jesus. They brought gifts to Him...gold, frankincense, and myrrh.

Grandpa: Remember, these wise men were not Hebrews from the nation of Israel. God was making it clear right from the beginning that Jesus came as the Savior, not only for Israel but for the whole world. (*He puts the star on the top of the tree.*)

(*A group, perhaps a men's ensemble or chorus, sings "We Three Kings of Orient Are." If they are to be seen as carolers, some of the family members could go to the window to look out at the singers. During each song, the children continue to hang various ornaments on the tree.*)

(*Grandpa returns next to Grandma. She is proud of him. She always is. She just likes to tease him a lot.*)

Tom: Okay, Grandma. It's your turn.

Shane: Yeah, Grandma. Come on! What did you pick this year?

Grandma: (*lifting some beautiful holly garlands with red berries from the knitting bag next to her rocking chair, she stands to her feet.*) Well, you know how much I love flowers. So this year, I selected the holly...(*good-naturedly teasing Allison*) before my daughter got her hands on it.

Allison: (*Making believe she is hurt*) Oh, Mother.

(*All laugh.*)

Grandma: The holly, with its dark green leaves and bright red berries, is very special to me. It ties together Christmas and Easter. Its sharp points and red berries are a reminder of the crown of thorns on Jesus' head when He died on the cross for us. Because it is a flower that blooms in winter, it reminds us of the resurrection of Jesus and of the eternal life God promises us. (*talking especially to Jeffrey and Shane*) And did you know that there is an old legend—not a real story, just a make-believe one—that a little lamb followed the shepherds when they went to see baby Jesus lying in the manger? When that little lamb was caught by the sharp thorns of the holly branches on that very cold night, some drops of the lamb's blood fell onto the holly leaves and froze there on the branches. And that is where the holly got its red berries.

Shane: That's not true, is it, Grandma?

Grandma: No, dear, just a fun kind of make-believe story.
(*Grandma hands Shane one end of the holly garland. Shane, Grandma, and Sherry drape the holly garland around the tree while a children's singing group—perhaps a choir or the third and fourth-grade classes—sing "Away in a Manger."*)

Grandma: (*following the song, just before returning to her rocking chair, she is drawn back to her youngest grandchild, Jeffrey*) My, my, Jeffrey. You certainly are quiet today. (*Jeffrey smiles and nods.*) Did you pick your symbol yet? (*Jeffrey smiles and nods again.*) Do you want to tell Grandma what it is? (*Jeffrey smiles and shakes his head.*) Oh, come on, Jeffrey. (*Jeffrey smiles and shakes his head again.*) Please, (*pleadingly*) for Grandma. (*Jeffrey smiles and shakes his head one more time.*)

Grandpa: (*lovingly but firmly*) Come on, woman. You're holding things up. You're taking so long; we're all about ready to fall asleep. (*Grandma laughs and returns to her rocking chair.*)

Jim: (*walking to the cartons next to the tree*) I guess it's my turn next. (*turning to his wife*)..."age before beauty," you know, dear. (*All groan while Jim chuckles.*)

Tom: (*to the audience, while his father, kneeling and choosing his symbol from a carton, has his back to the audience—in a loud stage whisper*) Dad says that every year. Every year!

Jim: (*straightening up and turning to the audience with a string of candles to be placed on the tree and then lighted*) Candles are always associated with Christmas. Obviously, they symbolize light...and Jesus is the light of the world. People proclaim this when they put candles in their windows at Christmas time. The candle is a favorite image of mine. At Christmas, when Jesus was born in Bethlehem, the light came into the darkness of the world. When I was born again, the light of the world took away the darkness in my life. Now Jesus says that I am to shine like a light in the darkness. It's just like that song I learned when I was a child in Sunday School—"This little light of mine, I'm gonna let it shine."

(*Jim puts the string of candles on the tree, then sits next to Allison. During this time, a group of nursery and/or kindergarten children may sing "This Little Light of Mine."*)

Jim: (*following the song*) Well, that was the "age." Now it's time for the "beauty." Allison, that's you.

(*All groan again.*)

Tom: (*to the audience*) He says *that* every year, too. *Every* year.

Jim: What was that, Tom?

Allison: Nothing important, dear. You know how he mumbles sometimes. (*standing to talk to the family and the audience*) There was another time when the light shone brightly at the birth of Jesus. Grandpa told us about the star, and Dad just placed the candles on the tree. But the brightest light of all was seen when some shepherds were out on the hillside—

Shane: (*jumping to his feet, distressed, and then running to Allison*) Mom! I picked the shepherds already. You can't talk about them!

Allison: (*consoling and comforting Shane*) Don't worry, Shane. I'm not going to talk about the shepherds. The ones who talked to the shepherds that Christmas night were surrounded by a brilliant light that was so bright it scared the shepherds. The symbol I picked is...

Shane and Jeffrey: (*together and loudly*) The angels!

Allison: You got it right, boys. Angels are God's messengers. That special night when God gave to the world the beautiful gift of His Son, Jesus,

I like to think the angels were so happy and got so excited that their loud singing broke out of heaven and right into the world, right there at Bethlehem. And that's when those shepherds, Shane, overheard the singing and were scared. (*Allison goes to a carton, picks out an angel ornament, and places it on the tree.*) You know, angels are not the only messengers God has. He expects everyone who knows about the miraculous birth of Jesus to tell everyone else about it. That would be a good thing to commit ourselves to this year...being messengers for God about His only begotten Son, Jesus.

(*At this point, another choir—perhaps children carolers—sing "Hark the Herald Angels Sing."*)

Sherry: (*following the singing*) Well, if we're going by age, I guess I'm next in line.

Tom: (*joking and teasing*) You know what they say, Sherry. "Age before beauty."

(*In rapid succession, Sherry playfully raps him on the head, Allison says, "Tommy!" and Jim speaks.*)

Jim: (*to the audience*) You know...he says that same thing every year. Every year! (*perplexed*) I wonder why.

Sherry: This is the symbol I picked this year—a bell. Bells have been used for centuries to tell the town of joyful or sad events. Slow-tolling bells were rung to announce someone's death. Brightly-ringing bells proclaimed a special birth. In England, it was traditional to ring the church bells each of the four Sundays in Advent and on Christmas Eve as well. The poet, Longfellow, wrote about the bells of London when he said:

"I heard the bells on Christmas Day

Their old, familiar carols play,

And wild and sweet

The words repeat

Of peace on earth, good-will to men!"

(*Just then, a teen choir sings "I Heard the Bells on Christmas Day," perhaps introduced or accompanied by a bell choir or bells on the organ console or synthesizer.*)

Tom: (*as the choir is introduced by bells*) Shh! Listen, everyone.

(*All listen. Some go to the window to see and listen. At the conclusion of the song, all clap and yell words of "Thank you" and "Merry Christmas" to the singers...that is everyone except Jeffrey, who is still sitting on the bar stool near the Christmas tree, hands behind his back. All return to their "places." Jim walks over to Jeffrey.*)

Jim: What's the matter, son? Didn't you like the singing?

Jeffrey: Uh-huh. (*all watch this dialog as it unfolds.*)

Jim: Then, why didn't you clap like everyone else?

Jeffrey: I can't.

Jim: Why not?

Jeffrey: My hands are busy.

Jim: Doing what?

Jeffrey: Holding on to Christmas.

Jim: You're holding Christmas in your hands?

Jeffrey: Uh-huh.

Jim: May I see?

Jeffrey: Huh-uh. (*smiles and shakes his head*) It's not my turn.

Jim: Okay, son. Well, Tom. I guess we won't know Jeffrey's secret until it's his turn. So, go ahead and tell us about your choice.

Tom: I picked the wreath, Dad. The wreath is an ancient tradition of Christmas and brings together in one symbol many of the other symbols. There is the holly that Grandma told us about. People often fasten bells and stars and angels on them. Our church has an Advent wreath with four candles that symbolize hope, joy, peace, and love. Lots of our families in church have Advent wreaths in their homes, too. And they light one new candle each week. I think the circle is a reminder of God's everlasting love...He just never stops loving us. And the evergreen branches in the middle of winter remind us of the eternal life God offers to those who believe in Jesus. (*Tom puts the wreath on the tree.*) Your turn, Shane.

Shane: Everybody already knows what I picked (*holds up a shepherd ornament*) the shepherd. I picked this because they were neat guys who worked hard. And they were the first people who knew about the baby Jesus being born. They were ordinary people like you and me. They were even dirty. But God invited them to come and meet Jesus.

(*He puts the shepherd ornament on the tree while a choir of carolers or a soloist sings "What Child Is This?"*)

(*As the song ends, Sherry goes to one side of Jeffrey and Allison to the other. He is "surrounded." All watch to see what mystery will be uncovered.*)

Sherry: Okay, little brother, let's have it. What have you been hiding behind your back?

Allison: He told Dad that he's holding Christmas back there. How about it, Jeffrey? Would you like to show us what you have?

Grandma: Yes, Jeffrey, I do believe it's your turn now.

Jeffrey: (*with a beaming smile, presents to the family his secret possession... baby Jesus in a manger*) I have baby Jesus.

All: (*All clap their hands and say*) Baby Jesus!

Grandpa: Why was that your choice, Jeffrey?

Jeffrey: Because you can't have Christmas without Jesus, Grandpa.

Grandpa: You are absolutely right, Jeffrey, absolutely right. We certainly can't have Christmas without Jesus.

Jim: You *were* holding on to Christmas, weren't you? (*Jeffrey nods and smiles. All laugh and clap their hands.*) This would be a good time to remember the story of Christmas. (*Jim reads Luke 2:1–7.*)

Allison: Okay, Jeffrey, you can put Jesus right here in the front of the tree where everyone can see Him. We want everyone to know that Jesus is at the center of our celebration of Christmas.

(*Jeffrey hangs the ornament on the tree.*)

Allison: (*speaking to the audience.*) Part of our family tradition is to finish our decorating party by singing together "Silent Night." Why don't you join us? After all, we are one family...the family of God. Let's sing as brothers and sisters in Jesus Christ.

(*The family and the congregation sing together.*)

Jim: (*down center stage, addressing the audience*) Well, we certainly do thank you for sharing in our preparation for Christmas this year. It always helps us to remember the real meaning of this special event...a day when God changed the history of the world. We hope Jesus will be at the center of your Christmas celebration this year. Merry Christmas to you all!

(*All shout,* "Merry Christmas!" "Thanks for coming!" *etc., and leave the stage together.*)

A Note about the Music: The songs sung and the groups singing are simply a suggestion. Each group that presents this play will have to choose the songs and singers they will use according to the gifts and abilities they have available in their church. In fact, the play can be presented with no music at all. But the carols of Christmas add a lot to the play and to the joy of the season this play celebrates. If singing groups are not available, recorded music is an option. Another option is to make the audience a part of the play by choosing carols they know and having them sing the first verses at appropriate places in the script. The players could watch them sing and applaud them each time as welcome carolers.

CPSIA information can be obtained
at www.ICGtesting.com
Printed in the USA
BVHW091945080223
658147BV00011B/138